The Second Empire Revisited

The Second Empire Revisited

Revisited

A Study in French Historiography

Stuart L. Campbell

Rutgers University Press
New Brunswick, New Jersey

Publication of this book was partially supported by the
Alfred University Research Foundation.

LIBRARY OF CONGRESS CATALOGING IN PUBLICATION DATA
Campbell, Stuart L   1938–
   The Second Empire revisited.
   Based on the author's thesis, University of
Rochester, 1969.
   Bibliography: p.
   Includes index.
   1. France—History—Second Empire, 1852–1870—
Historiography.   I. Title.
DC276.5.C35   944.07′07′2   77–20247
ISBN 0–8135–0856–8

To Sally and Isaac

Contents

Acknowledgments

This book owes much to many people who have contributed in a variety of ways.

Val Lorwin and Doug Legg many years ago at the University of Oregon first suggested that I undertake an historiographical study of the Second Empire. Temporarily set aside, the idea was eventually pursued as a doctoral dissertation at the University of Rochester under John Christopher and Jim Friguglietti, both of whom have been extraordinarily generous in their support over an extended period of time.

The transition from a dissertation to a published work was greatly aided by a host of people who have read and commented upon the manuscript at various stages in its development. Particular thanks are due Hayden White, Sanford Elwitt, Bob Hoffman, Bill Keylor, Warren Spencer, Joseph Moody, Theodore Zeldin, Stephen Graubard, Martin Siegel, Bob Zangrando, and John Rothney. I also wish to thank David Pinkney who read the manuscript for Rutgers University Press; his then anonymous and valuable suggestions were tendered in good spirit, and I truly enjoyed our dialogue through the offices of Herbert Mann.

Alfred University has contributed in several ways, two of which deserve special mention. A College Center of the Finger Lakes Grant made possible an extended period of research in France in

1972, and the Alfred University Research Foundation has provided a grant to defray partially the cost of publication.

Over the years, my good friend Joel Blatt has listened to and tested my ideas on French history and Marxism. I have learned much from him, and many of the book's virtues are the result of his hard questions. Note should also be made of my students at Alfred University who have endured and challenged my views on modern France. With the possible exception of Steve Rings, who has done the laborious task of compiling the index, and who knows very well the weight of his contribution, they have given more than they realize.

Special thanks are also due Joanne Droppers and Elizabeth Hoffman, whose efforts at the typewriter greatly facilitated the task of producing a manuscript.

Finally, my particular thanks and love to Sally, to whom, along with our son, this book is dedicated. It was she who years ago taught me a proper respect for the English language, who found the appropriate handle for a difficult administrative problem in 1971, and who allowed the historians of the Empire to become permanent guests in our household.

Introduction

At first glance, an investigation of the historiography of the Second Empire might seem excessively narrow, another example of erudition carried to its logical and questionable end. Further, until recently the French themselves have not shown a great interest in historiography, a condition which has led Charles-Olivier Carbonell to write that French historians have shown a "disdain" for the history of their discipline.[1] The question then becomes obvious: why should an American undertake a kind of study for which the French have shown little interest, and why should specific attention be given to the historiography of the Second Empire?

The answer, like the question, is twofold. On the general side, if the historian's craft can be likened to a mirror, it can be said to reflect the past in the light of the present, and as the latter assumes a new design or character, the historian necessarily discovers a new kind of past. Historians, like artists, create representations through which their particular time and cultural milieu can be seen, and to some extent, understood. As a statement, then, history is both individual and social, and cannot be treated apart from the historian or the society in which he lives. History, after all, is written by people who personify certain values and assumptions related to their own

1. Charles-Olivier Carbonell, *Histoire et historiens,* p. 45. Fortunately, recent developments, including Carbonell's book, would indicate a growing French interest in historiography.

time. The task of the historiographer is to investigate the relationships that join the historian, his work, and the context in which he writes. History so written—history explained historically, to use the words of Georges Lefebvre—properly allows history to become the object of historical analysis.

To answer the specific side of the question, it should be noted that during most of the modern period, the writing of history in France has largely been the function of the political divisions emanating from a revolutionary heritage. Until very recently, French politics and the writing of French history have been literally indistinguishable. Ernest Lavisse, who made the pilgrimage from Bonapartism to republicanism and who contributed so much to the character of both French education and the professional school of republican history, once called France's historiography a battleground for contending political ideologies. He wrote of historians that:

> The past of France is their battlefield: they study it like two armies in order to seize the accidents of a favorable terrain without any care for the character of the soil or the harvest it bears. We are polemicists, and the complete truth is jeopardized in the course of polemics. We plead a perpetual case, and what lawyer has never lied, at least by omission of the troublesome parts of the truth? Taking for our point of departure the time in which we live in order to unfold the prejudices of our political party, we demand from the past a proof that we think justly and that we act for the good.[2]

Lavisse's remarks, written in 1882, give some indication why the historiography of the Second Empire provides an accurate reflection of modern French political life. For one thing, Bonapartism was one of several competing ideologies designed to establish a national consensus. For another, and of particular significance to the present study, the regime's history was inseparable from the struggles that ultimately led to the establishment and consolidation of a parliamentary republic. The Empire, by discounting parliamentary political forms, by affirming the merits of a strong executive, and by

2. Ernest Lavisse, *L'Enseignement historique en Sorbonne et l'éducation nationale,* p. 4.

fostering economic growth to blunt the social question, was in many respects the antithesis of the Third Republic. As a result, any attempt to study the Empire necessarily raised questions pertinent to the Republic. It was therefore inevitable that when republican institutions fell upon hard times after World War I, the historiography of the Empire began to undergo a marked shift. Further, this shift was related to a larger struggle on the part of Henri Berr, Lucien Febvre, and Marc Bloch to renew historical study by enlarging it beyond mere politics, and by the attempt of Albert Mathiez and his students to push historical scholarship in the direction of Marxism. The overall effect of these changes upon the historiography of the Empire was indeed great. In particular, there was an increased emphasis upon the economic significance of the regime—an emphasis clearly related to the dilemmas of an interwar period marked by depression and class conflict.

Finally, the revisionism that began during the interwar years has since become near orthodoxy. Historians, however, remain advocates who take the present as their point of departure; it is significant that in contrast to their predecessors, the present generation of historians has granted less weight to the political disputes that found their source in the nineteenth century, and has paid less attention to the traditional criticisms leveled against Bonapartism. Instead, emphasis has been given to Bonapartist political economy and the so-called modernization of French society. This would indicate that the political issues that once divided the "old France" do not seem quite so relevant for what many consider to be a "new France." If so, then the historiography of the Second Empire charts the course of a fundamental reorientation in regard to how the French have treated their past and their politics.

Several particulars concerning this study deserve brief comment. First, the beginning chapter includes an analysis of Bonapartist political theory and the regime that followed, albeit imperfectly, from that theory. The questions broached by this chapter are important because Bonapartism was a political ideology with obvious historiographical implications, and because the political debates of the imperial period provided the sources of the regime's historiog-

raphy. A study of this nature necessarily begins with both Bonapartism and the republican and liberal criticisms of Bonapartist rule.

Secondly, I have employed an approach that is both generational
and chronological in order to outline the gradual shifts in historiographical attitudes. Strictly speaking, however, generational distinctions are not just a function of age and time. The boundaries
dividing generations sometimes overlap, given the demands of personal careers, the ties of friendship, and the effects of class and
family. Although only a few years in age actually separated Pierre
de La Gorce and Charles Seignobos, for instance, they were products of very different historiographical generations, and I have
treated them as such. La Gorce wrote in the well-established tradition of the leisured gentleman, while Seignobos was something of a
young turk, for his new methodology was associated with that of
the "professional" historians. In a similar fashion, I have included
Jean Maurain with his mentor, Seignobos, although in age he was
the contemporary of those discussed in the following chapter under
the heading of new historians. Despite his younger years, Maurain
clearly belonged to an earlier generation, and in some ways his
career was an example of institutional inertia. As an insider of both
the Republic and its University, he was far closer in outlook to
Seignobos than to the revisionist new historians, who were in one
sense or another outsiders and wrote their history accordingly. Had
Maurain lived longer, he might very well have made the transition
to a new kind of history—and there is some indication that he was
doing so—but his career was cut short by his accidental death in
1939.

Finally, I have omitted the historiography of the Empire's foreign
policy except insofar as it touches upon my major concern: the historiography of Napoleon III's attempt to heal France's political
divisions and the evolution of the regime toward liberalization. To
have included foreign policy would have entailed a second volume
and led me somewhat astray. Despite Gabriel Hanotaux's remark
that Bonapartism largely involved a foreign policy and although the
Empire received frequent criticism for the decisions that led to
1870, the regime acquired public support for reasons other than the

principle of nationalities. Whatever the importance of foreign policy in determining its evolution and destiny, on the domestic front the Empire represented a program of national reconciliation. Had Napoleon III suppressed his desire to upset the European balance, he might very well have postponed, and even prevented, France's third republican experiment.

Chapter I

Theory and Practice of Bonapartism

Louis Napoleon, sensing the possibilities of the Napoleonic legend and possessing a blind faith in his mission to restore imperial institutions, transformed the myth surrounding his uncle into a workable political program. An extraordinarily difficult figure to assess, the Prince has been called a simpleton by some, while others have thought him a devious Machiavellian who finally outsmarted himself. Madame Cornu, who probably knew him best, thought the Prince more suited for writing poetry than for directing the fortunes of a European state. He was, however, endowed with certain political capabilities. Although he possessed little originality of mind, Louis Napoleon did have a great capacity for absorbing other people's ideas and placing them into a vague system of generous and humane programs. He was also particularly sensitive to the climate of opinion of the 1830s and 1840s, and he understood the democratic aspirations of the period. Unfortunately, he completely lacked an administrator's attention for detail and execution, and thereby ran the risk of becoming entangled in the threads of his own designs. Willing and able to implement vast projects, he was also subject to periods of vacillation and passivity. When complications arose, he often as not met them with a fatalistic belief that events would sort themselves out for the best. This attitude finally proved his undoing, and a sympathetic observer might well have remarked that because he only managed to see clearly a distant future, Louis Napoleon stumbled over his own feet.

Historians have attributed the seemingly mysterious and contradictory policies of the Second Empire to the unpredictable character of its Emperor. The fact is that few pretenders have so thoroughly advertised their plans before taking power, and Napoleon III remained amazingly true to the proposals of Louis Napoleon.[1] Practically every major project implemented by the Emperor, including the catastrophic Mexican expedition, received embryonic expression in the Pretender's writings. During the 1850s, Napoleon III could see fit to have published an official, albeit expurgated, collection of his pre-1848 writings, thus establishing, at least in his own mind, that the Second Empire represented an honest reflection of his earlier beliefs. He certainly never repudiated them.

During the July Monarchy, Louis Napoleon fashioned a Bonapartism which included a progressive critique of Orleanism and allowed the Prince to present his own positive program. As such, Bonapartism consisted of two parts. The first Louis Napoleon drew directly from the Napoleonic legend, while the second represented the Prince's response to the problems of the 1815–1848 period. The meaning that Louis Napoleon attributed to the first part—the Napoleonic inheritance—is to be found in the *Political Reflections* and the *Napoleonic Ideas*. The latter, in particular, was an impressive piece of political propaganda. Well-organized and succinct, the pamphlet revealed the author's familiarity with important contemporary writers such as Thiers and Tocqueville. The most striking quality of the *Ideas*, however, was its democratic character. Louis Napoleon peppered Orleanism with the charge that it had proven unnational—meaning undemocratic—thereby revealing one of the Prince's major insights. More attuned to the temper of the 1840s than

---

1. He elaborated his ideas at some length in several pamphlets, the *Political Reflections* (1832), *Napoleonic Ideas* (1839), and the *Extinction of Pauperism* (1844) being the most important.

were the oligarchical Orleanists, Louis Napoleon asserted that any government foolhardy enough to ignore the democratic direction of history was simply building on sand, and would surely tumble.

The *Ideas* also indicated that Louis Napoleon held a set of preconceptions about the nature of history. Like everyone else dealing with the revolutionary heritage, he attempted to place the Revolution within the context of an historical pattern, and the result was a potpourri of contemporary commonplaces. This, however, was no handicap, as the Prince claimed to be relevant rather than original. He not only agreed with the republicans that the Revolution represented democracy, and with the liberals that it provided the basis for liberty, but he added that the Empire represented the Revolution's highest achievement. The Prince then proceeded to draw important conclusions from this assumption. He argued that history is essentially the story of progress, although periods of major change necessarily bring revolution, confusion, and chaos. Fortunately, society somehow provides or discovers great men—e.g., Alexander, Caesar, Constantine, Charlemagne, and Napoleon—who grasp the issues, prevent dissolution, and preserve the great ideas from which progress is born. History, then, is an interaction between heroes and humanity's development.

Louis Napoleon's vision of a progressive history dependent upon and acting through the agency of a chosen leader had obvious political implications. In both pamphlets the Prince argued that Napoleon I had saved the Revolution from its enemies and its own excesses. The First Empire itself had proven temporary only because of an undesired war and foreign intervention.

The message of the *Reflections* told a great deal about Louis Napoleon's program. Bonapartism was a political theory which in part emerged from the crucible of the Great Revolution, and therefore confronted the Revolution's historical problems. In specific terms, Bonapartism's fundamental political relationship was that which joined the Emperor and the people, and no space remained for a sovereign assembly or even a chamber with the role of mediator between the two ultimate powers. Government by assembly was unrealistic since parliaments consisted of deputies representing either petty or parochial interests which, when combined, hardly constituted the national interest. In a properly ordered Bonapartist system, a parliament's only function was advisory.

Louis Napoleon also assumed that the liberal program of parliamentarianism would result in either of two equally unhappy alternatives: if universal suffrage were implemented, the resulting assembly would be too divided to function properly; if the franchise were restricted to allow a consensus for governing, then the assembly would be unresponsive to the nation as a whole. Orleanists acknowledged the dilemma with their electoral distinction between a *pays réel* and a *pays légal*. The Prince, on the other hand, revealed his shrewdness in recognizing that most Frenchmen accepted the democratic implications of the Revolution. He was also aware of another possibility that escaped Guizot and his colleagues: with proper safeguards, a democratic regime could be established without threatening the stability of the community. In fact, Louis Napoleon realized that acceptance of the democratic principle provided the means of preserving stability. The real problem was how to implement universal suffrage without exposing and deepening France's political divisions. As was so often the case, the first Napoleon provided the answer and the nephew modified it to suit the needs of his own time. A Bonapartist government and its general policies would be ratified directly by the people in periodic plebiscites. Further, state and society were joined by the rather mystical link between Emperor and people, with the Emperor having the ability to discover and sense the needs and aspirations of the people, and the people trusting his ability to do so and to implement the proper programs.

Louis Napoleon's denial of the efficacy of liberal institutions did not render his program reactionary (unless one assumes that parliamentarianism was synonymous with progressivism, which it certainly was *not* in the France of the 1840s). The politics of Bonapartism, however, consisted of more than an authoritarian democracy. The Prince accepted his uncle's claim that the Empire would have eventually established political liberty with its accompanying parliamentary trappings. Until, however, France had achieved some kind of national agreement under the Napoleonic banner, liberalism remained impossible.

The *Napoleonic Ideas* provided a statement of Bonapartist political theory and justified the role of "great men" in history. Although some concern for the social problem was expressed, it was only later, while imprisoned at Ham, that Louis Napoleon attempted to extend Bonapartist theory beyond the political question. In later years, Napoleon III referred to his imprisonment as an education, and spoke of the University of Ham. While incarcerated, and thanks to Madame Cornu's willingness to supply him with books, the Prince immersed himself in the advanced thought of the period, and also established numerous contacts with the leftist opposition which was becoming increasingly socialistic in orientation. Sensitive enough to recognize the issues of the 1840s and the growing importance of the social problem, he remodeled Bonapartism accordingly. Indeed, Bonapartism became part of the current of social romanticism, and by corresponding with the likes of George Sand, by hosting Louis Blanc, and by contributing and subscribing to left-wing journals, Louis Napoleon established a reputation as something of a socialist.[2]

In brief, Louis Napoleon restructured Bonapartism to meet the needs of mid-nineteenth century France. The symbol of this accomplishment, a pamphlet entitled the *Extinction of Pauperism*, was a typical example of social romantic propaganda and shared a trait common to France's newly emerging social conscience: a belief that state intervention could better working-class conditions. The *Extinction* made reference to a need for savings banks and pensions, and suggestions were made that the national budget be employed in order to guarantee a more equitable distribution of wealth. The pamphlet also indicated that the Prince had read Blanc's *L'Organisation du travail*. Both Blanc and Louis Napoleon focused their attention upon the problem of unemployment, with the Prince in particular decrying a system that allowed men to be callously laid off for the sake of profit. To remedy the situation, Louis Napoleon

2. Louis Napoleon's reputation as a socialist still finds defenders. Hendrik Nicolaas Boon, *Rêve et réalité dans l'oeuvre de Napoléon III*, remains the most important work in this tradition.

advocated the establishment of agricultural colonies which would absorb the unemployed. Despite their military-like organization, these colonies would supposedly provide a healthy environment and pleasant surroundings. Although the Prince overlooked the obvious fact that available untilled land was of marginal use, he nonetheless argued that the program would solve both the specific unemployment and the general social problem. The colonies would theoretically support higher industrial wages since workers would not abandon the colonies for low-paying jobs. Secondly, the extra food production would lower the price of foodstuffs, thus increasing the buying power of wages. Finally, in times of economic crisis, workers could fall back upon the colonies, and the industrial work force would be both preserved and saved from the deprivations of an industrial slump.

Louis Napoleon's attitudes towards the working-class question were typical of those associated with social romanticism. Rather than emphasizing the role of conflict, the *Extinction* provided a plan for class harmony through state action. The paternalistic belief that the working class had to be led was the rule rather than the exception among pre-1848 social theorists; only Proudhon expressed distrust for programs manufactured by intellectuals rather than by the workers themselves. Likewise, most social theorists hoped to employ the power of the state to realize their goals. Again, Proudhon was the exception. That the *Extinction* was typical explains the favorable response it evoked from left-wing circles. George Sand wrote a letter to the Prince and expressed her approval by noting that the present Napoleon understood the sadness of the people whereas his uncle had personified their glory. Many criticisms have nevertheless been made of the borrowed quality of the program found in the *Extinction*. As for the obvious inadequacy of the policies outlined in the *Extinction*—e.g., the use of agricultural colonies for social reconstruction—they were typical of the utopian reformism of the 1840s. Louis Napoleon shared a general optimistic vision, based largely upon the assumption that historical progress would bring an end to social misery, and would do so within the context of progressive and generous political action. Whatever his shortcomings as a social theorist, by the time Louis Napoleon was Napoleon III, he understood more fully the implications of industrialization. The shift in attitude indicates both his realism and opportunism, and the Saint-Simonians, who believed industrialization to be humanity's salvation, may have influenced him. Although few direct ties between the Prince and the sect can be established for the period before 1848, some did exist. On the other hand, there may have been only a common set of attitudes shared by the Prince and the Saint-Simonians of the 1840s. The group's impact upon social romanticism alone would have proven sufficient to have influenced the Prince.

The *Extinction* also shared a point of view similar to the pragmatic Saint-Simonism of the 1840s. Rather than suggesting a complete renovation of the existing economic system, Louis Napoleon thought it more practical to insist that it operate in a more efficient and humanitarian manner. One major task was to provide the working class with a stake in society's operation. At the same time, the Prince wrote to the effect that the government should not try to absorb the economy, but should instead assume those tasks that individuals, or what is now called the private sector, were incapable of handling. Finally, Louis Napoleon's distrust of parliamentary government joined his cause to that of the Saint-Simonians. Both had little use for politicians, and both hoped to place the community's destiny in the hands of disinterested experts. If, on the other hand, Bonapartism was more democratic and less philosophical than Saint-Simonism, this merely indicated that the two were not identical.

The Prince's vague but real commitment to change and his tendency both to oversimplify problems and to inflate specific proposals into panaceas marked him as a man of '48. In later years, Sainte-Beuve supported the Second Empire by arguing that both monarchism and republicanism had been found wanting in a time when France needed enlightened and progressive leadership. A solution was to be found, he argued, by placing the power of Louis XIV in the hands of a socially-minded and democratically inspired ruler. Sainte-Beuve was the first to call Napoleon III a Saint-Simon on horseback, and many Saint-Simonians tacitly affirmed the judgment through their loyal adherence to the Second Empire.

------•-◄►◄-•◄------

The 1848 Revolution began inauspiciously with a series of banquets held to press for the broadening of suffrage. After riots sent Louis Philippe packing for England, Parisian radicals predictably proclaimed a Second Republic at the Hôtel de Ville, and Frenchmen embarked upon another political experiment. Events soon proved, however, that it was a difficult time for establishing a republic. While still living with memories of the Great Revolution, Frenchmen were just becoming conscious of social changes brought about by industrial development. The 1848 Revolution became an inept attempt to merge past and present into a vague compromise, as was exemplified by the two major figures of the Revolution's early stage: Alphonse de Lamartine and Louis Blanc. Both were historians. The first remained unresponsive to the social question and labored under the belief that politics ended with universal suffrage. The second tried to attach socialism to the new republic. That they both failed and fell into political disgrace tells a great deal about their revolution and their respective roles within it.

The men of '48 owed their failure in part to their own historical consciousness. Politically educated by the advanced historiography of the previous thirty years, the leaders of the Republic slipped into power with the belief that progress was somehow in the nature of things. They were ill-prepared to deal with the complex problems of democracy and social reform. At a loss for recent models upon which to pattern their action, the men of '48 frequently resorted to rhetoric and to mimicking the leaders of the Great Revolution. Marx and Tocqueville independently noted the prominence of sound over substance and the surprising degree of historical posturing. When these subterfuges failed, the 48ers either abdicated or resorted to force. In this latter instance, they finally shaped history rather than endured it, but even the history they made destroyed their republic.

The willingness to use force led to the June rebellion, which, in turn, gave rise to a period of reaction. The liberal-conservative offensive against the Republic and revolutionary principles was made possible because republicanism had fallen into disrepute with the mass of provincial voters. By 1850 the Assembly had gone so far as to pass the May Law which seriously restricted the franchise and certainly violated the democratic spirit of the constitution. As might have been expected, reaction increased the political polarization that the June Days so greatly intensified, and the striking quality of the 1849 elections was the decimation of the moderate republicans. Correspondingly, monarchists and red republicans experienced gains at the polls. France was being pulled apart, with the monarchists smugly holding their majority and the radicals alluding to the upcoming 1852 elections as a time when the left would correct the balance. Since radicals believed the May Law to be unconstitutional, those disenfranchised by it would troop to the polls and exercise their rights, and France could expect more revolutionary activity.

Politics, then, had failed, and if nineteenth-century historiography was a function of politics, it too left something to be desired, since nothing approximating a national consensus had been found by the mid-century. Perhaps historians had too closely served the demands of politics; or perhaps there were several French revolutions, each distinct from the other and mutually exclusive. Fortunately, the revolutionary tradition was fruitful enough to provide a way out of the tangle of 1848, and it was offered by Louis Napoleon, who was no less historically-minded than Guizot, Thiers, Blanc, or Lamartine. To escape the dilemmas of the First Revolution, Frenchmen had discovered a politics meant to transcend politics; the precedent was obvious, and everyone knew it. For this reason, political polarization played a major role in the fortunes of Louis Napoleon by allowing the popular set of myths surrounding the Napoleonic legend to intrude further upon French political life. The phenomenon began with a foreboding abruptness. Without even making an appearance, the Prince managed to win several by-elections (in-

cluding one in Paris) to the Constituent Assembly. He finally took a
seat despite some attempts on the part of the republican leadership
to deny it to him. The Prince then announced his candidacy for
President of the Republic; in December 1848 he defeated his opponents in a landslide victory that seemed unbelievable even though
a republican government counted the votes.

A Second Republic with a Napoleonic President and a royalist
Assembly proved unworkable. Political animosities threw the regime
into a massive stalemate, and the coup d'état of December 2, 1851
therefore came as no surprise. Predictions of its arrival had titillated
Paris since the election of December 10, 1848. If anything, public
expectancy was somewhat dulled by the long wait, and some won-
dered aloud whether the Prince lacked the necessary courage. The
expected finally happened. Louis Napoleon dissolved the Assembly,
arrested some leading politicians, placed Paris under martial law,
restored universal suffrage, and called for a plebiscite to approve his
actions. For the most part, Frenchmen heaved a sigh of relief, although some provinces in the south experienced uncoordinated uprisings. In Paris, a few persistent republicans formed a Committee
of Resistance in hopes of enlisting the support of the workers; although exaggerated, Victor Hugo's *Histoire d'un crime* chronicled
their failure. The working class showed little interest in defending a
monarchist Assembly which had labored to destroy universal suffrage. Moreover, the traditional links joining republicanism and
Bonapartism were still real. Almost thirty years later, Ernest Hamel,
by this time a Gambettist senator, admitted that his youthful reaction to December 2 was one of acceptance. "I did not yet have," he
wrote, "a decided preference for this or that form of government."[3]
The young man's latitudinarianism was no doubt reinforced by the
fact that Louis Napoleon's government was the first ever to have
jailed either Thiers or General Changarnier, an action that must
have warmed many a left-wing heart.

On the other hand, fear of radicalism allowed or forced most
liberals to accept the coup, at least for the moment. Indeed, the

3. Ernest Hamel, *Histoire du second Empire*, I, 5. Hamel did not mention the fact
that he publicly circulated a poem in praise of the coup d'état.

burgraves[4] registered some weak and very perfunctory protests while secretly wishing the conspirators well. Monarchist division between two royal houses precluded an early restoration, and thus Louis Napoleon seemed the only possible alternative. Repentant liberals like Mérimée and Montalembert simply despaired of parliamentary government, republican or monarchist, and called for a strong man. As early as July, 1848 Chancellor Pasquier had written his friend Baron Barante: "President of the Republic, Emperor or King, I am for whomever will establish security and return confidence."[5] The issue was further clarified by Thiers's remark to Senior in 1852:

> So little am I an Orleanist, that if Louis Napoleon after his coup d'état had founded a real constitution with an hereditary peerage and a House of Commons fairly chosen, and had handed over to it the government of the country, reserving to himself only the high place of a constitutional king, I should joyfully have adhered to him . . . He might have had Guizot and me for his ministers, or more probably Guizot alone—for I should have preferred standing apart, as a friend of the administration. . . .[6]

For his own part, the Prince admitted that he had broken the law, but he also argued that he had done so for the sake of a higher legality. A majority of Frenchmen seemed to agree. Despite obvious pressures, the results (7,440,000 *yes* votes to 646,000 *no* votes) were impressive, and contemporaries admitted the fact. In Bonapartist terms, the Prince was absolved by an expression of popular sovereignty. History seemed to have repeated itself, albeit in a somewhat telescoped and uneven fashion. Frenchmen moved from a constitutional monarchy to a republic, and then once again found themselves in an empire.

The Empire's immediate goals were obvious. The Prince hoped to join the old and the new, and to heal the wounds in French society. When Jules Baroche officially presented him with the results of the

4. Burgrave: a term frequently applied to the higher reaches of the monarchist political leadership.
5. A. Prosper de Barante, *Souvenirs*, VII, 342.
6. Nassau William Senior, *Conversations with M. Thiers, M. Guizot and other Distinguished Persons during the Second Empire*, I, 39–40.

plebiscite, Louis responded: "I hope to assure France's destiny by establishing institutions that will respond to both the democratic instincts of the nation and to the expressed universal desire for a strong and respected power. In effect, to satisfy present demands by creating a system which will reconstitute authority without damaging equality and without closing the road to reform. This will provide the basis for the one edifice capable of later supporting a wise and beneficial liberty." In the meantime Louis Napoleon asked Frenchmen to put aside their differences and accept a national program that would work for the benefit of the whole community. The appeal was certainly more attractive than that of the July Monarchy, and it also promised to provide the order and stability so obviously lacking in the Second Republic.

There were, unfortunately, indications that Louis Napoleon's self-appointed task of bridging the gulf between left and right might prove more difficult than first anticipated. Despite its preservation of order and universal suffrage, the Second Empire failed to rally republicans committed to a purity in political forms or liberals committed to the Charter of 1830. For both, Louis Napoleon seemed a usurper who had disrupted France's political development, and sent history down a tangential path. Despite such arguments, however, there was much about the new regime that was strikingly traditional. To take one example, enemies of the Second Empire never ceased to point out the predominance of the Emperor's position over that of the Legislative Body, and many echoed Guizot when he called the latter a "great eunuch." Furthermore, Louis Napoleon made no bones about discounting the role of the legislature; such had to be the case given the character of Bonapartist political theory, and the most authoritarian defenders of the regime—Haussmann, Persigny, and Cassagnac—argued that the Empire's greatness lay in precisely this. Bonapartist emphasis upon the executive was hardly revolutionary, however; in contrast with previous regimes, there was merely a change in degree. The *doctrinaires,* the spiritual forbears of Orleanism, had argued that ministers were completely dependent upon the king. They denied that the Crown and Chamber were rivals, and insisted that the latter was an auxiliary of the former. As for the Empire, ministers were defined as instruments of the executive; indeed, they were even prohibited from being deputies, and they did not officially present themselves in the Legislative Body.

It was the Council of State that theoretically mediated between the executive and legislative powers while acting as the former's representative. This peculiar role of the Council of State tells a great deal about the Second Empire. Amongst other things, preponderance of the executive power was meant to establish a formula enabling administrative expertise, rather than political partisanship, to direct the legislative process. More than one observer referred to the Council as the workhorse of the new regime.[7] It not only drew up legislation for the executive, but guided measures through the Legislative Body. Such a procedure, however, represented no major change in the Council's traditional function of technical counselor. The importance of the Council of State merely underlined the administrative continuity that linked the Empire with its predecessors, and this continuity contributed to the regime's character more than is generally recognized. Indeed, the new government was peculiarly dependent upon the administration. Having deliberately avoided a politics of vested interests, the Emperor necessarily looked to the administration to execute his program. In some respects, the Second Empire represented a partnership between the administration and Louis Napoleon. More abstractly, it was an alliance between the forces of bureaucracy and Bonapartism, and this alliance revealed another facet of Louis Napoleon's attempt to fuse the old and the new. No purge was made of bureaucratic personnel, and the administration retained its traditional functions. Louis Napoleon probably agreed with Louis Philippe, who was fond of commenting that France was a nation accustomed to being administered. The Emperor, however, expected that his more democratic and progressive leadership would allow the administration to overcome its traditional conservatism.

7. The role of the Council of State has recently been investigated by the English historian, Vincent Wright, in his *Le Conseil d'Etat sous le second Empire*. Wright concludes that the Council's predominant role was more theoretical than real.

To a point, administrative attitudes were extremely compatible with the Bonapartist outlook. Both viewed the community with some paternalism, and both expressed a marked preference for disinterested experts rather than doctrinaire politicians. Equally important, the administration saw in 1852 a potential crisis threatening France's very social fabric. In the circumstances, Louis Napoleon offered the only apparent viable alternative.[8] The administration, however, proved to be no mere rubber stamp. Its upper echelons were not easily bullied, and they regarded the state as an entity above any particular regime. Louis Napoleon's seemed a better choice than most simply because it allowed greater bureaucratic independence. The Council of State provided a good example of the regime's relationship with the administration. Although the Council's membership included men with varied and even nonadministrative backgrounds, the majority consisted of high-ranking and experienced *fonctionnaires*. These men, certain of their own competence, were quite prepared to resist what they thought to be the Emperor's ill-considered innovations. In any event, Napoleon III never established a Bonapartist administration. What emerged instead was a working partnership first organized during the Second Republic and then consummated by the coup d'état. Indeed, despite the need for the army's intervention in the Midi and left-wing assertions that the Empire was a praetorian regime, the coup was more an administrative than a military operation. Generals, in fact, proved less willing to make a coup than prefects.[9] Within the Bonapartist-administrative alliance, there were, of course, disagreements, but the Emperor was at a disadvantage, given his neglect of the details involved in the execution of policy.

A key post in the regime's administrative system was the Ministry of the Interior, and critics have made much of the supposed heavy-

8. Howard C. Payne, *The Police State of Louis Napoleon Bonaparte, 1851–1860,* p. 29.

9. Prefects did not even have to be discreetly polled by the government before the coup d'état. As for generals willing to make a coup, the government had to find new men, and even these showed a scrupulous concern as to whether or not they were covered by civilian orders. See Brison Gooch, *The New Bonapartist Generals in the Crimean War,* pp. 18–32.

handedness of the Imperial prefect who has become something of
an archetype.[10] The claims appear to be distorted, for the government, if for no reason other than political realism, was quick to
chastise those who engaged in what was officially called overzealous
activity. As the primary agents of the government, the prefects
oversaw the smooth functioning of the administration at the local
level, while cultivating a public opinion sympathetic and loyal to
the regime. This included the supervision and management of elections. The task was hardly new, as prefects during the July Monarchy had acted in a similar fashion. Nor for that matter did the
Second Empire introduce the system of official candidates who were
given active prefectoral support, as governments had traditionally
held prefects responsible for electoral results. The methods of operation employed by the Empire necessarily differed from those of the
constitutional monarchies. Given the demands of universal suffrage,
the nomination of official candidates became a completely open
practice. However, the Empire was not even original in trying to
influence the results of universal suffrage. During the presidency of
Louis Napoleon, the liberal monarchist ministry of Odilon Barrot
established the pattern with the elections of 1849. Official influences
notwithstanding, elections were run in a surprisingly honest fashion.
Moreover, the Empire granted universal suffrage the final say, and
even Napoleon III's most bitter opponents never charged that
official results and counts were fraudulent.

   Just as it made no attempt to establish anything approximating a
Bonapartist administration, the government also refused to organize
a disciplined Bonapartist party. Such an organization had existed
during the 1848–1851 period, but was summarily dissolved before
the 1852 elections. The Empire's approach to French political reorganization was to place the choice of official candidates for the
Legislative Body in the hands of the prefects. As Minister of the
Interior, Morny indicated what considerations the prefects should

---

10. On the prefectoral corps, see the important study by Bernard Le Clère and
Vincent Wright, *Les Préfets du second Empire*. The authors dispute the "préfets à
poigne" myth and emphasize the role of the prefects in adapting French administrative practice to the needs of a newly established democratic politics.

keep in mind while searching for candidates. In a circular of January 8, 1852, he suggested that nominations be given to "men held in public esteem, more concerned about the interest of the country than partisan political struggle, and sympathetic to the sufferings of the working class; men who have acquired influence and consideration through the beneficial use of their fortunes." A circular of January 20 added: "I wish to inform you of the chief of state's thoughts . . . When a man has made his fortune by work, industry, or agriculture, has improved the condition of his workers, and has made exemplary use of his property—he is preferable to politicians, because he will bring to the legislative process a practical spirit, and will second the government's task of pacification and reorganization." On the other hand, the government was willing to accept men associated with previous regimes provided their *ralliement* was genuine. Both wisdom and necessity imposed such tolerance. As Theodore Zeldin has pointed out, such a policy was unavoidable if the regime hoped to gather widespread support from the upper levels of society.[11]

The Empire, in short, placed its electoral fortunes in the hands of the prefects. Despite the oft-repeated criticism that Napoleon III subjected France to the authoritarian control of the Minister of the Interior, prefectoral power provided a certain diversity, and even reinforced local interests. No two prefects conceived of their task in an identical fashion. Although the prefectoral corps was agreed as to the need to preserve order and find loyal candidates, some prefects were more prepared to coopt traditional leadership while others showed greater interest in employing new men. In any event, prefects seldom tried to turn everything upside down. Rather, they chose allies according to their usually orthodox conception of the government's best interests. Prefects' reports, moreover, were filled with complaints about the power of "local influences," the term employed by the administration to designate established vested interests. Although the prefects were jealous of such influences and often tried to employ the newly enfranchised majority to dilute their

11. Theodore Zeldin, *The Political System of Napoleon III.*

power, they also found it necessary to ally with some interests at the expense of others. Finally, no two prefects faced identical problems. Each department had its own character, and prefects had to respond accordingly. In the West, for instance, Legitimist strength posed peculiar problems, whereas in parts of the Southeast radical republicanism remained a powerful force.

In the alliance between the regime and the administration, the Emperor was hardly a silent partner. Had the *procureurs généraux* and the prefects had their way, for instance, universal suffrage would probably have been a casualty of the coup d'état. The Prince's refusal to distinguish between a *pays légal* and a *pays réel* prevented the sacrifice of 1848's greatest democratic gain. Although the neutralization of the traditional parties left a clear field for Napoleon III, the Empire could hardly pose as a national regime and still ignore fundamental demands associated with the left. Herein lay the dilemma of those who remained loyal to republicanism. Their program was absorbed, at least in part, by their hybrid opponent. The Empire simply replaced the Republic, and for that matter the republicans, as the instrument for achieving democracy. It all seemed very unfair. If, however, André Siegfried is correct in his assertion that the left is a movement larger than any particular party, the Bonapartist venture was legitimate. And indeed, the Second Empire clearly indicated that republicans held no monopoly over the forces of the left. Louis Napoleon proved to be far shrewder than Louis Philippe, and to the very end of the Empire, Napoleon III managed to divide the left whereas Louis Philippe did the very opposite. Orleanism never rallied the likes of an Alfred Darimon or an Emile Ollivier.

There were difficulties, however. Bonapartism's democratic qualities provided the possibility of an aggressive policy designed to replace completely the power of the local notables. Philippe Vigier, who makes the strongest case since Persigny and Cassagnac for a popular Bonapartism, argues that any attempt on the part of the regime to compromise with the notables was bound to fail.[12] Vigier

12. Philippe Vigier, *La Seconde République dans la région alpine,* II, 364–379.

recognizes, nevertheless, the serious difficulties involved in implementing such a program in any complete fashion. Decisions of the prefects generally had a conservative effect upon the posture of the regime. Although the administration could hardly ignore the meaning and power of universal suffrage and the need to acquire the adhesion of the departmental majority, the democratic impulse was frequently diluted. For Vigier the proper course of action was perverted (or at least not carried through to its logical conclusion) by the prefectoral corps, which tended to identify the Empire with the forces of order. Prefects like Janvier de La Motte, who built the Eure—until then a virtual fief of the Passys and the Broglies—into a stronghold of democratic Bonapartism by his shrewd bonhomie and continual banquets, were not numerous enough.[13]

Personnel also reflected the regime's difficulties in establishing an opening to the left. The government hoped to rally men of talent regardless of their previous commitments. Although it manifested a high degree of tolerance, the government recruited most ministers and major advisors from among ex-Orleanists. Indeed, these advisors had frequently been figures of some importance—e.g., Magne and Fould—in the echelons just beneath the top leadership. Others, such as Baroche, were associated with the liberal opposition of Odilon Barrot. Given the Emperor's dislike for Orleanists in general, this choice of personnel appears strange until one recalls the *ralliement* of many monarchists to the imperial cause during the Second Republic. Some ministers, on the other hand, were decidedly more progressive: this was the case with Fortoul and Billault, both of whose earlier sympathies for republicanism were well known. In the 1860s the ministry even included Victor Duruy. The more typical minister, however, was not Duruy, but Jules Baroche. Rightly or wrongly, Napoleon III expected the support of upper-class political figures in implementing his program.

In some respects the Empire's greatest strength became its major

13. John Rothney in his *Bonapartism after Sedan* argues that Bonapartism's political demise after 1870 arose from a similar problem: the conservative nature of the Empire's deputies. The failure to construct an imperial party of truly new men as progressive in outlook as the Emperor gave the party a right-wing coloration, thereby ultimately allowing republicans to capture France's political destiny.

weakness. France of the 1850s demanded a regime characterized by some ambiguities. The result, however, frequently led to a certain confusion of purpose. The Empire never established a clear enough political identity outside of its authoritarianism, and even that authoritarianism was theoretically temporary. Napoleon III necessarily tried to accomplish too many things; he in fact accomplished much, but the confusion never abated. Consider, for example, the fate of Duruy. A thoroughgoing republican who had voted for Cavaignac and cast a *no* ballot in the 1851 plebiscite, Duruy was a history professor indirectly introduced to the Emperor by Madame Cornu. The two men immediately established a rapport, as they discovered in one another a common attachment to democratic principles. Duruy also agreed with the Emperor that a regime based upon universal suffrage demanded a literate citizenry, and that this could be achieved only through a complete state system of education with schooling available to everyone. In 1863 Napoleon suddenly and unexpectedly appointed his friend Minister of Education, a post Duruy held until 1869. During those six years the minister succeeded in laying the groundwork for an all-encompassing state system of education. Difficulties nevertheless arose. Although the Emperor seldom interfered with Duruy's work, he gave the minister little positive support. With his distaste for administrative details, Napoleon III allowed his ministers a relatively free hand. For Duruy this proved a handicap, as he found himself isolated in the conservative Council of Ministers. At one point he complained to his secretary, Ernest Lavisse, that his greatest hope was to "convince the Emperor to plead the case of my poor budget against M. Fould," and that he wished "the Emperor would speak to me in a loud voice so that M. Rouher could hear."[14] Duruy's problems, moreover, did not end with Fould or Rouher; he soon provoked the hostility of the clergy, who were important participants in the government's feast of national reconciliation.

Nevertheless, Duruy wrought some important changes. The Emperor accepted in principle the establishment of obligatory and free

14. Ernest Lavisse, "Victor Duruy," p. 53. On Duruy, see also Lavisse, *Un Ministre, Victor Duruy*, and Jean Rohr, *Victor Duruy, ministre de Napoléon III*.

education, although the Council of Ministers did not and prevented its implementation. Sizable increases were tallied in the number of primary schools. Communes with already existing schools were pressured into removing fees, and a system of technical schools was established. Finally, Duruy instituted a program of girls' education, which prompted Bishop Dupanloup not only to attack Duruy in a pamphlet entitled *La Femme chrétienne et française*, but to warn Frenchmen that the history professor turned minister presented a threat to public morals. But a regime that counted upon the services of the Church and the services of messieurs Fould and Rouher could not easily institute a modern educational program.[15] Indeed, when clerical and conservative outrage forced Duruy to dismiss Renan from the Collège de France, the minister could only avenge his aggrieved sensibilities by appointing a Jew to the post and establishing one of his girls' schools in Dupanloup's diocese.

There were other problems confronting the regime. The Second Empire necessarily depended upon a high degree of popular consent. A recent and sympathetic observer of Bonapartism has rightly commented on the difficulties posed by such a demand.

> To maintain a regime that was "democratic without being republican, representative without being parliamentary, and at the same time authoritarian and popular," it was necessary to gather at the very least constant adhesion, if not unanimous acceptance, from extremely broad areas of public opinion. . . . The overwhelming result of the two plebiscites of 1851 and 1852 left no doubt as to the degree of acceptance. This initial enthusiastic welcome, however, had to remain intact, even strengthened, for the regime to preserve its assurance and stability. It was important that imperialism, at that point totally accepted, was not later questioned in the details of daily execution. In the long run, nothing would remain of its original capital if, over a six year period, the country reclaimed from the Emperor in bits and pieces what it had granted him *en bloc*.[16]

The regime, in fact, functioned smoothly enough as long as the traditional parties and their respective constituents disliked one

15. This point is made particularly well in R. D. Anderson, *Education in France, 1848–1870.*
16. Marcel Prélot, "La Signification constitutionnelle du second Empire," p. 45.

another more than they resented the restrictions of authoritarianism. The razing of the authoritarian structure, however, appeared to be inevitable with the passage of time, unless the regime was prepared to employ brute force, which it was unlikely to do. Although the hatreds and fears which had divided the left and right since 1848 never disappeared completely, they eventually subsided in the face of new developments and certain Bonapartist policies. At the same time, it became increasingly difficult to satisfy the groups that had welcomed the Empire as an escape from the frustrations of 1848.

For this reason and at the most obvious level, Bonapartism proved a failure. The resurgent strength of opposition parties testified to the Empire's inability to bring about a permanent reconciliation on the basis of national goals. The 1860s clearly demonstrated the vitality of both the republican and liberal traditions. No less a part of the Great Revolution's heritage than Bonapartism, liberals and republicans managed to maintain themselves in spite of one another and of Napoleon III. Bonapartist theory aside, the Second Empire never succeeded in co-opting or absorbing either of its competitors. Indeed, Bonapartism was finally reduced to joining the political scramble.

Because it was ideologically opposed to partisanship, the regime did experience some important successes that otherwise would have been impossible. For one, Napoleon III managed to impart a greater dynamism to the administration. Despite the force of continuity, the *fonctionnaire* of the Second Empire played a more positive role in the nation's economic and social development. Bonapartist administrative action in this respect had more in common with the *ancien régime* (and with the Fourth and Fifth Republics) than with the constitutional monarchies. The source of this dynamism was the innovative spirit of the regime and Napoleon's willingness to place progressively-minded people on the Council of State and government committees. Michel Chevalier was only the most obvious example. The Emperor also imparted his influence through his concern for pet projects. In the modernization of Paris, administrative conservatism was circumvented by the simple act of placing Baron

Haussmann in charge of the project. The ex-prefect of the Gironde shared the Emperor's ideas and became one of the regime's most effective servants.

Napoleon III also managed to override the influence of economic traditionalists and to stimulate new forces that otherwise would have been restrained. In one particular case, the 1860 trade treaty, the Emperor revealed himself capable of acting by fiat, with a small group of like-minded aides, in order to circumvent the influences of conservative interests. The methods employed in 1860, however, were not typical. Instead, the government, by legislative and administrative means, established a milieu suitable for those who saw rapid economic growth as the answer for developing a new France. The Saint-Simonians in particular proved important for this policy, and they provided the Emperor with a lever outside the usual structure of politics. As we shall see, the Empire's contributions in this area frequently escaped the notice of nineteenth-century historians accustomed to viewing history as primarily a question of political institutions. Recognition, for the most part, had to await the twentieth century.

At the political level, Bonapartism's rejection of party politics provided the possibility of evolution. Not absolutely identified with any particular traditional party, the regime was open to public pressures. This allowed for a political flexibility that Orleanism never attained. Napoleon III was fond of commenting that no one understood the times better than himself, and he recognized the force of new developments in the 1860s. His willingness to accept the existing climate of opinion indicated a certain degree of shrewd opportunism. When a condition of political neutralization no longer existed as it had in the decade following 1848, fundamental changes in policy became mandatory; the Emperor avoided a direct confrontation by accepting change. Liberalization may not have been painless, but it did take place. It also provided an experience until then unique: Frenchmen saw a regime become more liberal with the passage of time, whereas every one of the Empire's nineteenth-century predecessors had moved in the opposite direction.

Despite republican and liberal accusations that the Empire represented a period of discontinuity in French political evolution, the reality would appear otherwise. The Empire may have been a mistake, but it was not unhistorical. Gambetta was more correct than he realized when he said that the Empire represented a bridge between two republics. By blending the new with the old, the Empire overcame the tragic failures of the Second Republic, and established the political base associated with the Third Republic. More precisely, the Empire succeeded in weaving both liberalism and democracy into the French political fabric. Before the Empire, democracy and liberalism represented two distinct political traditions, and the inability of the 48ers to join them had destroyed the Second Republic.

Napoleon III did not totally repudiate liberal political forms even though Bonapartism certainly contained strong overtones of anti-parliamentarianism. Though restrained, the legislative power kept the right of discussion and veto over legislation. In a fashion resembling its redirection of the administration, the Empire merely reshuffled the relationship between the executive and legislative powers. There was no massive break with tradition. As Zeldin's valuable study clearly indicates, a strong thread of continuity linked the Empire with France's experience in constitutional monarchy. The legislature contained not only so-called new men, but "old men" as well, who held liberal political values and saw authoritarianism as a temporary refuge from the radical storm. The seeds of liberalization existed in the Legislative Body elected in 1852, since it included a large number of men accustomed to participating in politics. And in fact the legislature almost immediately grew restive under the supposed tutelage of the Council of State. For this reason there always remained the possibility of extending the legislature's prerogatives. The government ultimately had no choice but to follow such a policy, since the authoritarian regime proved too demanding for the Emperor. He had no option but to share his powers, and the logical choice for such sharing was the Legislative Body. Finally, as increasing segments of the population emancipated themselves from government tutelage, they naturally saw the legislature as the object of reform. The regime, by its very structure, sublimated most protest into demands for a mere reorganization of the executive-legislative relationship. Frenchmen meanwhile became accustomed to thinking in terms of parliamentary politics and the interplay of parties.

The Empire was indeed a hybrid regime, and herein was the source of its political contribution. Universal suffrage provided the government's basic political support, but it was usually manipulated to elect prestigious individuals willing to accept the new regime. Napoleon's authoritarian guarantee of order promised to provide what had escaped the 48ers. By preventing disorder, the government preserved the principle of universal suffrage and joined it to the Legislative Body. Within the confines of his own regime, the Emperor found the elusive formula that merged democracy and liberalism. He also influenced the marriage of the two traditions in a more indirect fashion. The government remained a strong force at the polls right up to and including the 1869 elections. The Empire never actually lost a general election nor its majority. Separately, liberals and republicans lacked the strength to raise an effective challenge on the electoral field. Their only choice was for moderates in both camps to forge an alliance based upon common principles. The government's very existence forced liberals and republicans together into a coalition known as the Liberal Union. By the 1860s universal suffrage had become an integral part of French political life, and liberals dared not deny it. Napoleon III had impelled them to recognize what they had rejected in 1848. Thiers was instructive of the point: during the 1869 electoral campaign in Paris, to the very people he had once called a vile multitude he now promised to comport himself as a good citizen deserving of their votes.

The Empire did more than educate liberals. Napoleon III, unlike the republicans whose attention was fastened upon the urban areas, understood the demands of universal suffrage. A democratic regime had no alternative but to seek the support of the peasantry; with few exceptions, the republicans of '48 never successfully attracted rural votes. To the very end, Napoleon III's candidates rolled up large majorities in rural districts. An exasperated Jules Favre stood up in the Legislative Body in 1863 and questioned the merits of universal suffrage, suggesting that only those able to read and write be allowed to vote. In his pamphlet entitled *Les Elections de 1863*, Jules Ferry vented republican wrath against the peasantry's supposed political stupidity. Later observers, frequently writing with an urban bias, have assumed with Ferry that an uneducated peasantry simply and doltishly followed the government's dictates. Recent scholarship suggests otherwise. Although Jacques Bonhomme may have lacked formal education, he generally possessed a fairly clear idea of his interests. The name Napoleon implied a guarantee of certain revolutionary values, and the Empire frequently provided a lever against the notables, who represented the most important force with which the peasantry had to contend. Prestigious and important individuals may have been chosen by the Empire as official candidates, but these individuals were not usually drawn from the most powerful local families. Universal suffrage rightly dismayed the notables because it allowed for the expression of popular sentiment. Duvergier bemoaned the plight of gentlemen everywhere when he told Senior:

> Among the peasants he [Napoleon III] retains his popularity. My relation, the Marquis de Joubert, a liberal, that is to say a monarchist, though he has done much for his neighbors, for their church, for their schools, for their roads, and indeed for themselves, is ill-treated by a Bonapartist municipality. Among other petty vexations, they have just driven a road through his meadows, useless for all purposes, except teasing him. He threatened to appeal.
>
> "We don't care about your appeal," they answered. "L'Empereur aime le peuple, et il nous donnera raison contre un bourgeois comme vous."[17]

Geographic electoral studies bear out Duvergier's fears. Votes for the Emperor were an expression of an agrarian democratic impulse particularly strong where peasants were already fairly independent and becoming more so. Siegfried's study of the West indicates that Bonapartism made its strongest appeal to small and middling peas-

17. Nassau William Senior, *Conversations with Distinguished Persons during the Second Empire*, I, 91.

ant proprietors who showed little love for the clergy.[18] Some observers have argued that the Empire marked a necessary apprenticeship in peasant political action. Similarly, it has been noted that
peasant votes were later transformed into votes for Radicalism, and
that the peasantry provided one of the new social strata for Gambetta's republic. Rather than emphasizing the peasantry's growing
political maturity, however, one might do better to argue that the
Empire provided an apprenticeship for the republican party. In
1848 republicans proved incapable of selling their program on any
vast scale to the peasantry, even though the revolution brought the
peasantry into French political life. Given its urban orientation, the
party failed to establish a national following. The result was a Legislative Assembly noteworthy for its lack of republicans. Napoleon III,
on the other hand, never ceased to draw peasant votes. The republican party, to challenge the Empire in a democratic fashion, had to
capture a part of this broad electoral base. In the process, republicans became a bit more realistic and less doctrinaire. The change
was formidable, and not surprisingly, it necessitated a new generation of republicans. During the Empire, Sainte-Beuve frequently
commented that Napoleon III's great contribution was to have rid
France of its previous regimes. He was more correct than he
realized.

18. André Siegfried, *Tableau politique de la France de l'Ouest sous la IIIe République*, pp. 479–482. Such conditions were not limited to the West. See, for instance, the essays concerning rural departments in Louis Girard, ed., *Les Elections de
1869.* G. Palmade writes of Bonapartist strength in the Gers: "The Gers is therefore
an area with an egalitarian social structure, largely inhabited by a population of
small peasant proprietors, theoretically independent, masters of their means of sub-
sistence, and apparently capable of freely expressing themselves" (p. 188).

Chapter II

The Opposition

Throughout the Second Empire historical thought remained the handmaiden of political theory. Because Bonapartism in its authoritarian form failed to provide a permanent political settlement, it likewise failed to replace its two major competitors, the republicans and liberals, who employed already tested historical theories to prove their points. In many respects the Bonapartist period witnessed a continual restatement of the political-historical arguments heard before 1848. Now, however, Napoleon III rather than Louis Philippe or Charles X was under attack. The disillusionment and confusion emanating from 1848, however, thoroughly discredited those associated with socialism, except for the Saint-Simonians with their peculiar relationship to the regime. Frenchmen heard little from those once involved in social romanticism; Daniel Stern, for instance, retired from politics to write a history of the people's failure.[1] Her friend, Pierre Leroux, was on Jersey with Victor Hugo, and the exiled Louis Blanc completed his history of the French Revolution. The Blanquists dabbled in a radically fashioned history during the 1860s, but their output was small and the social content remained subordinate to the considerations of revolutionary tactics. Frenchmen, of course, were well aware of the social question, but

1. Daniel Stern, *Histoire de la Révolution de 1848.*

they lacked the ideological means by which to deal with it once social romanticism had proven so hopelessly inadequate. In France— once the center of social theorizing—the focus became surprisingly political.

During the 1850s liberals were more obvious than republicans in defending their case against the Bonapartist denial of politics. Liberal prominence arose from the heavy casualties republicans suffered at the hands of the government, since liberal cadres were never seriously threatened or damaged. They were, however, peculiarly isolated, as liberal and notable figures of the highest level, such as Guizot or Odilon Barrot, established a wide distance between themselves and the new regime. The comte de Saint-Aulaire expressed their sentiments when he wrote of the regime that "it's the most absurd and abominable in the world."[2] There were nonetheless ironies in this reluctance to embrace Napoleon III. The Empire was partially operated by ex-liberals who suddenly felt the need for stronger government. Guizot must have watched with some chagrin while one of his leading protégés, the duc de Morny, wielded the power necessary for the coup d'état.

Much has been written about the failure of the Empire to gain the active support of the monarchists and liberal elite.[3] The withdrawal of the notable uppercrust from political activity, however, arose as much from necessity as from taste. Thiers, for instance, did not enjoy being removed from power. However, Napoleon III never disguised his distaste for the burgraves—particularly those who were Orleanists—and he showed little interest in including them in the imperial feast of reconciliation. To make matters worse, the Empire's relative, but important, downgrading of the legislative function could hardly appeal to men who had once played a prominent and even dominant role in French politics through their parliamentary

2. A. Prosper de Barante, *Souvenirs*, VIII, 27.
3. See, for instance, Michel Mohrt, *Les Intellectuals devant la défaite, 1870*. Mohrt's position could best be termed neo-Orleanist; he argued that the Empire was so thoroughly democratic that it necessarily alienated the traditional elite and thus broke an established French pattern which joined literary and political activity. *Intelligence* was separated from politics, and the result was 1870. Mohrt continued the argument by suggesting that the Third Republic followed the imperial pattern; hence 1940.

skill. Finally, liberal leaders were ill-equipped to meet the demands of universal suffrage. Isolated from the larger community, they proved unable to match Napoleon III's popularity or political clout—particularly in the countryside—and therefore predictably cited the dangers of a peasant-based democracy disruptive of traditional hierarchies. The liberal elite thus found itself unemployed. Accustomed to ruling, its members were reduced to mere spectators. Those of a Legitimist bent frequently responded by retiring to their country estates; Falloux, for instance, devoted his time to remodeling the family chateau at Bourg-d'Yré and raising prize beef cattle. The more urban oriented Orleanists, ever mindful of history, followed the precedent of Madame de Staël during the First Empire: they withdrew to their salons. At the comtesse d'Haussonville's and Madame Bertin's, evenings were spent criticizing government policy, lauding the good old days, making *bon mots* at the expense of the Empress, and bemoaning the bad taste of the imperial court.

Although unemployed, the liberal leadership was nevertheless occupied in what contemporaries called a *petite fronde*. This opposition was naturally articulate and even erudite. Orleanism in particular exerted an attraction upon men of letters, and liberals had long before established a strong literary tradition. Moreover, during the July Monarchy, liberal literati had gained control of important institutions from which they could not easily be dislodged. Despite 1848 and 1851, it was still possible to speak of a liberal establishment which, not surprisingly, operated in large measure through the written word.

Platforms were thus available. The government's balanced press policy provided the most obvious with the *Journal des débats,* a newspaper owned by the Bertins and whose support Guizot had guaranteed during the 1840s with regular subsidies. The *Débats* staff was heavily weighted with academicians, in both the American and French senses of the word. Contemporaries called it a *petite académie,* and it provided a recruiting ground for the larger one. Salvandy and Saint-Marc Girardin were members before 1851. In 1853 the journal's chief editor, Ustazade Silvestre de Sacy, joined the Academy's gathering of Immortals. He was followed by Prévost-

Paradol (1865), Alfred Cuvillier Fleury (1866), and Jules Janin (1870). The *Débats*, with its cast of stars, necessarily moved cautiously during the 1850s as the regime allowed only the most restrained journalistic criticism. To make its point, the *Débats* twitted the regime by lauding English political institutions without, however, daring to suggest they should be transported across the Channel.

The liberal Catholics—more specifically, Montalembert, Dupanloup, Falloux, etc.—managed to launch their own periodical by resurrecting in 1855 the *Correspondant*. More direct political references were possible in the literary columns of a *revue* than in a newspaper, as the former were outside the government's press system. The *Correspondant's* most celebrated article came from the pen of Montalembert and appeared in the issue of October 25, 1858. Entitled "Un Débat sur l'Inde au parlement anglais," the article unfavorably compared a supposedly servile France and its lack of liberal politics with a free England and its parliamentary liberties. Montalembert, however, was realistic enough to recognize that not everyone shared his convictions. He sardonically commented, for instance, that, "I do not pretend to convert those progressives who regard parliamentary government replaced for the better by universal suffrage, nor those optimistic politicians who profess that democracy's supreme victory exists in abdicating into the hands of a monarch the exclusive direction of the country's internal and external affairs." Montalembert likewise repeated the common liberal belief that equated the Empire with a caesarism which too easily emerged from Frenchmen's democratic jealousy of superior talents.

The French Academy, however, provided the most prestigious sounding board for liberal concern about political liberty and parliamentary institutions.[4] Although it represented no dangerous threat to the Empire, the Academy was annoying, to the point that Napoleon III could complain to Lord Clarendon about a conspiracy of

4. On the political role of the Academy, see in particular Pierre Sechaud, *L'Académie Française et le second Empire*, Daniel Oster, *Histoire de l'Académie Française*, and Robert Reichert, "Anti-Bonapartist Elections to the Académie Française during the Second Empire."

letters against his regime. Indeed, the Liberal Union of the 1860s could be said to have partially developed within the walls of the Palais Mazarin as Guizot successfully implemented a policy of choosing academicians on the basis of their political credentials. Individuals primarily known as Orleanists, Legitimists, liberal Catholics, and nondynastic liberals joined the famed gathering. Room was even found for the moderate republican, Jules Favre. In contrast, Théophile Gautier was rejected for no other reason than his friendship with Napoleon III. The Academy became a club for the lettered opposition, and its membership represented a list of the Empire's major liberal enemies. Particularly intriguing was the weight the Protestant Guizot gave liberal Catholics. Montalembert and the Legitimist Berryer entered in 1852. Two years later, Dupanloup was elected. The political credentials of the Broglies were impeccable and their familial association with Madame de Staël undeniable; father and son entered in 1855 and 1861 respectively. For services rendered to Dupanloup and fusionism, Falloux received a place in 1856. To express distaste for the regime's foreign policy, the academicians then opened their ranks to Lacordaire, the first member of the regular clergy so honored in two centuries. Finally, the comte d'Haussonville joined the Immortals in 1870.

Most important, the Academy provided a tribune from which authoritarianism could be subjected to a restrained but public criticism. Liberals possessed in the Academy their own private parliament which somewhat replaced the loss of a more meaningful public Assembly. Receptions became minor political events eagerly awaited by liberal society. Indicative of the Academy's alliance of liberal forces was the fact that speakers drew no distinction between the Restored and July Monarchies. Montalembert, for instance, told his distinguished audience that the liberal ideal had included the Restored and July Monarchies, both of which provided an unparalleled period of liberty, prosperity and security. Victor de Broglie, in his reception of 1856, lauded Louis Philippe and commented that his own election recalled the time when

> France congratulated itself in having conquered at great price a system of institutions in which the word was in some way the soul and life. . . .

> During this time, literature and politics marched together. A close alliance joined them . . . from which public acts, state papers, and official documents assumed a character of gravity and authority, sober good sense, a severe simplicity which commanded while enlightening, and raised itself to the level of history. . . . I am the last product of this free exchange between literature and politics, the last in order of time as in order of merit, and the last vestige of what no longer is.

The liberal elite engaged in a scholarship of sublimated politics. Although direct attacks against the Empire remained difficult, indirect barbs were easily employed. Given the Emperor's known admiration for great historical figures in general and for Julius Caesar in particular, any admiring words for Tacitus expressed an ill-disguised dislike for Bonapartism. Removed from their usual employment, liberals reverted to a behavior pattern established during the Restoration. Unable to guide the present, they retreated into the past with the hope of employing it to shape the future. The result was a vast outpouring of historical literature. It was, however, not a literature primarily descriptive of the Second Empire. To write of the existing regime was still a bit too dangerous, and liberals were more interested in reaffirming historical principles denied by the present.

One liberal historian assumed that 1848 was partly an accident, and partly the result of his colleagues' stupid refusal to grant him the political support he fully deserved. Ever unimaginative, Guizot found it impossible to believe that his principles needed any reevaluation whatsoever. Rather than returning to his unfinished history of fickle France, he again took up his work concerning wise and stable England. It was probably reassuring to know that a proper politics was practiced on the other side of the Channel, and Guizot, as in his earlier works, lectured his reluctant fellow citizens. Unfortunately, the lesson remained unfinished. Aiming for the magic year of 1688, Guizot failed to get beyond General Monk—all of which must have intrigued the comte de Chambord.[5] Guizot in any case learned as little from 1848 as Frenchmen learned from his his-

---

5. François Guizot, *Histoire du protectorat de Richard Cromwell et du rétablissement des Stuarts.*

tory books, as the volumes written after the mid-century revolution in no way differed in tone from those written earlier.

Thiers, on the other hand, at least somewhat changed his tone if not his earlier project, and could thus more directly harass the new Emperor. Having contributed to the rise of the Napoleonic legend, Thiers made amends by returning to his history of the Consulate and the Empire. This time Thiers had Napoleon III rather than Louis Philippe in mind. The first Napoleon was still treated as a towering figure of the Revolution, but Thiers now emphasized the tragedy that emerged from his denial of necessary limits. For those to whom the newest message was insufficiently clear, the author ended the last volume with the liberal maxim: "In this great life [of Napoleon I] where military leaders, administrators, and politicians can learn so much, it is now the turn of everyday citizens to learn something: that it is never necessary to deliver the country over to a man, no matter what man, no matter what the circumstances! In finishing this lengthy history of our triumphs and dreams, it is this last cry that escapes from my heart, a sincere cry which I would like to impress upon the heart of Frenchmen, in order to persuade them that it is never necessary to surrender liberty; and in order not to be exposed to such a surrender, never abuse liberty."[6] Thiers's history nevertheless remained what it was from the beginning—as much a chronicle of the author's political attitudes as a history of Napoleon I. As such, the history of the uncle became an evaluation of the nephew. Indeed, just as the writing of history replaced the 1851 loss of politics, politics later took up where history left off. The history of the Consulate and the Empire was finished in 1862, and the following year Thiers presented his candidacy for the Legislative Body.

The political content of the *Histoire* was great enough to reflect not only the author's present-mindedness, but his future intentions. Thiers pretty well indicated that he was no irreconcilable enemy of Napoleon III, and the latter understood the profits to be gained from certain professional accommodations. Thiers, for instance, was al-

6. Adolphe Thiers, *Histoire du Consulat et de l'Empire*, XX, 795–796.

lowed privileged access to the archives and the correspondence of
Napoleon I. Tapping the little man's huge vanity, Napoleon III in
1855 shrewdly referred to him in a speech from the throne as an
"illustrious and national historian." Despite disclaimers of embarrass-
ment, Thiers was pleased with the compliment. He was soon telling
Senior that Napoleon III, unlike his uncle, knew the merits of flexibility, and that it was obvious the Empire would survive much
longer than first anticipated. Volume twelve, finished a year later,
contained the observation: "The greatest consolation for being
nothing in one's country is to see the country be everything it should
be in the rest of the world."[7]

The efforts of Guizot and Thiers were hardly unique. Expressing
the liberal fetish for things English, Charles de Rémusat wrote a
Histoire d'Angleterre au dix-huitième siècle. An indefatigable Montalembert published *L'Avenir de l'Angleterre*, which assured its
readers that England's example proved beyond a doubt that liberty
emerged from aristocratic rule. Frenchmen, of course, were to take
note of the fact and long for the better days of Louis Philippe. For
the sake of liberal Catholicism, Albert de Broglie and Falloux joined
the chorus. The former's *L'Eglise et l'Empire romain au quatrième
siècle* argued that Christianity had saved pagan Rome from its own
shortcomings, and implied that nineteenth-century France was in
need of a similar cure. Falloux's pious effort was of more dubious
liberal value; in 1854 he brought out a new edition of his *Histoire
de Pie V* which provided an apology for the Inquisition and Saint
Bartholomew's Day.

The most meaningful products of this liberal barrage of historical
literature were the works of Baron Barante and Alexis de Tocqueville. The first's *La Vie de Royer-Collard*, despite its topical defense
of liberal principles, remains to this day the finest work on the
father of the French *doctrinaires*. As for Tocqueville, he was convinced that he had found a democratic direction in history, a direction he equated with equality, a leveling process, and the destruction of pluralism. Tocqueville then pessimistically set about to find

---

7. Ibid., XII, xxxix.

the origins of this development. He was, in a sense, searching for the forces that made the Second Empire possible. Tocqueville's conclusions attested to his integrity and independence of mind, but *L'Ancien régime et la Révolution française* was not as revolutionary as many have argued. Something of a *doctrinaire* and thoroughly shaped by the historical tradition of Madame de Staël, Tocqueville was also an intellectual disciple of Montesquieu. He believed that centralized authority absorbs islands of autonomy and independent action, and thus destroys liberty. He concluded that the centralizing monarchy of the *ancien régime* had implemented the basic policies associated with democratic rule. The democratic tradition therefore represented no fundamental break in the operation and function of the French state. Madame de Staël, of course, had once said much the same thing about the old Bourbon monarchy although she perceived the Revolution as a drama about the establishment of liberty. Liberals were no longer sure that this was necessarily the case.

In any event, politics had changed since the time of Madame de Staël. The old monarchy—and monarchism in general—was no longer so clearly identified with nonliberal political goals. Some liberals even forgot their earlier complaints against the Restored Monarchy. The liberal Duvergier de Hauranne, who had been a member of the subversive society called "Aide-toi, le ciel t'aidera" and who had welcomed the July Revolution, could write a *Histoire du gouvernement parlementaire en France* in which he asserted that the Restoration Monarchy had represented an integral part of the parliamentary tradition and French liberal politics. This observation earned Duvergier a membership in the Academy in 1870.

----•◄►•----

In defending their principles during the 1850s republicans faced far more serious handicaps than confronted the liberals. Republicans were reduced to near silence for a number of reasons, the most obvious being the strategy and strong-arm tactics of Bonapartism. Louis Napoleon's reestablishment of universal suffrage and his dissolution of a monarchist controlled Assembly threw republican ranks somewhat into disarray. The party's leadership, moreover, was literally proscribed following the coup d'état, and its cadres were shattered. To complicate matters, the failures of 1848 cast republicans into disrepute; the adventure only reinforced the old popular belief that republics end in disorder. In sum, the attempt to recapture the republican experience of the Great Revolution provided a compressed, but on the surface a surprisingly faithful, reproduction of the original handiwork. Republicans, their regime a mere three years old, found themselves in a premature 1799 that quickly brought an early 1804. It was all very embarrassing, and republican participants were understandably squeamish. Their accounts of the 1848 Revolution became massive excuses designed to explain away republican responsibilities—to the point, for instance, that Garnier-Pagès attributed practically every republican mishap to the machinations of devious Bonapartist agents.[8]

Suffering repression, humiliation, and disrepute, the republican party temporarily disappeared as an active political force. No contest was possible in the 1852 elections, and refusal to take an oath of allegiance precluded participation in the new politics of Bonapartism. In 1852, the only electoral opposition encountered by the regime was raised by the Legitimists. Republicanism ceased to exist within France aside from a few plots organized by isolated young radicals and disenchanted Italians. Until 1857, the history of the party centered not in France, but in England, Belgium, and Switzerland where various exiles had taken up residence.[9] This proved to be an extremely melancholy period in republican history. As is so frequently the case with exile communities, homesickness and isolation led to incestuous bickering. Mutual suspicions fed one another, and were increased by Napoleon III's offer to permit exiles to return on the condition they no longer engage in politics.

Republicans, like their liberal rivals, retreated from the debacle of 1848–1851 into history; though generally less erudite, theirs was for the most part a history more varied and interesting than its liberal

8. L. A. Garnier-Pagès, *Histoire de la Révolution de 1848.*
9. The best source for this history is I. Tchernoff, *Le Parti républicain au coup d'état et sous le second Empire.*

counterpart. At one level, republicans returned to the Great Revolution to find a wellspring of inspiration and to discover what had gone amiss. Blanc, for instance, finished his *Histoire de la Révolution française* in London. Edgar Quinet, for his part, lost much of his earlier faith in both the people and in an historical providence which would guarantee the emergence of democratic liberty. With 1851 and Louis Napoleon's enormous plebiscitary victory, Quinet retracted his very republican belief that the will of the people corresponds to the will of God. Indeed, he labeled the idea a popular and crude form of idolatry. Quinet, who had actively resisted the coup d'état and fled into exile, eventually settled in Switzerland. Thoroughly disgusted with the turn of events in France, he set about to investigate the causes of the 1848 failure, and found them in the Great Revolution.[10] He attributed France's dilemmas to the revolutionary inability to establish a real basis for liberty and freedom. He attributed one problem to the Jacobin use of violence which had sown the seeds of future violence and ultimately placed the Republic under the dictatorship of Napoleon I. The final result was the rise of another Bonaparte. Quinet, an opponent of Napoleon III and once an admirer of Napoleon I, now became a critic of Robespierre who was blamed for both Napoleons. Quinet's second criticism concerned the Great Revolution's failure to uproot Catholicism. Never very friendly toward the Church, he argued that the Revolution unfortunately did not become a Reformation, and France thus remained the victim of its Catholic past.

Blanc and Quinet not only retreated into the past, they were in a sense voices from the past. Other republicans, who were necessarily exiles if they were to write their history during the 1850s, confronted the regime directly by attacking its origin: the coup d'état. Rather than reconsidering at length the past, they went straight to the mark of contemporary history. They engaged in an activity that never directly occupied the efforts of the liberal monarchists, who were less grieved by the Second Republic's demise. Victor Hugo, a man for almost any season—his political career had encompassed

10. Edgar Quinet, *La Révolution*.

Legitimism, Orleanism, Bonapartism and republicanism in that order—led the attack and established an orthodox republican treatment of the Empire that accompanied the regime into its grave.[11] Indeed, Hugo's interpretation has been repeated to this very day.[12]

On December 2, Hugo's vanity may have been somewhat injured by Louis Napoleon's failure to consider the poet worth arresting. If such was the case, Hugo spent the next eighteen years repaying the Prince for his oversight. After a fruitless attempt to raise up a revolt on the part of the Parisian workers against the coup, Hugo fled to Belgium and then to England whereupon he settled on the Channel Islands; from there, he and some like-minded colleagues directed a literary barrage against Louis Napoleon.

In setting the tone for republican historians during the Empire, Hugo discovered a clever ploy by which to avoid the embarrassing problems raised by 1848. He ignored them. He made Napoleon III into something of a red herring in order to draw attention away from the failings of the Second Republic.

Hugo's specific contributions to republican historiography were *Napoléon le petit*, *Histoire d'un crime*, and *Châtiments*. The first of these, published in 1852, remains Hugo's most important and extensive evaluation of Louis Napoleon. The title itself carried an obvious comparison meant to separate the nephew from his uncle. Written in a heat of rage, Hugo's purple prose lashed the Prince and his regime, and Hugo assured his readers that the condemnations were those of a universal conscience demanding retribution.

Napoléon le petit was a long diatribe and a call to action which contained little analysis, much diffuse thought, and many contradictions. Hugo first endeavored to represent the Prince as a man who

---

11. On Hugo's political career, see Pierre de Lacretelle, *La Vie politique de Victor Hugo*. Hugo's activities during the 1848 Revolution and his break with Louis Napoleon in 1849 are treated in Elliot Grant, "Victor Hugo during the Second Republic." Grant's sympathies rest with the poet; Lacretelle's do not.

Besides Hugo's efforts, there were: Charles de Ribeyrolles, *Les Bagnes d'Afrique;* Pascal Duprat, *Les Tables de proscription de Louis Bonaparte;* Victor Schoelcher, *Histoire des crimes du 2 décembre;* and Hippolyte Magen, *Mystère du deux-décembre.*

12. See, for instance, Henri Guillemin, *Le Coup du 2 décembre.* Although Guillemin uses Marxian categories, his approach is primarily that of Hugo—both in its tone and in the fact that he reduces the coup d'état to an act of piracy.

worked solely for his own self-advancement, and who was able to gain power only by "cunning and cash," the latter of which allowed him to purchase an entourage of paid adventurers and the loyalty of the army. Louis Napoleon represented no meaningful tradition or system of values. Thus Hugo could maintain that the regime was praetorian in nature, having no alternative but to rest upon the power of armed might.

Napoléon le petit was a highly successful case of character assassination. Hugo purported to show that Louis Napoleon stole governmental power by committing a massive crime against the French nation. He wrote: "This crime is the embodiment of all crimes,— treason in its conception, perjury in its execution, murder and assassination in the struggle, spoliation, knavery, and theft in the triumph."[13] Unfortunately, Hugo was unable to make much sense of the new government, which partially accounted for his praetorian theory. Faced with the ambiguities of Bonapartist rule, Hugo fell into confusion and ultimately confused his readers. He vaguely alluded to the regime's middle-class support, and then acknowledged the Prince's hostility toward the bourgeoisie. He made, however, no attempt to explain the existence of these two apparently contradictory qualities. Hugo likewise had difficulty with Louis Napoleon's extraordinary ability to gain peasant support, an ability that threw so many republican observers into despair, and the poet's first response was to condemn the peasantry in terms matching those of Marx.

Hugo nevertheless assured the reader that history is both meaningful and moral because Providence or God—like Guizot he used the words interchangeably—guarantees the final direction of history. It remained the historian's task to explain the relationship of specific events to the final goals of the cosmic process. Thanks to an historical guarantee, Europe since the sixteenth century had experienced a vast movement toward human emancipation, a movement that reached its greatest strength in 1789, and once again reappeared in 1848. Bonapartism became the latest political manifestation of the

13. Victor Hugo, *Napoléon le petit* in *The Complete Works*, XVI, 175.

forces of reaction which opposed the necessary march of progress. Fortunately, this opposition to history's movement meant Louis Napoleon's prompt disposal; Hugo believed the regime could not endure beyond a few months or at the very most, three years.

The *Histoire d'un crime*, written in 1852, was only published twenty-five years later when Hugo, then a republican senator, set about to warn Frenchmen of the dangers of Marshal MacMahon. In the *Histoire*, Hugo developed at great length a particular point he had made in *Napoléon le petit*. The former work, however, contained an introduction to the latter, with Hugo writing that he "has adopted the plan of a strict criminal enquiry; he has, so to speak, constituted himself the judge, and cited himself to appear at the bar." It should be added that the presentation of history as a criminal trial also involved the designation of Hugo himself as prosecutor. There was little chance of an impartial hearing, and Hugo admitted as much.[14]

In the *Histoire d'un crime*, Hugo described the coup as a three act play: ambush, struggle, and massacre. The scenario for the first act was the dissolution of the Assembly, the arrest of representatives, etc. Although Hugo admitted the immediate reluctance of the Parisian population to rise up in opposition, he added that the Committee of Resistance, formed by Assembly republicans, soon succeeded in gathering popular support. In the struggle or second act of the coup, Louis Napoleon began to lose ground to the forces of legality. To maintain themselves, the fomenters of the conspiracy against the Republic plied the army with cash and wine; drunken troops then engaged in an orgy of indiscriminate killing that terrified Paris into submission. Sheer wanton repression, in short, saved the coup d'état.

A felon who broke his oath, Louis Napoleon compounded the crime by instigating acts of murder to guarantee that his first felony would have no legal consequences. The third act of the coup, then, involved the terrorization of Paris. Hugo, as a literary *procureur*

---

14. "Impartiality is a singular sort of virtue, and Tacitus was without it. Woe be to the writer who would remain impartial in presence of the bleeding wounds of Liberty!" *Ibid.*, p. 250.

général, purported to show the regime for what it was by portraying its origins.

Hugo repeated, in short, the claim in *Napoléon le petit* that the Empire had no real historical content or relevance. The work of criminals, it necessarily represented a blank space in French history. The *Châtiments,* probably the longest tirade ever put to verse, continually sounded the same theme.

> Tu règnes par Décembre et tu vis sur Brumaire,
> Mais la Muse t'a prise, et maintenant c'est bien,
> Tu tressailles aux mains du sombre historien.
> Pourtant, quoique tremblant sous la verge lyrique,
> Tu dis dans ton orgueil: "Je vais être historique!"
> Non, coquin; le charnier des rois t'est interdit.
> Non, tu n'entreras pas dans l'histoire, bandit!
> Haillon humain, hibou déplumé, bête morte,
> Tu resteras dehors et cloué sur la porte.

As Providence would have it, the Empire finally toppled, though not as early as the predicted three years. The poet-historian returned to France in 1870, and added a fourth act to the *Histoire* entitled "The Fall." Hugo serenely argued that the Emperor, not France, was responsible for 1870. September 4 proved that retribution was in the very nature of things. Of Sedan he wrote: "The knot he tied on December 2, 1851 was untied on September 1, 1870. The carnage on the Boulevard Montmartre and the capitulation of Sedan are, we insist, two parts of a syllogism. Logic and justice are balanced. His terrible destiny was to begin with a black flag of massacre and to end with the white flag of dishonor."[15]

Providence aside, Hugo never revealed very much about the character of Napoleon III's Bonapartism. Mystified by their own failure in 1848, most republicans found it particularly difficult to comprehend their replacement. Their own inadequacies blinded

15. Victor Hugo, *Histoire d'un crime* in *The Complete Works,* XVI, p. 151. Another republican expression of history as a morality play is to be found in the role of the Roman question which supposedly prevented the Empire from gaining an Italian alliance during the Franco-Prussian War. Thus the Roman Expedition of 1849 was joined to the debacle of 1870. The most important expression of this point of view is that of Emile Bourgeois and E. Clermont, *Rome et Napoléon III.*

them to many of the Empire's greatest accomplishments. The current of protest from which republican historiography emanated could do little more than engage in a vindictive tirade. To do otherwise—to have recognized the meaningful qualities of the Empire—would have too clearly revealed the mid-century republican failure. For the moment, that proved too painful, and it was far easier to rail against a criminal conspiracy that erased republican responsibility. Sheer rage transcribed into words masqueraded as history.

Within France there were no public echoes to *Napoléon le petit* or the *Châtiments* during the 1850s. The quiet did not mean, however, that republicanism was dead. Nor, for that matter, did the government try to kill it. In its effort to reduce political parties to imperial tendencies, the government allowed the moderate expression of republican sentiments providing the regime itself was not subject to attack. Just as liberals retained their *Journal des débats*, republicans had their *Siècle* with its 36,000 subscribers. Edited by Léonor Havin, the journal tread a cautious path and yet managed to provide a counterweight when the government leaned very far toward the right. Rather than discussing immediate politics, however, Havin devoted his volumes to a philosophical defense of progress and modernity. Clericalism also came under frequent attack, much to the anger of Veuillot, while the democratic principles of '89 received favorable comment. Mérimée spoke for many when he commented that it was possible to live tranquilly only if one did not read the *Siècle*. Indeed, the journal so outraged conservative opinion that prefects pleaded for its suppression and people wrote unsolicited letters to the government demanding that something be done, while at the Council of Ministers, Billault's colleagues requested that he take a harder line against what the Ministry of the Interior itself acknowledged to be the *Siècle*'s "system of perfidious allusions."[16]

During the Empire, republicanism suffered from numerous weaknesses, not the least of which were its own divisions. In the 1850s the movement was small, and republicans necessarily ignored their

16. Archives Nationales, Ministry of Interior, Dossier *Siècle* (F18 417).

differences in order to form a solid front against the common enemy. The luxury of disagreement could not be afforded; by the 1860s the situation had changed. As republicanism revived and the Empire was liberalized, the party again broke into several groups and the question of tactics proved particularly troublesome. Moderates, such as Favre and Simon, had become accustomed to working with the liberal opposition. After having experienced success in pushing the Empire toward liberalization, they were anything but irreconcilable. Some, like Ollivier and Darimon, went so far as to attach themselves to the regime in order to reshape it accordingly. Less amenable republican groups employed the freedoms of the 1860s to contest the legitimacy of Bonapartist institutions. The most radical of these were the Blanquists, a circle primarily consisting of students such as Paul Lafargue and Charles Longuet. The Blanquists were the first to make their effects felt, and hoping to lay the basis for future discontent and activism, the group launched its own journal, the *Candide*. To avoid the press law, the journal dealt with historical and religious matters, and its columns were filled with praise for the most radical aspects of the Great Revolution.

The Blanquists were not alone in their glorification of the revolutionary and radical tradition. Ernest Hamel, the friend of Gambetta, redeemed his earlier enthusiasm for the coup d'état by publishing a 600-page *Histoire de Saint-Just* and a three-volume *Histoire de Robespierre*. Political history of this genre, however, was the exception, at least insofar as Gambettists and like-minded republicans were concerned. Gradual political liberalization and relaxation of the controls over the press gave rise to more direct republican participation in French political life. As a corresponding development, republicans hostile to the regime began engaging the regime in a less circuitous fashion. When the gradual liberalization of the press system was crowned with the 1868 press law, republican journalism and history became indistinguishable. There was a sudden plethora of republican journals, from Ernest Picard's *Electeur libre,* which remained on the edge of *ralliement,* to Delescluze's revolutionary *Réveil* and Rochefort's *Lanterne.* Republicans even managed to found their own *Correspondant:* the *Revue politique.* Relatively moderate in tone, its contributors included Spuller, Gambetta, and Taxile Delord. Through these and other periodicals, republicans—who had refused to rally or were reticent about doing so—launched a full-scale offensive against the regime, and generally returned to the themes established by Victor Hugo.

The first major salvo in this attack came from the pen of Eugène Ténot. An editor of the *Siècle*, which had become more aggressive following the death of Havin, Ténot had earlier been associated with the Blanquists, and then had moved into the more moderate, though still irreconcilable, camp. In 1868, with his *Paris en décembre*, Ténot reaffirmed Hugo's argument that Louis Napoleon's Empire was primarily the product of a military act that suppressed meaningful resistance. Moderate in tone, the book avoided Hugo's fantasies about secret graves, bayonetings, and drunken troops; Ténot even admitted that the Paris workers were noticeably reluctant to defend the Republic, and that the shooting on the Boulevard Montmartre had probably occurred because the troops panicked when insurgents had fired upon them. The book nevertheless had a tremendous impact, and immediately went through six editions. The Gambettist Arthur Ranc correctly described the situation when he said that *Paris en décembre* was more than a book: it was a political act. And in fact it was a conscious attempt to remind Frenchmen of the regime's illegal origins. As the author himself wrote: "Seventeen years have passed since December 2nd. A whole generation has grown up, a generation which does not know and cannot know how this celebrated coup d'état—origin of the regime under which we live—was accomplished."[17] Ténot had struck the regime on its Achilles' heel; Napoleon III himself had admitted to Eugénie his bad conscience over the coup and once confided to Nisard that it was no easy task to justify December 2nd.[18]

Paris en décembre stimulated further activity. Ténot's earlier and until then ignored *La Province en décembre* immediately became a

17. Eugène Ténot, *Paris en décembre*, p. vi.
18. Maurice Paléologue, *The Tragic Empress*, p. 24; Emile Ollivier, *L'Empire libéral*, II, 523. Bonapartist defenses of the coup d'état nevertheless existed. See P. Mayer, *Histoire du 2 décembre*, and Paul Belouino, *Histoire d'un coup d'état*.

best-seller. *La Province* argued with convincing simplicity that provincial resistance to the coup had been purely legal and motivated by nothing but a spontaneous desire to preserve republican political forms. Ténot denied the Bonapartist argument that France had been rescued from a premature *jacquerie*. As in Paris, the Empire established itself only by employing force against those prepared to defend the constitution.[19] Ténot's greatest influence, however, was upon contemporary political developments in Paris. In a sense, he set into motion a living history. *Paris en décembre* had mentioned the death of Baudin, a republican deputy killed on a barricade while resisting the coup d'état. Until then a forgotten incident, it was dramatized by Delescluze and Peyrat in their respective newspapers, the *Réveil* and the *Avenir national*. The two organized a public subscription to raise a statue to the fallen deputy over his grave, which

19. Eugène Ténot's *La Province en décembre* was first published in 1865. I have used the third edition. Ténot's argument concerning the provinces became a generally accepted republican truth which only now is beginning to be questioned by scholars. Philippe Vigier writes of the Alpine region, where insurrection and repression were heavy, that secret societies played a major role in the resistance. The societies, however, were poorly organized beyond the local level and had trouble coordinating their activities; hence, the disjointed character of the resistance, a quality that republicans have used to assert the spontaneity of those who acted against the coup. Vigier also finds that the resistance was neither a *jacquerie* in any full sense nor was it purely motivated by political considerations. Radical republicans, drawing support from peasants, were organizing for 1852 in order to foment revolutionary change. When the coup took place, they resisted with the intent of saving the Republic and then pushing it toward a *démo-soc* position. It was not, therefore, a simple case of defending the status quo against Louis Napoleon. It was instead the "inauguration at the local level of a veritable dictatorship of the montagnard party, on the order of the revolutionaries of 1793." See Philippe Vigier's *La Seconde République dans la région alpine*, II, 331. Vigier concludes that government repression in the Alpine region was anything but happenstance; it was, in fact, rationally directed against these secret society activists and particularly the leaders (pp. 319–339). Christianne Marcilhacy's "Les Caractères de la crise sociale et politique de 1846 à 1852 dans le département du Loiret," reaches similar conclusions for a different area. Similarly, Maurice Agulhon in *La République au village* argues that the serious uprisings in the Var clearly had a social content related to economic difficulties. However, Ted Margadant, an American scholar, has recently written that Vigier underestimates the political factors involved in at least one department. His "Modernisation and Insurgency in December 1851" portrays economic considerations in the Drôme as giving rise to political impulses that assumed a life of their own through conspiratorial organizations. Margadant's arguments also parallel the conclusions of Roger Price, *The French Second Republic*, who reaffirms the military character of government repression in the Midi while treating the uprisings as both political and social in inspiration. Finally, and for a survey of the more traditional arguments, see Maurice Agulhon, "La Résistance au coup d'état en province."

was conveniently rediscovered for the event. The hope was twofold:
to embarrass the regime with a granite monument of accusation
against the coup d'état and to arouse further public excitement in
the wake of Ténot's books. The gambit proved more effective than
expected. Conservative and moderate journals joined the subscription and pushed it beyond the boundaries of republicanism. The last
political act of a dying Berryer was to contribute his royalist francs
to the project. The government managed to ride out the storm, but
not before its own miscalculation raised Gambetta into a public
figure of major proportion. Pinard, the Minister of Interior, foolishly
brought charges against Delescluze for troubling the public peace.
He was defended by Gambetta who was, until then, relatively un-
known outside certain republican circles. A presiding judge of Orleanist sympathies allowed the defense to thunder against the
illegality of the coup, and thus turn the trial into an eloquent con-
demnation of the regime.

Still, it all came to naught. Republicans were divided amongst
themselves, and the more moderate ones had obviously joined their
destinies with the liberals in accepting a liberal Empire. Many
feared the dangers of radicalism more than they disliked the accommodations involved in making peace with Napoleon III. Furthermore, once the journalistic wave passed in 1868, it became increasingly obvious that France was not in a revolutionary mood, a fact
that became even more evident with the 1870 plebiscite. As a result,
republicans continued their drumbeat of literary opposition with a
new intent in mind. They now campaigned for the 1869 elections and
for the plebiscite of the following year, when republicans were thrown
on the defensive. Ténot, for instance, tried to call attention to another period of imperial heavy-handedness. He and Antonin Dubost
described the operation and effects of the Law of General Security,
passed during the repression that followed the Orsini bomb plot.[20]
Ténot's new effort was indicative of another development in republican historical mindedness. For the first time republicans began

20. Eugène Ténot and Antonin Dubost, *Les Suspects en 1858.* For a more recent
treatment of the 1858 action see Vincent Wright, "La Loi de sûreté générale de
1858."

to focus their attention upon considerations beyond the Empire's origins. Taxile Delord, another editor of *Siècle*, in 1869–1870 published the first two volumes of his *Histoire du second Empire*, a work that was temporarily interrupted by the unexpected catastrophe of 1870.[21]

Ténot was peculiar in his moderate tone and his scrupulous attempt to establish the facts of a particular case. The Gambettist Spuller was far more typical of republicans who tried to assess the Empire during the 1860s. Writing a *Petite Histoire du second Empire* to advise voters to cast a *no* ballot in the 1870 plebiscite, Spuller launched into a diatribe. He apparently foresaw the possibilities of a Bonapartist victory, and replied by employing both Hugo's basic argument and his tone. Bonapartism, he argued, represented the most dangerous threat to republicanism because it was successful in gathering popular support through fraudulent methods. In Spuller's own words, the regime was a "hybrid mixture of democracy and caesarism—which suffocates liberty while appearing to serve it—a bastard and corrupt system of government, which has no other restraint than the personal will of the Prince who operates under the cover of popular consent."[22] Spuller, like Hugo, could not account for the Empire's longevity nor for its apparent popular acceptance. Irreconcilable republicans, in short, had not yet escaped the restrictions of either Hugo's rhetoric or his limited analysis. Nor would they succeed in doing so until later. For the moment, the stakes were too high.

21. Delord's work is discussed in the following chapter.
22. The *Petite Histoire* is reproduced in E. Spuller, *Histoire parlementaire de la seconde République suivie d'une petite histoire du second Empire*. The quotation is from page 341.

Chapter III

Traditional Statements

Napoleon III's reputation suffered irreparable damage as a result of 1870. In March of the following year, the National Assembly officially declared the Emperor "responsible for the ruin, the invasion, and dismemberment of France." As an indication of national sentiment, the editors of the *Grand Larousse dictionnaire* took over Hugo's cry of Napoleon the Little and expressed confidence that he would be Napoleon the Last. With the aid of physiology, they explained how a single man could have led a whole nation astray. The editors described the Emperor as a peculiar type known as a "lymphatico-nerveux," and for the uninitiated, the *Grand Larousse* contained the following explanation:

> Where the nerves dominate, the mind is quick, comprehensive, rich in projects; the imagination inclines toward pleasure.
>
> If it is the lymph [that dominates], the mind is slow, and the senses are dull . . .
>
> Suppose that these elements are united [as in the case of Napoleon III]: from their fusion arises a new character which shares in the two principles and modifies the one with the other. Then a man is both intelligent and numb, rash and calculating, modest and dull, quick and slow, sensual and insensible, mystical and skeptical, curious and indifferent, inconsistent and tenacious, indiscreet and secretive, credulous and scornful, affable and distant, unyielding and irresolute, stuttering and verbose . . .

The editors confirmed popular belief that Napoleon III's many-sided character confused Frenchmen and that he fell victim to the contradictions of his own personality and dragged an unsuspecting France into ruinous defeat.

Both republicans and liberals echoed the attack, and their criticisms carried a moral judgment. Sedan became the price of tyranny, with republicans emphasizing the crime of December 2, and liberals emphasizing the dangers incurred by a community foolish enough to ignore its natural leadership. Both groups attacked the Empire's frivolity, and accused the regime of having corrupted the nation and destroyed national strength. For republicans, the argument dated from the time of the Empire, as indicated by E. Pelletan's pamphlet of 1862, *La Nouvelle Babylone*, which emphasized the ill effects of financial speculation and material progress. Liberals, on the other hand, joined their despair over 1870 with previous doubts concerning 1848 and the Second Empire. Prévost-Paradol's *La France nouvelle* (1868) was prophetic of things to come; Paradol questioned the future of liberal political institutions in the face of a rising democracy, and doubted continued French predominance in world affairs. After 1870, Renan's *La Réforme intellectuelle et morale* spoke of the same doubts, which by that time had become little more than liberal commonplaces.

Following 1870, Frenchmen resumed their traditional debate on how the community should be politically organized. The discussion, amongst other things, provided a restatement of the liberal and republican cases against the Empire. These arguments were transcribed into historical form and became part of the older discussion concerning the Great Revolution and the nature of French history. While one of these efforts, Taxile Delord's *Histoire du second Empire* was of no great merit, another, Pierre de La Gorce's multivolume work of the same title, has rightly been called a classic.[1] Finally, Emile Ollivier published his provocative and highly personal *L'Empire libéral*. Frequently underrated—probably because Ollivier's

---

1. I have used the twelfth edition of Pierre de La Gorce's *Histoire du second Empire;* the seven-volume work was originally published during the years 1894–1905.

critics never bothered to read it—*L'Empire libéral* was of far greater merit than is generally recognized.

In their own fashion, the three authors were products of the imperial period. They all lived under the Bonapartist regime, and each employed history to justify the political commitments he carried from the Empire into the Republic. As such, all three were dealing with issues raised by the Bonapartist regime, but issues nonetheless relevant to the Third Republic. Even Ollivier, who was more than a mere defender of Napoleon III, had much to say about republican institutions. In a fundamental sense, however, the three multivolume works represented nothing new. They were extensions of the traditional arguments that emerged from the period following 1815. Insights were astute or nonexistent, the tone moderate or emotional, depending upon the particular author. There was nothing approximating a new approach to the basic material. For each writer, Clio remained a creature of the old politics.

Taxile Delord

Born in Avignon in 1815, Taxile Delord began his career as a journalist of the Midi before moving into the upper echelons of the republican party. He first wrote for the mildly Orleanist journal, the *Sémaphore*, which attracted the progressive youth of Marseille during the 1830s. A liberal Protestant background guaranteed his anticlericalism, and he soon became a member of the republican party and a friend of Demosthenes Ollivier. In the late 1830s Delord moved to Paris and by 1842 had become editor-in-chief of the *Charivari*, the iconoclastic and left-wing journal made famous by Daumier's caricatures. During the Empire, the journal became particularly well known for its criticism of Parisian worldliness and corruption, a theme that later reappeared in Delord's *Histoire du second Empire* and which apparently influenced Zola's treatment of the imperial era.[2] Meanwhile, Delord became a prominent figure in Parisian republican gatherings; he was, for instance, a good friend

2. Roger Ripoll, "L'Histoire du second Empire dans *La Curée*." Ripoll suggests

of Jules Simon, a regular visitor to the salon of the comtesse d'Agoult, and a frequent guest at the home of Emile Ollivier.

Although Delord originally intended to make his mark in literature, he was inevitably drawn to republican politics; during the 1850s, however, he was not an irreconcilable opponent of the imperial regime. A close friend of Havin, who saw much good in the Empire, Delord left the *Charivari* in 1858 to become literary and then political editor of the *Siècle*. Delord's own articles for the journal primarily involved literary criticism, and he soon gained some notoriety for his insulting attacks upon Sainte-Beuve.[3] As political editor, he guided the *Siècle* in its defense of the government's foreign policy and in its affirmation of anticlericalism, all of which brought a series of clashes and a lawsuit with Bishop Dupanloup. Like Quinet and other republicans, Delord identified progress with the destruction of Catholicism, and he viewed the Reformation as a source of democratic inspiration. For these and similar reasons, Delord also played an active role in progressive Protestant circles that unsuccessfully challenged Guizot's conservative influence in the French synod.

During the 1860s Delord edged closer to the republicans who thoroughly opposed the Empire, and he broke with Ollivier in 1863. With Havin's death, he and Ténot took charge of the *Siècle* and quickly moved the newspaper toward an editorial position openly antagonistic to the regime, and at one point, Delord even joined the staff of Alphonse Peyrat's *Avenir national*. Delord, however, was no revolutionary, and he returned to the *Siècle*. A supporter of the Liberal Union, he belonged to the advanced contingent that demanded republican adherence to legal methods.

---

that because the republican party drew its leadership and literary spokesmen from the petite bourgeoisie, it was ideologically unprepared to confront France's economic development and the accompanying social difficulties. The attitude of the party was that of a group, "that resents the pressure of change brought to French society by the rise of capitalism and that remains blind to the real contradictions of this society." For Ripoll, then, the corruption theme expressed a petit bourgeois concern over status and represented an attempt to confuse real political-social issues in a cloud of moral, classless republicanism.

3. Delord's literary criticism for the *Siècle* is collected in Taxile Delord, *Les Troisièmes Pages du journal Le Siècle*.

Delord's early ideas revealed him as a man of '48. He shared the normal assumptions of the 1840s, particularly in respect to foreign policy and the historical role of the first Bonaparte, and during the mid-century revolution Delord openly supported Ledru-Rollin. He was, however, one of the few republicans of that vintage to shift successfully from pre-1848 attitudes to the opportunistic radicalism that did so much to establish the Third Republic. Furthermore, Delord took part in the republican offensive that began in 1868. While the *Siècle* supported the subscription to raise a monument to Baudin, Delord presented his candidacy in the Lot and Vaucluse for the elections of 1869. His vote-gathering abilities apparently left something to be desired, and he was defeated in both districts on the first round. Meanwhile, he began writing his *Histoire du second Empire,* and the following year actively campaigned for a *no* vote in the plebiscite confirming the liberal Empire.

Like most republicans, Delord was caught unawares by the events of 1870. To make matters worse, he was burdened with the demands of a long desired position as deputy (he had also run in the elections of 1857 and 1863; the Vaucluse finally elected him to the Assembly in 1871) and an unfinished history of the Second Empire. He fulfilled both tasks. The *Histoire* was enlarged from a projected three to six volumes, and transformed into a general warning against the dangers of tyranny. The work nevertheless failed to establish the author's reputation with the voters of Apt, and in the elections of 1876 they retired him on the first round of a three-way race. The republican journalist turned historian and deputy died the following year.

The *Histoire* is actually two separate books, written under different conditions, and with different objectives in mind. The first, inferior to the second, briefly discussed Louis Napoleon before 1848, the problems of the Second Republic, and the authoritarian Empire of the 1850s. The projected third volume was to deal with the 1860s. The events of 1870, however, forced Delord into an unexpected reevaluation as the Empire's success during the 1850s suddenly seemed less important than the difficulties of the following decade. A new situation called for a new book, and Delord wrote it. On the other hand, nothing was done with the first two volumes; they were left intact, and neither revised nor shortened. Delord plunged ahead as if to imply that his earlier observations had once and for all settled the problem of the 1850s. As for Volume III, it was inflated, until it became Volumes III, IV, V, and VI.

Although the two books of two and four volumes respectively were linked by an obvious dislike of the Empire, history written by an opposition journalist was not identical to history written by a loyal republican deputy. For instance, none of the various opposition fantasies which were frequently found in the first book appeared in the last four volumes. Before 1870, Delord suggested that the Empire rested upon twin agents of despotism: a permanent army and a centralized bureaucracy. Republicanism of course would remove these institutions, so that liberty and freedom might better flourish. The later volumes conveniently ignored such issues, since the new government had no intention of dismantling the administration nor of establishing a defense system patterned after the Swiss militia.

Aside from blackening the Empire's reputation, it appears doubtful Delord knew exactly what he hoped to accomplish when he started writing the *Histoire*. The first two volumes were noteworthy for their lack of direction; indeed, a failure to include an introduction indicated that Delord had no clear idea of what he was about. Lacking a precise goal, the author never discriminated between the relevant and the irrelevant. He wandered about piling trivia higher and higher, and he followed no pattern except that of chronology. The result was a case study of narrative history at its very worst. To take one example, Delord provided copious information about Napoleon III's marriage and wedding ceremony. The two volumes also failed as political history. Although he assured the readers that the Empire represented a form of tyranny, Delord never explained its operation or how it was organized. The constitution of 1852 received little attention and virtually no analysis; Delord likened the

Legislative Body to a *conseil général* appointed by the administration and placed under the control of the regime's "workhorse," the Council of State. This, of course, was old hat and hardly informative.

The only question addressed with any consistency in the first book concerned the failure of 1848 and the ensuing success of Louis Napoleon. In explaining the Republic's failure, Delord blamed the monarchists; to destroy the Republic, they had allied with Louis Napoleon and in the process destroyed liberty. Delord nonetheless recognized the inadequacy of this explanation, and he later confronted the problem from a different perspective. Not wishing to emphasize the June Days, the author commented that confusion, rather than disorder in the streets, had ruined the experiment in democratic liberty. The political and intellectual inheritance of the 1840s was so diverse that Frenchmen lost their way in a maze of republicanism, democratic Catholicism, socialism, etc. Delord had a point, of course, but he failed to explain why the confusion should have led to a resurgence in Bonapartism. He did, however, acknowledge the obvious attraction that Bonapartism exerted in the election of December 10, but weakly attributed it to a popular ignorance of both the revolutionary heritage and the nature of history. He wrote:

> The Napoleonic idea consists of two elements: bonapartism and imperialism. The one represents dictatorship exercised to the profit of the people; the other, the series of civil and political institutions established by the Emperor Napoleon I. Bonapartism has never existed except as an aspiration for the uneducated classes . . . Bonaparte did nothing for the people; the people frightened him when it was not in uniform . . . The Revolution had been made against a greedy and extravagant monarchy, against a corrupt nobility, against an intolerant clergy, against censorship, *lettres de cachet*, the *corvée*, ignorance and misery. Bonaparte restored all this. The people believed that Bonaparte had really destroyed the institutions of the old regime, whereas he had only changed their name. The people did not know that the Revolution was preceded in history by the Renaissance, by the Reformation, by the eighteenth century.[4]

The assertion that Bonapartism represented a disguised form of counterrevolution arising from popular ignorance unfortunately

---

4. Taxile Delord, *Histoire du second Empire*, I, 120–121.

raised another problem: Delord came within an ace of denying popular sovereignty.

The second book and last four volumes of the *Histoire* proved more satisfactory than the preceding volumes, simply because Delord found a more coherent theme. Despite continued obsession with trivia, Delord underlined the republican truism that the Empire could never redeem itself. The crime of December 2 made true liberalization impossible and the whole idea of a liberal Empire was an attempt to square the circle. Accordingly, Volume III began with the reforms of 1860 which Delord summarily dismissed as the first act in a ten-year comedy. By the last volume, he had written off the liberal Empire as a mere facade for authoritarianism, and he refused to grant that there had been any transformation whatsoever in the regime's character.

Delord's limitations as an historian, excluding his unimaginativeness, were the result of an absolute antagonism toward the Empire. Because Delord could not accept the Empire's relevance, his own *Histoire* was largely irrelevant. Instead of describing the dynamics of Bonapartism, Delord preferred to emphasize the impact of tyranny upon the nation's moral fabric. Indeed, this theme pervaded all six volumes, and Delord discussed the regime's efforts in public works and economic development only within the context of moral decay. Except for the evils incumbent in the loss of national territory, and a temporary national decline into tyranny and decadence, the Empire apparently vanished without a trace in 1870. The republican historian denied everything and therefore explained nothing. He did, however, deserve a prize for perseverance. It was no small feat to write two thousand pages of history devoted to the proposition that the very subject of that history was worthless.

Delord never really understood what the Empire accomplished, nor did he even try to do so. In a similar fashion, the accomplishments and careers of the regime's personnel were ignored. Haussmann, for instance, was merely labeled a second-rater deserving no real attention. In an even less excusable fashion, the author refused to investigate the personal role of Napoleon III. The Emperor was treated as little more than a phantom mysteriously linked to the operations of a tyrannical regime. The reader brave enough to suffer through all six of Delord's volumes would surely agree that the good citizens of Apt in 1876 had displayed a discriminating awareness about the nature of French historiography. History and politics had traditionally gone hand in hand in nineteenth-century France; it was fitting that a mediocre historian should experience a short, undistinguished political career.

Pierre de La Gorce

Aside from atypical modesty and self-effacement, Pierre de La Gorce was in background, attitudes, and career the epitome of a liberal notable. The La Gorces were a family from the Nord, known for their austere, almost Jansenist, Catholicism. The family traditionally gave its sons to the magistracy and the army, and Pierre's father served in the officer corps of the Restored and Orleanist monarchies. Unashamedly royalist, the La Gorces surrounded themselves with mementos of the *ancien régime* and the young Pierre was nurtured on the novels of Sir Walter Scott and tales of revolutionary atrocities. Born in 1846, the boy received an education proper to the family's beliefs and situation. He attended a Catholic school at Douai, the Collège of Saint-Jean, where the program was designed for young noblemen, and Pierre showed an appropriate love for literature and history. Later, he would make a major contribution to an impressive tradition which assumed that historical literature followed from the reflections of liberal and lettered gentlemen.[5]

Following the family pattern, La Gorce attended law school in Paris during the 1860s and prepared for the magistracy. These were important years. La Gorce witnessed many of the events discussed in the *Histoire du second Empire*. He also became intimately involved in a gathering of young liberal Catholics who looked to Augustin Cochin and Montalembert as guides for reconciling Christianity with political liberty. La Gorce was particularly attracted to

5. The best single biographical source concerning La Gorce is Agnès de La Gorce, *Une Vocation d'historien.*

Montalembert in whom he saw proof that Catholicism and liberty were synonymous. Whatever the merits of the idea, La Gorce, unlike many royalists, never abandoned his liberal Catholicism, and by the time of his death in 1934 he had become something of a political anachronism.

La Gorce's political sympathies lay with Orleanism, although he supported the program to merge the two royal houses, primarily because he feared the possibility that a republic might be established by default. La Gorce, in brief, subscribed to the French liberalism that arose after 1815 and which associated its cause with constitutional monarchy. His personal career and attitudes indicated a great deal about the direction and fate of this traditional liberalism in the post-1870 period. During that time, the strong, underlying conservatism of French liberals became more evident, to the point that even the worth of the Great Revolution was questioned. Liberals, of course, feared the increasing power of the left throughout the late nineteenth century, and the Revolution's democratic thrust seemed to threaten liberalism's narrow conception of liberty. La Gorce—and again he was typical—believed democracy to be a dangerous expression of a French egalitarianism that refused to recognize the need for or importance of *capacité* in directing the nation's destinies. He was, however, no member of what could be termed a "radical right," and Jules Simon appropriately called him the most liberal of conservatives. La Gorce criticized reactionaries for merely exacerbating a bad situation and inciting the left to revolutionary activity. The nationalist right he found repugnant, largely because of its violent tone and its attempt to arouse mass emotions.

La Gorce accepted the Third Republic, but he did so with little faith. As a magistrate, he swore allegiance to the Republic, only to resign his post in 1880 to protest the administration's dispersion of unauthorized religious congregations. He was hardly alone. Over 600 magistrates did likewise in opposition to the alleged lack of due process in the government's action. Faced with unemployment, La Gorce followed a well-established liberal pattern; he retired to the writing of history.

As an historian, La Gorce was noteworthy for his judicious fair-mindedness. He frequently disapproved of the actions and even motives of those he described, but he understood that politics involves shades of gray. He employed a moderate tone, seldom engaged in diatribe, and he was as capable of lauding republicans as he was of criticizing monarchists. Indeed, he was generous toward all except those he thought guilty of evil intentions, and this charge was primarily reserved for the Blanquists. If his histories were any indication, he probably made a kind and humane judge.

La Gorce rightly saw himself as belonging to the historical tradition of Thierry, Guizot, and Thiers, although he hardly shared the latter's admiration for Napoleon I. He retained Guizot's belief in a history guided by Christian providence, and he assumed that a moral pattern was built into the very nature of things. Unlike his three models, however, La Gorce belonged to the generation irretrievably marked by the catastrophe of 1870. Accordingly, his works reflected a profound sense of pessimism, and he frequently referred to Prévost-Paradol's morbid prophecies in *La France nouvelle* as the most thoughtful observations to have emerged from the 1860s. He was particularly impressed with Paradol's despair over the fact that revolution had divided France against herself and therefore prevented national unity and political evolution through gradual change.[6]

Like so many of his generation, La Gorce feared for France's capacity to maintain her national vigor. The events of 1870 reinforced liberal fears that French history might be something other than the story of progress. La Gorce, for instance, shared Renan's belief that France had to recapture her past strength by carefully husbanding her resources and restructuring the community around traditional institutions. History accordingly provided a form of knowledge which, if properly understood, would allow France to salvage her destinies from the wreckage of 1870. La Gorce's writing was therefore replete with references to the need for a return to older values,

6. On La Gorce's perception of historical change, see Jean-Francis Gervais, "Une Théorie du changement en histoire: l'oeuvre historique de Pierre de La Gorce." Gervais emphasizes La Gorce's conservatism and argues that the royalist's vision of history was pessimistic in spirit and cyclical in conception.

and he supported a program of decentralization meant to recapture the strength of the true France—the provinces. He likewise emphasized the urgent need for replacing the decadence of an urban, materialistic society with the simpler, spiritual values of Catholicism.

As a liberal historian, La Gorce was largely concerned with political affairs, and he dealt with his subjects accordingly. His first work, the *Histoire de la seconde République* was solid and coherent, but a bit wearisome, and La Gorce honestly admitted that it made dull reading. The two-volume work nevertheless established the author's reputation in conservative circles. He wrote when the Third Republic's future was still uncertain and his references to the Second Republic reflected a concern for contemporary politics. He argued persuasively that republican adherence to revolutionary principles and the 48ers' inability to maintain order ultimately brought about the destruction of political liberty. Yet, he was a reluctant critic. He believed that the 48ers were largely the victims of their own idealism. Never before had so many good intentions proved so fatal, an ironic point that he returned to in the *Histoire du second Empire*. And indeed, the *Histoire de la seconde République* ultimately served as a preface of sorts for the work on the Second Empire.

The *Histoire du second Empire* brought La Gorce deserved fame. The work received the Academy's highest award, the Gobert prize, in part through the friendly efforts of a Broglie. La Gorce's third and next work, the *Histoire religieuse de la Révolution française*, was his favorite, and it absorbed twenty years of his life. La Gorce's other works, of which there were four, were written after the author was over 80 years old. They were shorter, more topical in approach, and beautifully succinct. The first three, *Louis XVIII, Charles X,* and *Louis Philippe* together comprised a *Histoire de la monarchie constitutionelle*. The underlying argument was the obvious one: the three reigns represented a single era of French liberal government. Finally, La Gorce returned to the Second Empire and managed to complete his *Napoléon III et sa politique* just before his death. Both a restatement and a reassessment, the small volume—it numbered a mere 180 pages—was a very astute evaluation of the Emperor.

To complete the liberal pattern, La Gorce contributed to the *Cor-*

respondant and the *Revue des deux mondes*.[7] Having devoted his life to defending order and liberty, La Gorce joined the Immortals in 1914; the Academy still remained a foyer for the notable elite despite the Third Republic. He assumed the seat formerly held by Thureau-Dangin, who was something of a mentor for La Gorce, and who was himself another liberal Catholic with a penchant for writing history. Patterned after a time-honored model, La Gorce's was a distinguished career. On the other hand, it seemed reminiscent of things past, and perhaps its most redeeming feature was the quality of the man himself. According to Louis Barthou who delivered the Academy's tribute at the time of La Gorce's death in 1934, the historian was ". . . austere without being severe, firm without being rigid, and profoundly indulgent and good."[8]

———————

The preface to the *Histoire du second Empire* presented a clear statement of the author's goals—to escape political partisanship and to provide Frenchmen with an objective appraisal of the Napoleonic regime. In La Gorce's own words: "The reign of Napoleon III has until now only been judged by favoritism or hate. It has twice undergone the test of falsification: the falsification of adulation in its days of power, the falsification of calumny in its days of misfortune. In this reign at once brilliant and inauspicious, superficial and tragic, I would like to apply the customary rules of criticism which establish the facts according to witnesses and as a result, put men and events in their true place."[9] La Gorce's goal was meritorious, but he hardly transcended the attitudes of French liberalism. Instead, he reaffirmed his political principles with a moderate tone and in a fair-

7. The most important articles were collected by his family and published under the title of *Au temps du second Empire.* La Gorce also made occasional contributions to, and the year before his death became an honorary editor of, the *Revue des questions historiques,* a journal of Catholic and monarchist persuasion.

8. Archives de l'Académie Française, dossier Pierre de La Gorce. It was the description of a judge whose colleagues on the bench fifty years earlier had noted that La Gorce seemed to fret continually over the possibility of condemning an innocent man.

9. La Gorce, *Histoire du second Empire,* I, i.

minded fashion. Although thoroughly committed, the author remained judicious, and this no doubt explained why the *Histoire* has
been employed as a model by other writers.[10] Later specialized
studies have also underlined the astuteness of the *Histoire*'s conclusions. La Gorce, for example, comprehended the ambiguous character of the provincial resistance to the coup d'état, and he recognized that it was motivated, in some instances, by republican
concern for legality and in others by a desire to push France into a
form of red republicanism.

La Gorce's use of source material revealed the nature of his work.
He generally relied upon the papers of contemporary figures, and
primarily liberal ones, such as Daru and Montalembert. He also
utilized the papers of Walewski, and spoke at great length with
Ollivier, for whom he had had great admiration since his student
days.[11] It was a political history and emphasis was understandably
placed upon foreign affairs, a feature that explained the apparently
disproportionate number of pages devoted to the 1860s. To take one
example, the first volume covered the period from 1852 to 1856,
while Volumes V through VII concerned the four years between
1866 and 1870. La Gorce, with some justification, treated internal
policy as an auxiliary of foreign affairs, even though he admitted
that this represented something of an oversimplification.

The *Histoire* contained several themes. The first and most obvious
was that the republican failure to maintain order brought about a
national relapse into authoritarianism. For this reason, La Gorce
displayed mixed emotions about the coup d'état. He acknowledged
and deplored the fact that it had destroyed liberty, but his conservative sense of order led him to condemn those who apparently

10. In his *La Société française sous Napoléon III*, for instance, André Bellesort
acknowledges his debt to La Gorce, and indeed, the little book is in many respects
a shortened version of the *Histoire*. J. M. Thompson's *Louis Napoleon and the Second
Empire* for all practical purposes provides a restatement of La Gorce's observations
and conclusions, and Thompson even follows the Frenchman in moving back and
forth between an attachment for the idealistic Emperor and a distaste for the slightly
vulgar adventurer. If anything, Thompson is a bit more severe than La Gorce.
11. The admiration was not entirely reciprocated. Ollivier, so incensed by La
Gorce's failure to absolve him completely of any responsibility for the 1870 war,
fought to prevent the liberal Catholic's entry into the Academy. As a result, La Gorce
only joined the Immortals after Ollivier's death.

condoned illegality through their willingness to perpetrate, or their inability to prevent, disorder.

There was no doubt in La Gorce's mind that the Empire rested upon dictatorial principles. He carefully scrutinized the 1852 constitution, and judged it a document providing for "legal authoritarianism." The system was weighted in favor of the executive power that operated either under its own direct auspices or under those of the Council of State. La Gorce nevertheless asserted that from the very beginning the regime possessed a capacity for liberal evolution. Most important, the Legislative Body retained the right to pass or to veto laws and taxes, and thus maintained the nucleus of political liberty from which other freedoms could emerge. Further, the government chose for its official candidates men of enough independent stature that the Legislative Body soon began striving to extend its powers against the restrictions of the ministers and the Council of State. La Gorce also argued that Louis Napoleon had neither the capacity nor the taste for operating a despotic regime. Indolent by nature, the Emperor could not fulfill the demands made upon an efficient autocrat. Apparently believing inefficient autocracy an impossibility, La Gorce then concluded that liberalization was inevitable. As for the Emperor's preferences, La Gorce saw no reason to deny that the Prince honestly believed that liberal political forms would arise from an authoritarian settlement. He accepted Napoleon III's good faith and referred to the tempered quality of the Empire's authoritarianism during the 1850s.

In assessing the 1852 constitution, La Gorce concluded that two principles obviously inspired those who designed the Empire: respect for universal suffrage and distaste for parliamentary political forms. La Gorce admitted that the Empire managed to guarantee political democracy by imposing controls upon it, and that such an accomplishment carried a certain price, the discounting of parliamentary political forms. As a result, the traditional elite associated with parliamentarianism either withdrew from public life by preference, or failed to overcome the difficulties encountered in a system of universal suffrage. Indeed, La Gorce unhappily acknowledged that the old liberal establishment became somewhat irrelevant in the face of new conditions. He wrote of the regime's alliance with French popular sentiment, and the effect of that alliance upon the liberals:

> But here would appear their true condition, at once very brilliant and very precarious. Everything which assured to them fame and even glory in Paris—in the midst of political society, escaped them with the brutal and powerful blast of universal suffrage. They were unaware of what pleased the masses, and they most often offered what the masses were unable to understand . . . They personified liberty, a word somewhat abstract, the sense of which is difficult to understand without culture and study. They represented all aristocracies: the aristocracy of education and taste, of talent and birth—a poor situation from which to conquer democratic societies, rebellious to all superiorities, outside that of gold . . .[12]

The Empire, however, did more than set democracy against the forces of liberty: it also employed economic development as a foil against political activity. The various groups within the community were diverted from their quarrels as they enjoyed the regime's guarantee of order and economic progress. La Gorce called Bonapartism a form of enlightened despotism that stimulated public works programs and economic development in a fashion impossible for a truly liberal regime. As a result, the Empire had vision enough to comprehend the importance of railroads and to complete the long overdue task of constructing a national network. As for the rebuilding of Paris, La Gorce expressed approval while wondering whether or not a good thing might have been carried too far. In fact, La Gorce believed that the Empire's very success in furthering economic and material prosperity was, at the same time, the source of many difficulties. France became something of a massive bazaar, as meaningful issues were ignored for sheer frivolity and financial speculation. The Jansenist La Gorce echoed the puritanical Delord to the effect that a one-sided concern for material wealth led to a decadence not unrelated to 1870. Indeed, La Gorce did the republican one better; he claimed that Offenbach's *La Grande-duchesse de Gérolstein* and French refusal to accept the sacrifices of military

12. La Gorce, *Histoire du second Empire*, IV, 195–196.

reform indicated moral decay and an accompanying deterioration in civic virtue.

While straightforward and to the point, La Gorce's description of Bonapartist authoritarianism during the 1850s nevertheless recognized the subtle character of the Empire. At the same time, he recognized that the regime was highly personal and that anyone trying to comprehend its meaning had to confront its Emperor. Previous authors had fallen into one of two traps: Delord wrote as if there were no Emperor while Hugo never really escaped the criminal metaphor. La Gorce, while comprehending that more was necessary, nevertheless proved unable to resist the personal attraction of Napoleon III. La Gorce suffered the fate he attributed to others: "Napoleon, by his simple goodness, rarely failed to seduce those who met him."[13] While never explicitly saying as much, La Gorce obviously believed the Emperor to be a man of '48. For the pessimistic royalist, one of the Emperor's two great faults was his idealism; the other, a bent for conspiracy, joined the first to make an impossible situation. A dreamer with utopian visions, Napoleon III employed his tremendous powers to put into motion secret projects that frequently raised insoluble problems to which he responded by engaging in further conspiracy. Without the magic of physiology, La Gorce reached a conclusion not very different from that of the editors of the *Grand Larousse:*

> It seems then that the judgment of public opinion will never place the Prince in his proper place. In the midst of many vicissitudes, it is still possible to recover the web of this strange existence. In the adventures of his youth, he had wrapped himself in dreams. This double tendency penetrated him so well that it absorbed everything else. Dreamer and conspirator, he was such on the throne and always remained so: an extraordinary conspirator who, having in hand all the resources of official power, preferred subterranean intrigues to open negotiations . . . Everything about him provided a contrast. One saw him conduct some intrigues as if he had studied Machiavelli, and then caress humanitarian utopias as if he had wished to copy Don Quixote. He brought . . . to the same enterprises calculation to the point of duplicity and disinterestedness to

13. Ibid., III, 110. La Gorce, however, hardly thought the Emperor simple—just the contrary. At another juncture, he wrote that Louis Napoleon had as much trouble being simple as most men had in being complicated.

the point of dupery. His dreams, at once ambitious and weak, were those of neither a mediocre nor a sane mind; what horrified him most was routine . . . He had many faults, but a triumphant manner and airs of profundity that dazzled his friends and sometimes disconcerted his enemies. Even when his acts were contradictory or wretched, his language was always of high rank which well surpassed that of the average man. Following the Napoleonic tradition, he affected disdain for theory, of ideology, and yet betrayed himself as the greatest of theoreticians . . .[14]

The *Histoire's* treatment of the regime's second and less authoritarian decade was more ambiguous than its treatment of the 1850s, which were described as superficially successful years carrying the seeds of later difficulties. The 1860s were portrayed in a completely different light. For one thing, numerous chickens came home to roost. Secondly, La Gorce accepted the proposition that, dating from the reforms of 1860, liberalization was constant and real. Indeed, he called the decree of November 24 the most important single change in the process that transformed the authoritarian Empire into an acceptable regime, this despite the fact that the essential outline of the 1852 constitution remained intact. La Gorce even reserved some harsh words for liberals who failed to rally at this juncture. By their reticence, he believed that they merely slowed the liberal process.

Had La Gorce confronted a particular issue, he might have had less difficulty with the problem of liberal reluctance. As it was, he never adequately explained the forces behind government reform. Instead, he oscillated between two theories which, while not mutually exclusive, nevertheless had to be weighed separately and given their due. Specifically, La Gorce, at times, argued that reform was necessarily the result of increased conservative resistance to government policies, particularly in foreign affairs. Having angered his conservative supporters, Napoleon III tried to reassure them by enlarging the powers of a generally conservative legislature. La Gorce continued the argument of reform from necessity beyond the decree of November 24. Of the liberalization announced in 1867, La Gorce alleged that further difficulties forced the Emperor to include the nation in the responsibility of future developments. Yet, La Gorce

14. Ibid., I, iv–v.

also employed the theory of a generous Napoleon III who granted reforms in an entirely voluntary fashion, and who did so in 1860 before Frenchmen really desired them. Something more needed to be said if La Gorce was to reconcile his good Emperor with a bad political system.

Because he portrayed the 1860s as a period which saw the re-emergence of liberalism, La Gorce was faced with yet another problem: how to explain the government's hedgings and hesitations in implementing reform. Rather than placing direct blame upon Napoleon III, La Gorce emphasized the role of the Empire's personnel. La Gorce gave the impression—a questionable one unless carefully qualified—that Napoleon lost control over his own agents who deliberately sabotaged or at least weakened the whole liberalization program. A case in point was Rouher, and La Gorce, with some justification, attributed to him a policy of accepting liberalization in principle, and then subverting it from within governmental councils. The result was a confused state of affairs that weakened liberal faith in the regime and catastrophically postponed the inevitable reforms, which if implemented sooner, might have prevented the events of 1870.

In assessing the whole eighteen-year period, La Gorce was less indignant about the loss of political liberty in 1851 than grateful for its gradual restoration after 1860. With each volume La Gorce made it increasingly evident that he would have preferred to live under a liberal Empire than a Third Republic. In contrast to some Frenchmen who found the idea of a republic especially enticing during the Empire, La Gorce had experienced enough of the Republic to long for its predecessor. As a result, La Gorce's tone underwent a marked change in the later volumes as he discussed the rise of both radical sentiment and republicanism. He exhibited particular hostility toward the republican refusal to rally to the reforms of the late 1860s. La Gorce accused republicans of being unable to agree amongst themselves on a positive program and of attempting to overcome their divisions by means of a purely nihilistic criticism. Finally—and with the Commune in mind—he denounced left-wing extremists in general and Blanquists in particular. As enemies of man and God, they hoped to use their opposition to the Empire for an attack upon both society and civilization. For the first and only time in seven volumes, La Gorce cast aside his moderate tone and engaged in diatribe. With the lines so drawn, La Gorce naturally placed himself on the side of the Empire.

While arguing that Bonapartist foreign policy ultimately proved fatal, La Gorce implicitly denied Delord's contention that the Empire was necessarily doomed. In the realm of internal developments, the government achieved a major success. Liberalization redeemed the Empire, and provided the basis for a workable solution within existing institutions. This was possible because, among other things, the liberal *tiers parti* did not demand a pure parliamentary system that would have emasculated the executive power. In discussing the 1869 reforms which substantially enlarged the authority of the Legislative Body, La Gorce assured the reader that the edifice had been properly crowned. Led by Ollivier, who placed liberal values above partisan dogmas, Frenchmen rightly entered 1870 with a sense of hope and national well-being. To use his own words:

> With a remarkable return of confidence, the enlightened turned toward the Emperor. His nobility in relinquishing power was lauded, his bold magnanimity in seeking old adversaries and admitting them to his counsels was admired, his generous initiative which tried to join all parties in a grand national party was touching. France not only judged things thus, but all Europe did so. Until then, Napoleon had above all guaranteed order; if he also assured liberty, what good citizen could refuse his support.[15]

The 1870 ministry, then, was a great experiment. La Gorce likewise emphasized the number of liberal *ralliements*, as reflected both in the ministry and the various extraparliamentary commissions meant to investigate fundamental problems of the community—the role of local government, education and administrative organization. Equally important to the regime's apparent success was republican disarray. Frightened by increased radical activity, moderates in the party began to fear the possibility of disorder. Even Gambetta, for

15. Ibid., VI, 2.

whom La Gorce had a great deal of admiration, showed a new hesitation in the face of possible revolutionary disturbances. Finally, the 1870 plebiscite proved beyond a doubt the regime's popular strength. Despite republican and right-wing Bonapartist attempts to misconstrue its meaning, the referendum above all indicated French desire to maintain the Empire. The nation seemed well on the path toward an orderly liberalism.

It was with a sense of melancholy that the liberal historian described the catastrophic events leading to September 4. Sedan was the price for earlier mistakes that fate, had she been more generous, might have done better to forgive or overlook. "True history," he wrote, "will place its severities upon the epoch when faults were committed, and not upon the epoch when they were paid. The faults, they were the unbelievable series of aberrations, stupidities, ambitious and wretched dreams which had brought everything to this final abasement. Sedan was only the expiation."[16] Be that as it may, La Gorce indicated his belief that providence had been a bit too unrelenting. To use his own words: "Posterity will understand that the people of Paris, sacrificing wisdom to rancour, on September 4 reversed the Empire."[17]

For La Gorce, the Empire almost succeeded in restoring the political balance disrupted in 1848, an appraisal that raises a major criticism of the *Histoire*. The work divided the Empire into two parts, broadly defined as the 1850s and the 1860s, or more appropriately, the authoritarian period and the era of liberalism's re-emergence. La Gorce failed to link the two adequately, leaving the reader with both two Empires and two Emperors. For the 1850s, La Gorce portrayed the regime as a form of authoritarian democracy, and Napoleon III was accordingly described as a democratically inspired leader naturally opposed to the traditional leadership of the notables. While discussing the 1860s, La Gorce presented a somewhat different Emperor for an obviously changed regime. Still generous in character, Napoleon became less democratic, more liberal, and able

16. Ibid., VII, 368.
17. Ibid., pp. 429–430.

to work with the liberal forces he had once denied. At the risk of
overlooking other considerations, La Gorce was perhaps too persistent in trying to establish Napoleon III's liberal credentials. Likewise,
he too easily blamed government personnel for any difficulties in the
reform program. One suspects that for the 1860s a greater distinction
needed to be drawn between the Emperor and his regime. La Gorce
was somewhat reluctant to draw this distinction, and he therefore
ran the risk of not recognizing the long-run democratic impact of
the Empire. Napoleon III may have been willing to accept the im-
position of liberalization, but like Gambetta, he believed that democracy was the historical means by which Frenchmen would
escape the exclusive social forces associated with liberalism. Given
his dislike for the Third Republic, La Gorce treated the Empire of
the late 1860s as a liberal regime pure and simple. But the Empire
was also democratic, a fact which did not necessarily bode well for
the liberals with whom La Gorce identified. Ollivier was not a figure
easily associated with the notables or the liberal elite despite their
attempt to capture him and his own efforts to rally them. From the
unhappy perspective of the early twentieth century, La Gorce employed the liberal Empire as a yardstick of sorts against the Republic. It was not an altogether fair comparison. Although he discovered
the Empire's liberal contribution, La Gorce failed to explain adequately its democratic guarantee, or how liberalism was finally
joined with that guarantee. He instead wrote two histories linked by
a generous Emperor who somehow inauspiciously slipped from the
role of an authoritarian democrat into that of a liberal leader. The
change was treated less as an historical transformation than as an
unexplained case of political transubstantiation.

The magistrate turned historian obviously agreed with J. J. Weiss,
a leading liberal publicist during the Empire, who acknowledged
that when he compared Louis Philippe and Napoleon III, he preferred the government of the first and the person of the second. La
Gorce in 1933 consequently returned to the Second Empire with his
Napoléon III et sa politique. Evidently fearing that he had perhaps
been too harsh with the Emperor in the *Histoire,* he wrote: "I have
been unable to resist, in my old age, a re-evaluation of this compli-

cated man whose reign I previously described. Although he was fatal, I have with difficulty written that word which I would now like to soften, since he was so good and even enlightened . . . "[18] La Gorce called Louis Napoleon a man with the temperament of a philosopher, who was totally inadequate for the tasks of a statesman. He would have done far better to have presided over an academy devoted to humanitarian projects. Further, the life and fate of the Emperor contained a great irony; a well-meaning and thorough-going idealist, he set into motion the very forces that ultimately destroyed him. It was La Gorce, in fact, who coined the idea of a tragedy of good intentions, and he specifically alluded to *Napoléon le bien intentionné.*[19]

Despite certain shortcomings, La Gorce accomplished several impressive tasks, not the least of which arose from his ability to comprehend the political forces that gave rise to the regime, his willingness to accept the humanity of the Emperor, and his understanding that the regime possessed a flexibility that separated 1851 from 1869–1870. Because he assumed the Empire deserved serious study, La Gorce provided that which eluded Delord. The liberal Catholic may have written with a conservative bias, but his work explained something and was thus what it purported to be: history.

Emile Ollivier

Emile Ollivier's *L'Empire libéral* was a personal testimony by an active participant in the politics of the Second Empire. Charles Seignobos argued that for this reason it should not be called history, but instead a literary defense by an eloquent but incompetent politician. Seignobos, however, missed the point. Ollivier's choice of a subtitle, *études, récits, souvenirs,* indicated the author's awareness

18. La Gorce, *Napoléon III et sa politique,* p. 179.
19. La Gorce's theme of *Napoléon le bien intentionné* has been echoed by Roger Williams, "Louis Napoleon: A Tragedy of Good Intentions." An American, Williams has contributed a great deal to the recent social, political, and literary history of the Empire. See his *Gaslight and Shadow: The World of Napoleon III; Henri Rochefort, Prince of the Gutter Press; The Mortal Napoleon III;* and *Manners and Murders in the World of Louis-Napoleon.*

that the work was not a mere *histoire*. Amongst other things, Ollivier described his long pilgrimage from the republican to the moderate opposition and then beyond to a complete *ralliement*. *L'Empire libéral* was both a debate with historians as well as a response to the numerous attacks made upon its author.

Emile Ollivier was above all a man of '48—sentimental, overly optimistic, given to posturing, democratic, a little confused, and confident that Frenchmen could resolve their differences. He was greatly influenced by his father, Demosthenes, who had been a Carbonaro, a leading republican, a socialist, something of a Bonapartist, and a close friend of Mazzini, Armand Carrel, Ledru-Rollin, and Pierre Leroux. It was also through his father that Emile entered politics. In 1848, at the age of 22, he was catapulted into prominence by Ledru-Rollin, who appointed the young man republican commissioner at Marseille. He proved a faithful servant of the Provisional Government and quickly suffered its fate. By patterning himself after Lamartine, whom he greatly admired and resembled, he dazzled angry crowds with eloquent tributes to fraternity and reconciliation, accomplished little, and ultimately pleased no one. When Marseille experienced a workers' revolt, Cavaignac promptly demoted him to the prefecture at Chaumont. This post also proved temporary, as the Barrot government in 1849 began purging republicans from the administration. Ousted from Chaumont in January, the young man of 23 resigned, refusing Louis Napoleon's offer to intervene and find another prefecture. For Ollivier, the revolution was over.

During the eight years before he reentered public life, Ollivier devoted much effort to rethinking his politics in the light of the 1848 failure. The result was a vague system of ideas that remained true to mid-century aspirations, but included certain accommodations with the new situation. On the one hand, Ollivier retained his democratic commitment and a belief that France could achieve unity through reconciliation. On the other, he was less sanguine about the power of "fraternity." Indeed, he argued that fraternity would be the result of reconciliation and not vice-versa. In a similar fashion, he alluded to the problem of extreme idealism; the France of 1848 needed practical men but instead received *penseurs* with no concrete program for achieving a permanent settlement. He confided to his journal that, "facts and practical possibilities must modify, or rather regulate, contain, and moderate the flight of boundless theory . . . "[20]

Ollivier concluded that stability could only emerge from a synthesis incorporating the community's several political traditions. He unfortunately provided few specifics beyond the idea that a national program would have to incorporate the liberal program for parliamentary liberty and the conservative concern for preserving order. This national republicanism, then, would have to be at once democratic, liberal, and nonrevolutionary. As to the organization of this vague program, Ollivier was correspondingly vague. His journal was replete with references to Constant and Royer-Collard, and to the idea of balanced government—i.e., a system including republican and monarchical principles. What these principles were and how they might be implemented was not clear. One point, however, was obvious: before 1860, Ollivier had settled upon a republicanism that was conciliatory to practically everyone except those who believed in revolutionary activity. In his own fashion, he resembled Louis Napoleon.

Ollivier's confused hopes for a national government led to his eventual *ralliement* to the Empire. If nothing else, his diffuse theorizing implied that general programs should take precedence over specific policies, all of which explained his later defense that he was a man of principle placing substance over political forms. Further, his attitudes during the 1850s and the fashion in which he returned to politics were indicative of the future. His journal showed that he had little animosity for Napoleon III, and unlike most republicans he refused to dwell upon December 2. The journal even contained sympathetic references to the Bonapartes, and he remarked that for all his faults, Napoleon I had represented the Revolution. Ollivier also moved in a republican circle that was not altogether hostile to the regime. He frequented, for instance, the salon of the comtesse

20. Emile Ollivier, *Journal*, I, 61.

d'Agoult—soon to become his mother-in-law—who had temporarily lost faith in the republican mission. Although she refused to rally, the comtesse cooperated with left-wing Bonapartists in order to serve the progressive cause. Moreover, her attitude was rather typical. The demand for complete disengagement largely came from the exiles who made an understandable virtue of an absolute necessity.

The leading figure of republican accommodation during the 1850s was Léonor Havin. Editor of the *Siècle,* he was a man of notoriously flexible principles and he was perhaps little more than a natural collaborator. A nominal republican, Havin found the July Monarchy acceptable and the Second Empire even more so. A personal friendship with Prince Napoleon and financial ties with Morny contributed to the government's choice of the *Siècle* as the republican representative to the official system of a balanced press. As publisher of the only semi-independent left-wing newspaper, Havin carved out an autonomous position by occupying the ground that separated the government and the republican opposition. It was a tricky game, but Havin played it successfully throughout the 1850s, and until he faced the added problem of competition. Indeed, Havin quickly became a major power in progressive circles, and in 1857 decided to support republican candidacies for the upcoming elections. The party—or movement—immediately fell into turmoil. To assume a seat in the Legislative Body, a deputy swore allegiance to the regime, an unacceptable condition for the republican leadership. Havin, however, blithely charged Ernest Picard, Ollivier's best friend, to find some young candidates whose ambition would guarantee their pliability on the question of taking the oath. Ollivier, in short, entered the legislature through the manipulation of Havin. From the beginning, the Cinq (Ollivier, Darimon, Picard, Hénon, and Favre) consisted of men representative of the most conciliatory wing of the republican party, and even Daniel Stern expressed dismay over her son-in-law's poor judgment.

Thirteen years later Ollivier completely rallied, only to be identified with a war that destroyed his reputation. Sedan overshadowed or became indistinguishable from the liberal Empire, and the traditional link between politics and history guaranteed Ollivier's bad press. He provided republicans with living proof that opportunism bears bitter fruit, and they joyfully used him as a convenient stick for thrashing the defunct Empire. With calculated viciousness, Rochefort even suggested that if Ollivier were murdered, no jury would convict the assassins. Bonapartists, meanwhile, proved equally vindictive; in both Cassagnac's *Pays* and Dréolle's *Drapeau,* many columns were written at the expense of the ex-minister. Things worsened with Napoleon III's death in 1873 when the Empress and Rouher, who blamed Ollivier and liberalization for the regime's demise, assumed control of the party. For once, republicans and Bonapartists agreed, and when Ollivier announced his candidacy to the Assembly in 1876, they promptly joined forces against the common enemy.

Aversion for Ollivier was more than a partisan affair. As late as 1918, Henri Bergson ignited a minor uproar by defending Ollivier in the Academy as the victim of prejudice and the national desire for a scapegoat. For most Frenchmen, Ollivier remained the fatuous, but eloquent, incompetent with a light heart.[21] Historians have generally echoed public opinion, though much has depended upon the particular writer's attitude toward the Empire and its liberalization. Both Delord and La Gorce, who knew Ollivier, judged him differently. For the republican, he was a traitor whose efforts to realize a liberal Empire were nothing more than an attempt to achieve the impossible. The ever judicious La Gorce described him as a man of substance, who recognized that France had more to gain by affirming liberal values than political partisanship. Historians in general have exhibited a tendency to dismiss the liberal Empire as irrelevant, because of its short duration. Such an appraisal placed Ollivier in the position of devoting his political career to a useless and vain experiment. That historians affirmed the futility of it all is indicated

21. Ollivier's unfortunate phrase has been studiously—and it would seem deliberately—miscontrued by his enemies, including Delord. La Gorce, on the other hand, portrayed the remark for what it was: Ollivier's affirmation that France's position vis-à-vis Prussia was justified. As of now, Ollivier has had the last word: see Pierre Guiral's new edition of *Histoire d'une guerre* (Paris: Martineau, 1970), originally published in 1910, and Ollivier's defense of his role in 1870.

by the fact that only two authors, one of them an Englishman, have thought Ollivier deserved to be treated as the subject of a political biography.[22]

In 1870 Ollivier was only forty-five years of age, and he was to live another 43 as a pariah, spending much of his time secluded in a small villa in the Midi. Despite stoic disclaimers of fatigue for the glories of this world, Ollivier was obviously grieved by his ostracism. With ill-disguised belligerence he attended sessions of the Academy even though its members subjected him to continual affronts. He likewise badgered the reading public with a never-ending flow of books and pamphlets that few, if any, read; still confident of his political wisdom, he wrote *Principes et conduite* (1875) and *Solutions politiques et sociales* (1894), both of which indicated his reserved *ralliement* to the Republic. More conservative after 1870 than before, he grew increasingly dubious of an "atomized" universal suffrage, and he supported numerous techniques for blunting the power of sheer numbers. He also remained convinced that the Third Republic should copy certain features of the liberal Empire, and on democratic grounds he adamantly defended the principle of a strong executive with plebiscitary powers. As for assemblies, he accused them of encouraging an oligarchic rule unresponsive to popular demands; for this reason, he greeted Boulanger as the harbinger of a new and better politics.

It was, of course, the older Ollivier who wrote *L'Empire libéral.* Finally recognizing that he would never return to politics, he set about at the age of sixty-five to write his own defense. The task absorbed the remaining years of his life and was only finished in 1913, the year of his death. The motives for *L'Empire libéral* were two: to explain how a principled statesman rallied to the Empire, and to show how the regime in fact had deserved France's support. The apology proved remarkably ineffective. Some blamed its shrill tone, the author's too frequent use of the pronoun *je,* and a supposed lack

22. Theodore Zeldin, *Emile Ollivier and the Liberal Empire of Napoleon III,* and Pierre Saint-Marc, *Emile Ollivier.* There is also a biography by Ollivier's second wife: Marie-Thérèse Ollivier, *Emile Ollivier, sa jeunesse,* which follows Ollivier's career to 1857.

of balance. In actual fact, few read *L'Empire libéral*, and the publisher suffered a loss on the venture. Perhaps it was simply too massive. Seventeen volumes of text and three million words make for heavy reading, particularly when events had apparently decided against the defendant. Even Ollivier had to admit that his efforts were to no avail; approaching the end of his labor, he wrote: "However convincing be my demonstrations and whatever is the force of the irrefutable documents supporting them, they will not destroy—except with a small elite—the legend of cleverly engineered lies by which the parties have infected public opinion."[23]

———————————————

The title, *L'Empire libéral*, was misleading, and merely reflected the climax of Ollivier's career. In actual fact, the multivolume work was a history of the Second Empire, and Ollivier only reached the liberal period with Volume XII. To complicate matters, the seventeen volumes contained several books with overlapping themes, the predominant principle of organization being the author's demand for vindication. Volume I, amorphous and somewhat superfluous, described the nature of European progressivism during the 1840s and provided a vague outline for the following tomes. The next three volumes concerned Louis Napoleon and the early years of the Empire; with much animation, Ollivier portrayed the Emperor as a great leader employing authoritarian methods to achieve progressive and democratic goals.[24] Ollivier then shifted his ground with Volume V; the story no longer concerned so much the democratic Napoleon III as the principled Ollivier struggling for the reinstitution of a liberal politics. Meantime, the story became a narrative history describing the emergence of liberal forces in response to the policies of authoritarianism. Thereafter, and with Volume IX, Ollivier provided less a narrative history than a description of his own efforts against the background of French politics. With Volume XII, the story be-

23. Emile Ollivier, *L'Empire libéral*, XIV, 4–5.
24. The English historian, F. A. Simpson, has borrowed the ideas found in these three volumes for his *Louis Napoleon and the Recovery of France;* this includes Ollivier's analysis of French goals in the Crimean War.

came increasingly personal, the author treating the liberal period as a triumph for Emile Ollivier.

To this day, *L'Empire libéral* remains the most important work concerning the political evolution of the Bonapartist regime. Likewise, Ollivier's career reflected the Empire's journey from authoritarianism, through liberalization, and into catastrophe. Indeed, Ollivier's political position in 1851 was similar to that of Taxile Delord. Ollivier, however, moved gradually in a different direction and accepted the liberal Empire. His ultimate assessment of the regime resembled that of La Gorce, although the two men wrote from different perspectives. La Gorce's literary *ralliement* in the *Histoire* was motivated by a liberal monarchism; the *ralliement* described by Ollivier was that of a liberal democrat.

The ex-minister correctly perceived that his own history could not be separated from that of the regime. The seventeen-volume work therefore made fascinating reading, to the point that Toynbee could compare Ollivier with Thucydides and Machiavelli.[25] History as a reflection upon Ollivier's career narrated an eventual marriage of democracy with liberalism, and Ollivier portrayed himself and the Emperor as the brokers who arranged the union. Unfortunately, the ex-minister became overly engrossed with his own tragedy, and failed to comprehend the full extent of the imperial contribution. Like La Gorce, he thought September 4 a catastrophe bringing all good things to an end. Because he had failed—through no fault of his own, however—Ollivier assumed that both the Empire and France had done likewise. For the disgraced politician, history went astray; it was only other commentators, with no personal stake in the matter, who recognized how much of the liberal Empire survived into the Third Republic.[26]

25. A. J. Toynbee, *A Study of History*, III, 287–290, 296–298.

26. The first of these defenders of the liberal Empire was Henry Berton, *L'Evolution constitutionnelle du second Empire*. A republican, Berton nevertheless argued that the Empire educated Frenchmen to liberal politics and would have survived except for the tragic events of 1870. Like Ollivier's work, of which it provided a summary under the guise of a doctoral dissertation in law, Berton's volume has been studiously avoided by most historians. Another defense is that of Marcel Prélot, "La Signification constitutionnelle du second Empire." Prélot's political position is actually quite similar to that of Ollivier, in that both men affirm the positive qualities of a strong executive.

Haunted by the events of 1870, Ollivier devoted a great deal of space to a discussion of foreign affairs. At one point he observed that foreign rather than domestic policy was the key issue in the Empire's history, and he defended the nationalities' program on the ground that a revolutionary tradition demanded support for less fortunate peoples and that any such program worked to the disadvantage of France's enemies. As for the 1870 war, it arose not from the logic of the nationalities' principle, but from Bismarck's perversion of the democratic ideal. Except insofar as these observations cleared his name of any responsibility for the 1870 debacle, they were not germane to Ollivier's primary concern. During the Empire, his real attention always remained fastened upon internal rather than foreign considerations, as evidenced by his journal's lack of comment about issues unrelated to domestic matters. The journal revealed that Ollivier saw himself as a philosopher in search of a solution to the division separating left and right; only when the philosopher assumed the role of an historian did he take into account foreign policy, and his defense of the nationalities' principle merely confirmed public belief that he was a man with a light heart—and possibly an empty head.

Like La Gorce, Ollivier argued that the Empire was incomprehensible unless one understood the Emperor, and while the royalist portrayed Napoleon as merely well-intentioned, Ollivier justified his *ralliement* by depicting Napoleon as unquestionably beneficent. Like so many others, Ollivier was thoroughly seduced by the Emperor, whom he portrayed as a man of reconciliation struggling to provide a national program of progress and order. Always exuberant and seldom judicious, Ollivier even described Napoleon as a realist tempered by a philosophical wisdom comparable to that of Marcus Aurelius. Whatever the merit of his flights of enthusiasm, this one amounted to a major insight, and one Ollivier probably reached less through reflection than through a kind of empathy with the man he had come to admire. To the point, Ollivier argued throughout *L'Empire libéral* that Napoleon III was a man of '48, shaped by the progressive movement and the milieu of the 1840s.

While acknowledging that his views had undergone radical change since 1851, Ollivier found the Prince blameless for the short

duration of the Second Republic. The problems of 1848 only manifested the dilemma that arose from a national division separating
left and right. In the ensuing paralysis, Frenchmen naturally sought
a national figure who would maintain order and preserve the progressive gains of the revolution. As for the Prince, he entered the
Elysée with no thought of a coup d'état, but the very forces that
paralyzed France before December 10 continued to do so after the
presidential election. On the one hand, the left fell into a blind opposition that prevented any cooperation with the President, while
the monarchists hoped to employ the executive as a tool with which
to destroy the Republic. The result was both ironic and ridiculous.
The man who represented a national desire for an end to extreme
partisanship found himself incapacitated by the exclusive ambitions
of the various factions. The Prince had two alternatives: either abdi-
cate and allow France's divisions to bring further chaos, or somehow
grasp the nettle and institute a national policy. For Ollivier, the
coup d'état was an unfortunate necessity, and he likewise called the
plebiscite an expression of national sovereignty vindicating the
Prince's action. "No vote in our history," he commented, "has expressed more sincerely the thought of the people."[27] Those, on the
other hand, who refused to accept the outcome of December, 1851
merely manifested the very problem that rendered the coup d'état
necessary.

Ollivier's assessment of the authoritarian period from 1852 to
1860 was equally sympathetic. Indeed, Ollivier the historian proved
more amenable than had Ollivier the young republican, and the
author of L'Empire libéral condemned his earlier disapproval of the
regime's railroad program and the remodeling of Paris. As for politics, the historian claimed for the 1852 constitution the achievement
of joining order with progress; he also called the decennial republic
established immediately after the coup d'état a nearly ideal regime
and one superior to the Third Republic. Having thus defended the
decennial republic, Ollivier was nevertheless at some difficulty to
explain its rapid transformation into a Second Empire. While calling

27. Ollivier, L'Empire libéral, II, 518-519.

the change a mistake, Ollivier refused to hold Louis Napoleon accountable. He instead blamed the President's advisors for cooking up the scheme in order to serve their own interests, an argument that was not altogether convincing, and which reflected Ollivier's tendency to hold Louis Napoleon responsible for only those acts which Ollivier was prepared to defend.

Decennial Republic, Second Empire, or whatever, Ollivier saw no reason for fearing the regime's obvious downgrading of representative institutions. Louis Napoleon intended to restore full political liberty, and the constitution of 1852 retained enough vestiges of parliamentarianism to guarantee basic liberties and political evolution. Ollivier believed that the germ of the liberal Empire was to be found in the authoritarianism of the 1850s.

> As long as there are elected deputies, even chosen by money as in England, even deliberating behind closed doors in a celler as was also the case in England; as long as deputies have the full power to refuse subsidies without which no war, no expense whatever can be engaged; as long as true liberty—social, civil, and individual liberty—is not infringed, the nation is not in servitude, it is master of its destinies; there is no despotism.[28]

After establishing to his own satisfaction that the Empire was not inimical to liberalism, Ollivier employed the 1857 elections and the policies of the Cinq to justify his future *ralliement;* from the beginning, he argued, the Cinq had stood for a responsible opposition designed to achieve certain goals. Their criticism in the Legislative Body was directed not against the regime's title of Empire, but against its inadequate provision of liberty. The tiny group stood for liberal values larger than any particular political system. Ollivier thus implied that the very logic of the Cinq's position imposed an eventual *ralliement* if and when the Empire granted authentic reform. He likewise established his credentials as an *honnête homme* in contrast to Favre, who refused to rally in 1870. *L'Empire libéral,* in short, portrayed Ollivier as desiring to heal French divisions with democratic liberalism. The task involved pressuring the Emperor to

28. Ibid., III, 18.

reinstitute a liberal politics within the confines of the regime. As we shall see, this was a difficult task, calling for two Olliviers. The first, Ollivier the democrat, understood the progressive character of Bonapartism, while the second, Ollivier the defender of liberty, ultimately allowed Napoleon III to crown the edifice.

L'Empire libéral treated the years 1859–1860 as the crucial period in the regime's development. The reform of November 24, 1860 and conservative hostility to freer trade and the Italian affair changed the character of French politics. In the one case, Ollivier called conservative opposition a major source for liberty's revitalization. His attitude toward the November 24th decree was equally clear; he attributed the reforms to Napoleon III's generosity, and the volume in which he discussed them was accordingly entitled the "Inauguration of the Liberal Empire." He likewise noted that his own *ralliement* really began in 1860, as he first saw the possibility for the regime's transformation. Ollivier, on the other hand, resembled La Gorce in his failure to weigh the separate roles of the Emperor's generosity and the pressures of conservative dissatisfaction in the movement toward liberalization.

There was, however, another consideration. Fully aware of conservative anger over the government's Italian and tariff policies, the Cinq saw an opportunity for harassing tactics. While basically agreeing with governmental policies, the Cinq nonetheless mounted an attack against the authoritarian manner in which these policies were enacted. Led by Favre and Ollivier, the Cinq rather unscrupulously tried to shake the government majority. Such a policy, unfortunately, had certain drawbacks, not the least of which was to aid conservatives. The events of 1859–1860 had alerted clericals, protectionists, and assorted conservatives to the dangers of authoritarianism. Ollivier, who theoretically desired liberty for its own sake, must have felt some discomfort when he allied with the newly disenchanted. Moreover, any attempt to jar loose the conservative majority in the legislature ran the risk of undercutting the progressive Emperor, whose authority had thus far pretty much kept the Legislative Body in line. Ollivier was caught in the contradictions of Bonapartism. While Favre remained untroubled over the prospect of embarrassing the government, in part because he was more conservative than his colleague, Ollivier had second thoughts. Although he never mentioned the fact in *L'Empire libéral*, he began fearing the possibility of a conservative offensive. His journal, for instance, contained an entry for March 13, 1861, in which he reflected upon the attacks of the clericals and protectionists against the government. He wrote:

> I fearfully think of the counterrevolution invading the world if this man [Napoleon III] was overthrown, and for the first time I understand and excuse Béranger and the liberals of the Restoration; I also understand how, with the Republic's demonstrated impotence, revolutionary France had blindly thrown itself into the arms of the first Bonaparte. Up to the present, Bonapartism has been the single, regular obstacle that the revolution has been able to pose against reaction—hence its popularity.[29]

Ollivier wanted his Emperor and his liberty too.

Ollivier's ambiguous position was indicative of things to come. *L'Empire libéral* traced Ollivier's endeavor to construct an independent position in the political no man's land somewhere between the government and the moderate opposition. Ollivier argued that liberty could only be served by an alliance of all parties committed to its enlargement. He therefore labored for the Liberal Union which in 1863 presented liberal candidates of every political stripe, and he openly collaborated with the so-called liberal elite and worked for the candidacies of Thiers, Buffet, and Montalembert. To offset the impact of the conservatives, however, he reached something approximating an accommodation with the regime, and did so through no one less than the duc de Morny. As Ollivier described the matter, the shrewd president of the legislature recognized that all was lost unless the government established a working partnership with the forces of liberal democracy. That is, Morny hoped to achieve liberalization without appealing to the traditional and conservative forces of liberalism. He therefore saw Ollivier as a likely ally, and tried to rally the young republican, even tempting him with a possible ministerial position. When this blandishment proved to no

29. Ollivier, *Journal*, II, 12.

avail—Ollivier, after all, was incorruptible—Morny accepted Ollivier's suggestion that the regime undertake a program of civil reform. The beguiling Duc accordingly set the stage for the government's coalition or strike law of 1864, for which Ollivier acted as the official reporter. With Morny's help, he was working both sides of the street, which involved a risk that Ollivier never adequately comprehended. A politics of nonpartisanship, it ultimately accounted for Ollivier's repudiation in 1864 by the republicans, who, if they were anything, were partisan.

Despite tremendous prestige in government councils, Morny failed to carry the day for his liberalization program before his abrupt death in 1865. Ollivier was immediately confronted with a dilemma. He had reckoned upon his own influence with the regime to forge an independent but loyal and liberal Bonapartism. Morny's death disrupted the gambit and left Ollivier isolated. His bridges with the republican party were burned, there was certainly no place for him in the majority, and the *tiers parti* remained more enamored with Thiers than with Ollivier. In typical fashion, he confused his personal interests with those of the Emperor, and called Morny's passing a catastrophe: "no misfortune so grave had yet struck the sovereign."[30] With Morny gone, liberalization was postponed for nearly three years, and for four years the regime was guided by the inept and authoritarian Rouher.

L'Empire libéral described the period 1865–1867 as Ollivier's journey through a political wilderness. Fortunately, a stoic dedication to principle allowed the future minister to endure the burden, and the historian noted that, "to think of myself alone is an error I have never committed."[31] Under Rouher, meanwhile, the regime fell into disarray, but Ollivier never criticized Napoleon III's stubborn refusal to retire the minister. In any event, difficulties in foreign affairs and the inability of a sick Emperor to provide adequate leadership caused a malaise to sweep over the regime's personnel. The only choice was a renewal through further liberalization, and Napo-

30. Ollivier, *L'Empire libéral*, VII, 277.
31. Ibid., XI, 111.

leon III accordingly promised more reforms in his letter of January 19, 1867. Ollivier, in turn, reemerged from the wilderness, once again playing his double game, or, as he called it, the politics of reconciliation. Through Walewski, for instance, he opened a channel to Napoleon III, and even influenced the content of the January 19 letter. On the other hand, during the 1867 legislative session, he attacked Rouher for blocking and delaying the promised reform. He referred to the minister as a vice-Emperor, and flatly called for new personnel equal to the task of transforming the regime. The attack served two purposes: it indicated Ollivier's willingness to assume a ministerial position and reaffirmed his liberal commitments. As the historian pointed out with obvious satisfaction, Ollivier the liberal had established himself as a man of reform acceptable to the democratic Emperor.

According to his own account, Ollivier alone could implement the liberal Empire. He was indispensable because no one else held the trust of both the liberal opposition and the democratic Napoleon III. Indeed, given his decision to avoid a ministry controlled by the conservative *tiers parti*, Napoleon III had no other choice. While Ollivier acknowledged the problem of reconciling liberty with democracy, he never adequately recognized that he became something of a hostage. The ministry of January 2 merely continued Ollivier's balancing act between the liberal opposition and the Emperor. On the one hand, Ollivier's majority in the Legislative Body remained dependent upon the *tiers parti*, or as it was called after 1869, the center left. A grab bag of independents, clericals, protectionists, and liberals, the center left hoped to enlarge parliamentary powers and institute a conservative program. Ollivier proudly noted that he rallied the center left to his great experiment, and therefore gathered the support of the liberal elite. Buffet and the comte Daru even joined the ministry as symbols of the *ralliement*. Meanwhile, the extraparliamentary commissions brought a swarm of notables, including Guizot, Falloux, and Barrot, into open collaboration. To seal the pact, the Immortals in 1870 elected Ollivier to its august membership, an event Ollivier recorded as, "a testimony of an infinitely precious adhesion . . . given to the Cabinet through my person by the French Academy, one of the most ardent foyers of war against the Empire."[32]

Yet, it was no easy task to work with the forces represented by the center left. In Ollivier's words:

> Their distrust had two causes: all were loyally devoted to the government to which they willingly became servants, but their past was monarchical while I was basically republican . . . Moreover, my colleagues were protectionists, I was a free trader; they were irreconcilable enemies of Italy, and in spite of my disagreements on Rome as a capital, I remained its devoted friend. But all this, although serious, was only a kind of accessory. They felt an involuntary distrust of the Emperor, and no personal affection for him; I had confidence in him . . .[33]

The center left, however, did not exhaust Ollivier's difficulties with the legislature. He also needed the support of the center right, a group even more amorphous than the *tiers parti*. Ostensibly consisting of official candidates rallied to the idea of a liberal Empire, the center right included a large number of disenchanted clericals and protectionists. Many held political convictions indistinguishable from the center left. Ollivier's majority in the Legislative Body rested upon a bloc far more conservative than himself, and he became a hostage forced to surrender a great deal in order to guarantee his majority. Haussmann, for whom Ollivier in 1870 had real admiration, was one of the first sacrifices, and Duruy, who greatly resembled Ollivier, was permanently lost, given the strength of the ministry's clericals. Meantime, the ministry set out to dismantle the Empire's so-called free trade program. As many have pointed out, a liberal Empire greatly resembled an Orleanist Empire.

Ollivier had some harsh words for both centers, and accused them of frequently placing factional interests above those of the nation. He nevertheless minimized the extent of his sacrifices, and focused the reader's attention upon the Emperor's role in the national quest for liberal democracy. In 1870 Napoleon was in fact Ollivier's ace in the hole against the conservative majority in the

32. Ibid., XIII, 221.
33. Ibid., XII, 226.

legislature. *L'Empire libéral* therefore contained an eloquent defense of an executive power which Ollivier claimed he had no intention of dismantling—just the contrary. Ollivier likewise expressed distrust for pure parliamentarianism and doubted an Assembly's ability to provide an adequate response to democratic demands.

Indeed, Ollivier argued that assemblies strengthen cabals which impose an oligarchic rule, and he posed a hypothetical question: what remedy exists in a pure parliamentary system when a legislative majority is intent upon imposing an unpopular law? Fortunately, the office of the Emperor provided an answer. The constitution of 1870, according to Ollivier—and it was his constitution —organized a "parliamentary republic." The term was Ollivier's strange appellation for a system in which the executive acted as a responsible agent operating through a ministry dependent upon the legislature. Ollivier had constitutionalized his delicate balancing act. In the case of an unresolved conflict between the legislature and executive, the Emperor could call for a dissolution and new elections, or for a plebiscite, which Ollivier insisted upon calling a referendum and which he defended as an irreproachable republican institution. A balanced system with a strong executive therefore guaranteed democratic participation whenever a stalemate disrupted the ministry's precarious task of mediation. The expression of popular wishes received further protection with a proviso that all constitutional change would thereafter be subject to plebiscitary approval. The 1870 constitution was tailor-made for the situation in which Ollivier and his ministers found themselves—a regime with a still powerful executive and a newly strengthened legislature.

L'Empire libéral portrayed Ollivier's political career as a case of disinterested civic virtue on the part of a statesman who never received due credit. He described his efforts of 1870 as identical to those of Benjamin Constant in 1815—that of bringing liberty to a national regime with inadequate representative institutions. The ministry of January 2 liquidated authoritarianism, established true liberty, saved the dynasty, and in the process preserved the Empire's democratic structure. The precarious balancing act, in short, brought a national reconciliation, and some observers have confirmed Ollivier's conclusion. Henry Berton, operating from a democratic commitment, noted that whatever the strength of conservative forces in the new arrangement, the Legislative Body emerged from universal suffrage, a feature separating it from any Assembly ever convened under the auspices of Louis Philippe. Theodore Zeldin, focusing upon the other side of the program and echoing La Gorce, has argued that Ollivier's great insight was to recognize that the Empire contained within itself the makings for liberalization.[34]

Ollivier naturally affirmed that the liberal Empire was viable and would have proven permanent except for a war which was everybody's fault but his own. He devoted the whole of Volume XIV to discussing the problem of responsibility. There is no need to pursue the matter here, except to point out that Ollivier portrayed himself as blameless. The culprits were Bismarck and Ollivier's unscrupulous political enemies, particularly Thiers, who excited anti-Prussian public opinion and forced the ministry into a corner. Gramont also received some criticism; the Emperor was treated as a victim of conservative influences within the court, an argument that avoided the major issue.

Aside from enumerating various liberal *ralliements*, Ollivier took particular pleasure in pointing to the 1870 plebiscite as evidence of national confirmation. Indeed, Ollivier treated the vote as a vindication for his own policies and an absolution for the coup d'état.[35] *L'Empire libéral* did more than tell of a redemption; it provided a statement by the redeemer. Despite his self-righteousness, Ollivier had a point. The result of the plebiscite (7,336,000 *yes* votes and 1,560,000 *no* votes) threw the opposition into total disarray.

Some commentators, however, have argued that a Bonapartist regime could not truly be liberalized, and that Ollivier therefore attempted the impossible. This was Delord's argument. He called the liberal Empire a hoax and assumed that nothing really happened

---

34. Berton, *L'Evolution constitutionnelle*, p. 745; Zeldin, *Emile Ollivier*, p. 110.

35. Ollivier, *L'Empire libéral*, XIII, 400. In his journal, an overjoyed Ollivier was even less restrained. "I have absolved Napoleon of December 2; I have imposed only one condition: a liberal constitution. He has given it to me. Then I have turned toward the people and have said to them: Do you confirm my absolution? And they have responded to me: yes . . . " (*Journal*, II, 448).

throughout the eighteen-year period. Others, while admitting the possibility of liberalization, have asserted that it meant the death of Bonapartism. To share authority with a legislature negated the regime's meaning and established a completely different kind of government. Such was the assumption of La Gorce, and because he thought the liberal Empire was truly liberal, he found it acceptable. Ollivier viewed the matter somewhat differently. The 1870 regime represented a compromise for a nation unwilling to endure the probably fatal effects of another revolution. The liberal Empire was, as it were, having half a cake by eating only half. Although he never used the words, Ollivier obviously thought that a liberal Empire divided Frenchmen the least.

It all nevertheless proved temporary. Unfortunately, vanity prevented Ollivier from comprehending that his disgrace was partially the result of his own system. He rose to political power by avoiding partisanship, only to find that a crisis left him without reliable support within the legislature. Forced to play to the gallery, he quickly bowed to the majority's wrath against Prussia. Further, Gramont, either because he envied Ollivier's preeminence in the ministry or because he thought crises demanded quick action, short-circuited normal procedures and dealt directly with the Emperor. The two powers between which he was to mediate simply overwhelmed Ollivier, and in the 1870 crisis he never succeeded in implementing a policy of his own. Events took control, and the regime slid into the abyss. Few governments, of course, would have survived the defeat of 1870, but it was Ollivier's that fell and it was Ollivier who paid the consequences. With a little exaggeration and much melancholy, he wrote of what had been and what might have been:

> In 1857 I had taken the oath and in 1858 I had constituted the Cinq, in order to impede the prohibition against liberty and to maintain the burning torch transmitted by our masters. When the amnesty of 1860 had appeased my heart and when the decree of November 24 had shown me a sovereign capable of comprehending liberty, I had believed that it would not be impossible to transform the Empire, and that transforming it would be easier and above all more profitable than reversing it . . . I had found this a good task and consecrated myself to it for ten years, without allowing myself to be halted . . . I had formed a responsible,

parliamentary ministry, and by successive stages, had substituted the liberal Constitution for the authoritarian Constitution. Now the people said to me with more than seven million votes that I had not deceived myself . . . Suppose that I had been carried away at that point by a fever like Cavour? I would have been unanimously celebrated as one of the rare statesmen of the nineteenth century . . .[36]

Had Ollivier been a second Cavour, he would not have written *L'Empire libéral*. Unfortunately, his bitterness was so great that he underestimated the accomplishments of the liberalized regime. He mistakenly assumed that French history started anew simply because his own career came to an end, and herein lay a shortcoming of history written as personal testimony. Like La Gorce and Delord, he thought 1870 represented a watershed of major proportion, and he refused to grant his achievements a survival greater than his own career. The marriage of liberalism with democracy, however, did not vanish with the 1870 experiment—just the contrary. Although the Bonapartist tradition suffered an eclipse, Morny actually had his way, and one suspects that the wily duc would have prospered during the Third Republic. In any event, liberal adherence to the January 2 ministry included an acceptance of democratic principles, and that acceptance carried over into the next regime; France spent the 1870s under a monarchist republic that was not so very different from Ollivier's liberal Empire.

36. Ollivier, *L'Empire libéral,* XIII, 402–403.

Chapter IV

The Professionals

During the first thirty years of the Third Republic, history as a discipline underwent a major change, the effects of which are still very real. The transformation represented a shift away from the idea that history is best written by literate men of the world employing their wisdom to draw lessons from past experience. Although such history continued to appear, it was superseded by the work of a new breed of historian who denied the relevance of history written by dilettantes and amateurs. Emphasis was instead placed upon credentials, and historians became professionals concerned with the mastery of proper method.

Professionalization involved a series of related developments, the most important of which was the attempt to establish the writing of history as an objective and supposedly scientific endeavor. Although a precise idea of what constituted scientific history was never fully agreed upon, it did entail a scrupulous reliance upon documents and critical analysis. Such a reliance arose from a sense of detachment and the use of skills acquired in seminar training adopted from the German universities. Proper technique theoretically guaranteed the elimination of bias, thus allowing the historian to tell it as it is—or was. The truth of the documents found expression through the historian who, as a priest with the proper method, unlocked what was hidden from the uninitiated. Alphonse Aulard was typical of a whole generation when he concluded his history of the Revolution with the assertion that he had no thesis to prove; he merely recounted the Revolution's history. Similarly, there was skepticism about any attempt to reach general conclusions and distrust of those who hoped to cover the broad spectrum of French development. General histories were viewed as the work of nonprofessionals who imposed their political prejudices and preconceptions without proper regard for the facts. Such history was labeled metaphysical, meaning unscientific, and Charles Langlois accordingly commented that Michelet could not be truly considered a man of learning. The concern for facts and documents demanded topics narrow enough to permit intensive study. As Gabriel Monod commented in his famous introductory article in the *Revue historique,* historians should limit their generalizations to the modest conclusions allowed by the study of particular areas in which the facts are thoroughly established. The result, of course, was specialization, with the monograph representing the historical endeavor *par excellence;* indeed, the doctoral dissertation with its breathtaking, or perhaps suffocating, erudition became the model for proper scholarship.

The impetus to transform history into a formal discipline originated in the 1860s and in the larger work of Victor Duruy. Like so many on the left, the minister admired Prussia's educational program and thought it guaranteed an enlightened citizenry. He hoped to establish in France a similar system of obligatory and universal education; such a program, however, called for a general reform of higher education if the community was to have an adequate number of qualified teachers. For the moment, the numerous *facultés des lettres* were inferior to the task. As an example, in the teaching of history each of the provincial faculties had only one professor, whose job was to lecture to the public rather than to serious students. To make matters worse, these professors were lettered gentlemen in the tradition of Guizot and Cousin. Duruy's plan included a reform of higher education designed to provide a source of competent teachers in a system of state secondary education. The minister accordingly commissioned an investigation of German universities, and began searching for a way to introduce the techniques of German scholarship. Unfortunately, immediate reform within the faculties was well-nigh impossible given the ministry's lack of funds and the inertia of an already established system. A partial answer, however, was found in 1868 with a separate institution designed to act as a model—the Ecole Pratique des Hautes Etudes.

After 1870, Duruy's protégés introduced German scholarship and adapted the curriculum for the needs of public education. The Ecole Pratique des Hautes Etudes played a particularly significant role as its methods were adopted by the Ecole Normale. The two major figures in the reform were Ernest Lavisse and Gabriel Monod. Lavisse, formerly Duruy's secretary and tutor to the Prince Imperial, was left unemployed by the events of 1870. Convinced that an inadequate educational program accounted for the French defeat, he undertook a study of German schooling. By 1878 he was teaching at the Ecole Normale. His major efforts were directed toward educational reform, and while writing numerous textbooks, he filled the *Revue internationale de l'enseignement* with articles concerning various proposals; he also organized like-minded professors (e.g., Monod, Georges Weill, Fustel de Coulanges, and even the sociologist Durkheim) into the Société pour l'Etude des Questions d'Enseignement Supérieur, an educational lobby highly respected by government officials. With some justification Lavisse has been called the major architect of the Republic's educational policy. Monod, on the other hand, epitomized the professional concerned with critical method. Like Lavisse, a *normalien* who studied in Germany, Monod in 1868 was appointed by Duruy to the historical section of the Ecole Pratique des Hautes Etudes. A founder of the *Revue historique*, Monod also served as its first editor, and employed the journal to propagandize for the new history. With the Ecole and the *Revue* at his disposal, Monod exercised an influence that few dared challenge in the narrow circle of higher education.

The practitioners of professional history, however, were less original than they imagined. Their quest was an old one: a true history. Like their "amateur" predecessors, they thought history primarily involved politics, although a concern for documentation supposedly allowed the historian for the first time to describe political life accurately. Yet such an affirmation merely demonstrated the failure of the professionals to comprehend fully what they were about. Documents or not, the very connection between German scholarly technique and public education belied the idea that historians were nonpartisan. Jean Macé, a moving force behind the new educational system, had established the important Ligue Française de l'Enseignement during the 1860s simply because he believed that an uneducated electorate too easily voted Bonapartist. Indeed, the whole gamut of educational reform was largely prompted by political considerations: the republican desire to establish a new political order, and the larger national response to the humiliating defeat of 1870 and the social divisions reflected by the Commune. Republicans could therefore agree that a democratic politics called for an educational program designed to shape a citizenry with a common set of loyalties and symbols; otherwise, national cohesion remained doubtful. Many observers, remembering 1870, recalled with despair the apparent Prussian sense of unity as opposed to an excessive Gallic individualism. Such anxieties accounted for the prominent role played by historians in establishing the new educational curriculum. Monod argued and others agreed that history had a "national importance" because it revealed to Frenchmen their common ties and destinies. Lavisse, an ardent nationalist, frankly referred to history as an instrument for instilling young citizens with a sense of civic virtue and national pride, and he established the pattern by which textbooks in history taught the value of military preparedness.[1]

The professionals owed the Republic a great deal, and they correspondingly exhibited great loyalty to the regime. Without a republican educational program, their conquest of the University would have been slower and less complete. Further, they generally shared the republican leadership's aggressive laicism—or more appropriately, anticlericalism—and their educational structure was built at the expense of the Church. Always an anticlerical, Lavisse

---

1. See in particular Pierre Nora, "Ernest Lavisse: son role dans la formation du sentiment national"; and Jacques and Mona Ozouf, "Le Thème du patriotisme dans les manuels primaires." Lavisse's militarism may have been a bit exaggerated, but it was not extraordinary; Jean Macé in 1885, for instance, drew up a *Manuel du tir à l'usage des écoles primaires, des lycées et des bataillons civiques.*

abandoned Bonapartism and rallied to the Republic in part because of his admiration for the policies of Jules Ferry. As for the Republic, its leaders showed little sympathy for erudition when it conflicted with proper politics; to take one example, Fustel de Coulanges failed to receive a chair in medieval history at the Ecole Normale because some attributed to him clerical sympathies. The President of the Republic outlined the terms of academic employment when, in 1896, he told the professors at the Sorbonne that they were the "resolute and devoted servants of the republican and national idea."[2]

Professionalization brought the development of a huge academic apparatus which included bibliographical projects, research institutes, prescribed courses in historical method, and numerous journals patterned after the prestigious *Revue historique*. Given the professionals' role in the University, the academic structure was partially integrated or absorbed into the state. Amongst other things, the new historian was a *fonctionnaire*. At times he became something more; Alfred Rambaud, a colleague of Lavisse, became *chef de cabinet* for Jules Ferry in 1879, a senator in 1895, and later Minister of Public Instruction. When World War I struck, Lavisse took charge of a massive effort to organize French historians in a propaganda program against the Germans, and his cry for academic warriors did not go unanswered.

There may or may not have been a republic of professors, but there certainly was a university of republicans. The Third Republic defended itself against unfriendly scholarship by hiring and patronizing its own historians; avowed enemies were found in the ranks of the amateurs, not within the University. Professional history therefore proved more conservative than its practitioners dared to acknowledge. Wedded to republicanism, the professionals generally shared the values and prejudices associated with liberal democracy.

2. Cited by Gaston Rouvier, *L'Enseignement public en France au début du XXe siècle*. Rouvier was an assistant to Louis Liard, the Director of Higher Education.

For the links joining professional history and republicanism, see in particular Charles-Olivier Carbonell, *Histoire et historiens*, and William Keylor, *Academy and Community*. Also, the commemorative edition of the *Revue historique*, 518 (1976) has the following articles: Charles-Olivier Carbonell, "La Naissance de la *Revue historique*"; Alice Gérard, "Histoire et politique"; and Madeleine Rebérioux, "Histoire, historiens et dreyfusisme."

As a result, the idea of universal education became as central to the Republic as economic progress once was to the Second Empire, and it was no accident that the young regime enlarged and renovated the buildings which housed the University of Paris, a public works program which provided a contrast to that of Haussmann. Since they operated a system at least partially designed for social pacification, republican teachers taught the virtues of social solidarity and economic individualism in a democratic society that allowed for both mobility and progress through education. As a further measure of safety, textbooks destined for rural schools propagated the idea that life in the provinces and on the farm was preferable to that of the capital and in the factory. With real justification, a recent observer has noted that the republican school system provided a major support for the so-called stalemate society which remained unchallenged until the years following World War I.[3]

In the meantime, the professors of the Sorbonne, while establishing policy and setting educational standards, fulfilled the demands of their discipline. The results were impressive. Objective history meant measured, if modest, conclusions, and monographs provided intensive studies of major importance. Duruy seemed to have had his way: scholarship ministered to the needs of both democracy and truth.

Charles Seignobos

Charles Seignobos has been called the perfect example of the empirical or scientific historian, and at least one observer has portrayed him as a period piece, who was more important for what he represented than for what he accomplished. Whether justified or not, the judgment indicated much about Seignobos, since his career

---

3. John Talbott, *The Politics of Educational Reform in France, 1918–1940*. Other works which deal with the conservative impact of the Republic's educational system are: Mona Ozouf, *L'Ecole, l'église et la République*; Antoine Prost, *Histoire de l'enseignement en France, 1800–1967*; and two articles by Gérard Vincent: "Les Professeurs de l'enseignement secondaire dans la société de la 'Belle Epoque'," and "Les Professeurs du second degré au début du XIXe siècle."

revealed the bonds that joined the Third Republic and the new history.[4]

The Seignobos family, from the Ardèche, Protestant and moderately well off, produced a line of republican figures. While a student at the Ecole Normale (1874–1877), Charles engaged in political affairs, and he proved a loyal son; his later views never extended beyond the boundaries of French radicalism, as evidenced by his approach to history. He continually reaffirmed that politics was history, and once wrote that, "I am convinced that political authority and political accidents . . . have always exercised a decisive action on the evolution of the French people."[5] He likewise thought Marxism inadequate for describing politics, and believed socialism in general a threat to individual liberties.

While a student at the Ecole Normale, Seignobos studied under Fustel de Coulanges and Ernest Lavisse, both of whom convinced him of the importance of documentation. Lavisse also obtained for his student a two-year government grant to study the German university system; it was something of a national mission given French concern for educational reform and scientific methodology, and in 1881 Seignobos published his findings in the *Revue internationale de l'enseignement*. Despite the critical tone of the article, Seignobos greatly admired German erudition, and his doctoral dissertation, *Le Régime féodal en Bourgogne jusqu'en 1360* (1883), was a model of proper scholarship.

The upper reaches of the University were very much an insiders' club, and success demanded patronage. Before entering the ranks of the elite, men were judged by both whom and what they knew. Seignobos's credentials were in order and his rise was accordingly rapid. A grandson of a 48er and the son of a republican deputy, he had also been chosen by Lavisse as the old master's successor at Paris. While still in Germany, Seignobos received a post at Dijon, in

---

4. Gordon McNeil, "Charles Seignobos." In the *Etudes de politique et d'histoire*, selected writings of Charles Seignobos, there is a nearly complete bibliography of Seignobos's huge body of writings. For an appraisal of Seignobos as the political democrat-historian, see André Siegfried, "Charles Seignobos."

5. Charles Seignobos, *Histoire sincère de la nation française*, p. vii.

part through the intervention of his father who wrote letters of support under the Chamber of Deputies' letterhead.[6] Seignobos's clout at the Ministry of Public Instruction was such that he apparently ignored with impunity the rules which restricted the behavior of his less fortunate provincial colleagues. He disappeared for weeks at a time, missed classes, and failed to answer the queries of the rector, who desperately complained in vain to Paris. By 1883 Seignobos obtained a post at the Sorbonne where he remained until his retirement a half century later.

Like so many at the pinnacle of higher education, Seignobos adhered to a Radical politics of anticlericalism. The historian viewed France's modern history as a contest between an incipient democracy and a retrograde Church, and in this contest the University played a singular role. Seignobos commented to the *Petite République* in a published interview of January 5, 1899 that, "the Church holds men in domination by dominating women and educating children." Indeed, laicism remained Seignobos's governing principle. An important figure in the Ligue des Droits de l'Homme, he organized Dreyfusard demonstrations at the Sorbonne and viewed the Jewish officer as a victim of a clerical plot against democracy. In a similar vein, he told the *Petite République* that Marxists and socialists, with their emphasis upon the social question, muddied France's political waters and thereby diverted attention from the real challenge—clericalism.

A member of the important Société pour l'Etude des Questions d'Enseignement Supérieur, Seignobos frequently advised the government on matters affecting the University. Official responsibilities enlarged in 1914 when Lavisse included his old protégé in the propaganda office operated by historians. The man, however, who once studied in Germany and admired its erudition was anything but a chauvinist and he proved much less pugnacious than his colleagues. As early as 1916, Seignobos joined the Société d'Etudes Documentaires et Critiques sur la Guerre, an organization of intellectuals critical of the official interpretation of the conflict. When

6. These letters are contained in Seignobos's Ministry of Public Instruction dossier, now located in the Archives Nationales, F17 23801.

appointed to a government committee on war aims, Seignobos became a minority of one, opposing a policy of annexations and arguing for the need to build a new Europe through international reconciliation.

No one contributed more than Seignobos to introducing the critical method into French higher education. He and Charles Langlois in 1898 wrote the *Introduction aux études historiques* which became a handbook for the new history. The manual proved extremely influential both within and without France, and the authors managed to set the style for a whole generation of historical scholarship. They reaffirmed the principle that history could be scientific; documents provided raw material, and the historian employed a critical attitude in order to establish the facts. More than anything, being critical implied a hesitancy to draw conclusions and a certain mental reservation.

As an historian, Seignobos adhered to the strictures of the scientific method. He wrote in a dry and precise style, and in a reference to Michelet, criticized any attempt to merge science and literature. Seignobos's approach emphasized the importance of particular events, and even accidents, and critics frequently accused him of stubbing his toe on Cleopatra's nose. Something of a nominalist, as behooved a defender of Alain's republic, he once denied the relevance of institutional history, calling such entities as the Church and Crown mere abstractions with no real life, or history, of their own.[7] Ever unimaginative, he also questioned the judgment of his old master, Fustel de Coulanges, whom he thought was given to devising abstractions.

Despite the assertion that Clio served no other master than truth, Seignobos nevertheless thought history politically useful. In an article entitled, "L'Enseignement de l'histoire comme instrument d'éducation politique," he called the historian an agent for enlightening the population to the duties of democratic citizenship, and commented that, "since history is true civic education, the mission of

7. See Charles Seignobos, *La Méthode historique appliquée aux sciences sociales*, p. 149. For a criticism of Seignobos on this count, see Henri Berr, "Les Rapports de l'histoire et des sciences sociales d'après M. Seignobos."

fulfilling the public education of future citizens has fallen to the professors of history."[8] In another context, Seignobos affirmed that prior to the Third Republic, the University "had above all been an ecclesiastical fortress, built in order to maintain clerical domination over a lay society,"[9] and in true republican fashion, he later added that history, if it does anything, teaches that Burke and Taine erred on the side of pessimism. In some measure the objective historian-republican had managed to objectify his prejudices.

Although Seignobos wrote his dissertation in medieval history, he found repugnant the Church's institutional role during the Middle Ages. As a republican, he preferred nineteenth-century France to that of the *ancien régime,* and therefore shifted his attention to more recent events, becoming a professor of modern history. An authority on the political affairs of post-1815 France and an author of numerous articles, he made his major contribution to the collaborative histories that naturally followed from specialization. Since no one man was thought erudite enough for the affairs outside his particular field, scholars pooled their resources in joint efforts designed to provide the benefits of both scholarship and general history. Seignobos first contributed appropriate chapters to the Lavisse and Rambaud *Histoire générale du IVe siècle à nos jours.*[10] More important, however, was the famous *Histoire de France contemporaine* written under the direction of Lavisse, and the classic cooperative work of the early professionals. Unlike monographs, the *Histoire contemporaine* was written for the educated public; in Lavisse's words, it provided a history for twentieth-century men. The work made available to the public the benefits of scholarship, and Seignobos's contribution consisted of three volumes, two of which concerned the Second Empire.[11] As an historical effort, they represented a limited,

8. The article is reproduced in *Etudes de politique et d'histoire,* pp. 109–132. The quotation is from page 132.

9. Charles Seignobos, "L'Organisation des divers types d'enseignement," p. 117.

10. Charles Seignobos, "La Révolution de 1848 et la réaction en France" and "La Troisième République."

11. Charles Seignobos, *La Révolution de 1848—Le second Empire (1848–1859);* and *Le Déclin de l'Empire et l'établissement de la 3e République.* The republican professionals treated the Empire as an interlude in French political development; as a result, the regime was not granted a volume of its own in the *Histoire contemporaine*

general study by an expert employing both his own research and that of others. The results were predictable. Always moderate and seldom original, Seignobos provided a measured defense of liberal-democratic values.

Like most republicans, Seignobos approached the Empire by emphasizing its origins. For Seignobos, the coup d'état set the stage for a morality play only a little less crude than the dramas of Hugo or Delord. He described the coup as an executive revolt against constituted authority, slighted the fears concerning 1852 which theoretically justified illegal action, and portrayed provincial resistance as being politically motivated, perfectly legal, and in no way socialistically inclined. According to Seignobos, the Mixed Commissions, which oversaw the repression that followed the coup, set the style of the new regime. He wrote that, "the *coup d'état* made against the Assembly in the name of the sovereignty of the people became a war against the republicans in the name of the principle of authority . . . Authority above all and in the future a limited liberty: this formula came to be the program of the reign."[12] Most important, repression guaranteed republican animosity which limited the Empire's alternatives and prevented the regime from becoming "definitive."[13]

Seignobos's discussion of the authoritarian period was brief. He thought that the constitution of 1852 repudiated the very essence of representative government, and he denied the relevance of Bonapartist executive responsibility. His judgment echoed that of La Gorce, but was even more severe as no mention was made of the

(the series to which the two above volumes belong), but was divided between two volumes which, as a set, began and ended with a republic.

12. Seignobos, *La Révolution de 1848*, pp. 215–216. See also Seignobos's "Les Opérations des Commissions Mixtes en 1852."

13. Vincent Wright confirms Seignobos's conclusion on the effect of the coup in later hindering an accord between Napoleon III and the republicans. Wright argues that although the coup was a technical success, it politically alienated the regime from the left and made Napoleon III the leader of the Party of Order with which he had little in common. See Wright's "The Coup d'état of December 1851."

regime's potential for liberal development. In the realm of practical
politics, Seignobos argued that the government never succeeded in
establishing firm support, and that the history of the Empire primarily concerned this dilemma. The authoritarian regime seemed
stronger than it was, given the numerous controls exercised over the
legislature and press. There remained, however, an opposition consisting of the republicans and others who were politically enlightened. To complicate matters, the regime lacked the full support of
conservatives. Although Orleanist rank and file rallied to the government, its leaders refused to do so, while Legitimists in general followed an abstentionist policy. The 1857 elections were indicative of
the government's problem: the opposition, despite official pressures,
received 665,000 votes. In Seignobos's words:

> The Empire had succeeded in neither rallying nor destroying its ad-
> versaries. It did not run the risk of being overturned, because all the
> organized forces—the army, the civil service, the clergy—supported it,
> and the enormous majority of the electors obeyed it. But, those who voted
> for it were the peasants and bourgeois, indifferent to politics; it had
> against it almost everyone interested in political life.[14]

The argument, however, was unconvincing. The regime's 5,471,000
votes against the opposition's 665,000, and its support by the peasantry and bourgeoisie represented no small accomplishment—few
regimes, including the Third Republic, have asked for more. Further, as Seignobos admitted, things went smoothly for the government until the Italian affair, which he acknowledged to have been
of Napoleon's own making.

On the other hand, Seignobos found Napoleon III far more ad-
mirable than the Empire, and the historian drew a sharp distinction
between the two.[15] He likewise distinguished the Emperor from his
advisors, and blamed the latter for the Empire's more questionable
policies. Seignobos apparently dismissed Bonapartist theory as being

---

14. Seignobos, *La Révolution de 1848*, p. 275.
15. Seignobos's sympathetic attitude toward the Emperor is found in *La Révolution de 1848*, pp. 245–246. In his preface to the French edition of H. A. L. Fisher's
work, *Le Bonapartisme*, translated by H. H. Duncan (Paris: Plon, 1909), Seignobos
was even more indulgent, calling Napoleon III a democratic leader toward whom
Frenchmen had not been altogether fair.

irrelevant, since the Emperor's advisors, drawn largely from the ranks of Orleanism, had gained control of the regime. Bonapartist theory had called for an executive able to manage the operations of the state, and it could not compensate for Louis Napoleon's woeful lack of administrative ability. According to the historian, Louis Napoleon's own government dominated him; he never learned to control it.

Many have alluded to the tendency of the early professionals to treat economic and social history as a kind of remnant which remained after political matters had been considered. It was in precisely that manner that Seignobos, following his lengthy discussion of the politics of the 1850s, added a section entitled "French Society." Slightly over fifty pages in length, this section completed the first volume and apparently represented a political historian's concept of social history. Limited to economic affairs and class structure, it included virtually no discussion of such matters as social theory, or more surprisingly, of the Church, except for a brief comment that universal suffrage increased the political power of the clergy. Worse, the matters Seignobos did consider were not related to the previous sections concerning politics. "French Society" was a separate piece, an unlabeled appendix, the major thesis of which was that mid-nineteenth-century France more closely resembled a society of the *ancien régime* than that of the turn of the twentieth century. Political democratization had not yet weakened old class distinctions and barriers, since the community's economic organization remained traditional. The French were still a nonurban people, and poor transportation guaranteed rural isolation and primitive agriculture geared for local markets. Similarly, industry was dispersed and decentralized. Once these points were established, however, "French Society" provided no direct allusion to the economic changes associated with the Empire. Seignobos's only reference to the regime's contribution in economic affairs appeared in four pages of a chapter concerning authoritarian politics, and he noted that Bonapartist strategy called for a policy of transferring community attention from an obvious loss of freedom to the benefits of material welfare. Seignobos likewise mentioned with favor the prominent role played by the Saint-Simonians, and he referred to the railroad system as the *oeuvre capitale* of the regime. Yet, the implications of all this were not carried over into the addendum on social history. For whatever reason, politics remained separate from any other consideration, and the Empire as a result never received its due.

Seignobos's second volume, *Le Déclin de l'Empire et l'établissement de la 3e République,* was pure political history. Divided into four parts, the volume covered the internal politics of the 1860s, the Empire's foreign policy during the same decade, the war of 1870, and the establishment of the parliamentary Republic. The treatment of the Empire's internal history, however, was less than satisfactory. Seignobos seemed intent upon exaggerating the regime's weakness, even at the cost of misrepresenting the opposition's strength. Secondly, he was hesitant to acknowledge the reality of liberalization, and never quite decided how to evaluate the 1860s. The result was a discussion marked with ambiguities and not a few contradictions. To make matters worse, Seignobos frequently revealed more by what he refused to mention than by what he actually considered. Possibly exasperated and apparently aware of the problem, he resolved his dilemmas with a leap into the faith of his republican predecessors.

On one point Seignobos was clear: foreign policy, because it alienated government supporters, set in motion the process of liberalization. The years 1859–1860 therefore represented a boundary separating the Empire into two distinct periods.

> The conservatives, the Catholics, the bourgeois and the peasants who supported the internal politics of the Emperor, condemned his foreign policy; the adversaries of the imperial regime, workers and republicans, approved his external politics. The role of authority's champion against liberty in France clashed with the attitude of liberator in Italy. He had discontented all the parties, none of which any longer supported him.[16]

Isolated, the government was reduced to moving awkwardly back and forth between liberalization and authoritarianism, and the resulting instability merely quickened the pace of liberal reform.

16. Seignobos, *Le Déclin de l'Empire,* p. 6.

Beyond the obvious evaluation of 1859–1860, Seignobos devoted his major efforts to contrasting the regime's electoral support during the 1860s with that of the opposition. He misconstrued the situation, however, by refusing to clarify it. When discussing the elections of 1863 and 1869, he tended to treat the opposition as if it were one. The election of 1863 was thus described as a government defeat, given the combined vote of Catholics and republicans. The conclusion was a bit too facile. Catholics and republicans were in fundamental disagreement, and if faced with a choice between a Republic or an Empire, Catholics would—and did—choose the latter. Napoleon III, after all, held some important cards. The meaning of the electoral defeat remained problematical when the opposition was in fact a diverse coalition. The government in 1869 received 4,438,000 votes to 3,355,000, the latter being almost evenly divided between conservative liberals, many of whom had once been official candidates, and republicans. There were, in fact, three major political blocs: the government supporters (including the authoritarian Arcadians, intransigent and more Bonapartist than the Emperor), the *tiers parti,* and the republicans. The government, of course, struck a bargain with the *tiers parti,* and isolated the left. Seignobos neglected the dynamics of this maneuver by writing of a "widespread" opposition. Before 1870, opposition was indeed widespread, but much of it was also amenable to a *ralliement.* And indeed, almost in spite of himself, Seignobos had to grant the liberal Empire broad support in all political quarters except those of the far right and the republicans.[17]

When it served the function of emphasizing government weakness and underplaying the prospects for liberal evolution, Seignobos proved capable of more clearly distinguishing republicans and conservatives. He portrayed the former as a hostile force whose antagonism kept the regime off balance. Conservatives, on the other hand, were described as having weakened the regime by their disengagement, but their role was apparently negative as opposed to that of the more aggressive republicans. Seignobos, perhaps because he wished to exaggerate the role of the republicans, never consis-

17. Ibid., p. 86.

tently acknowledged the conservative contribution to a liberal politics, and he therefore neglected the very development that allowed Ollivier's experiment. The Italian question accomplished both something more and something less than the separation of the Empire from its early supporters. Rather than completely denying the government, conservatives, including clerical ones, demanded the dismantling of authoritarianism. Herein lay the possibilities for a liberal regime.

Seignobos likewise experienced some difficulties in appraising liberalization. While admitting the Empire experienced profound changes in the period from 1860 to 1870, he never reached a consistent appreciation of what those changes meant. On the one hand, he argued that Napoleon III remained opposed to parliamentary government; forced to implement reform, the Emperor tried to lessen the regime's authoritarianism without repudiating Bonapartist principles. The historian argued that an authoritarian apparatus remained intact although restraints upon the legislature were slightly relaxed. Seignobos also believed that the reforms represented a major breach in the earlier system, and that they established a regime reminiscent of the constitutional monarchies. Further, the decade as a whole brought, little by little, a return to parliamentarism. In the last analysis, however, Seignobos showed little willingness to grant liberalization any fundamental reality, and he remained ambivalent toward the experiment of 1870. He seemed to believe that the Legislative Body had become a parliament, but refused to allow the Empire the status of a parliamentary government. In his own words:

> Piece by piece Napoleon had re-established the parliamentary regime, always under the pretense of "improving" the regime of 1852. He pretended to have maintained "the fundamental bases of the Constitution," in adding liberty as the crowning of the edifice. This fiction left his authority intact. The Cabinet, formed from deputies of the majority, was after all only an experiment: it depended upon the Emperor to end it . . . The Emperor alone remained responsible before the people and was president of the Council of Ministers.[18]

18. Ibid., p. 85.

Seignobos was no more decisive about the plebiscite of 1870. In one instance, he argued that the referendum strengthened the Bonapartist right while discouraging republicans and exacerbating their divisions. Then he added that the plebiscitary results of 1870 reflected the regime's failure: government support had merely returned to the level of 1851–1852. Such a conclusion revealed little more than republican astigmatism on the part of Seignobos; to recapture the support of the early Empire was a major accomplishment. As for the observation that the plebiscite worked to the benefit of the Arcadians, it hardly corresponded with the idea that the plebiscitary vote indicated a Bonapartist failure. The historian had lost his way by once again ignoring the obvious.

Seignobos is reputed to have said that it is useful to pose questions, but dangerous to answer them. In the *Histoire contemporaine* he followed his own advice, thereby avoiding a few of the pitfalls inherent in the republican vision of history. Seignobos nevertheless remained somewhat ambivalent and, in the end, simply moved to the events of September 4 after discussing the foreign policy of the 1860s. The French defeat was attributed to insufficient military preparation, and he made no attempt to call Sedan the inevitable result of December 2. Empiricism apparently excluded any mention of Hugo's republican providence. Yet, so strong was Seignobos's republican bias, that the brief conclusion of the *Histoire contemporaine* seemed almost incompatible with the preceding two volumes. With a one page summation, Seignobos finally overcame his equivocations:

> The Empire, imposed upon France by a military *coup d'état,* had in its service no other force of action but the army. The nation had not become imperialist and only lent the government the support of inertia. Electors voted for the Empire because it was there. The government was only a group of functionaries superimposed upon the nation without becoming a part of it. The government remained an official machine without moral authority. The mass of indifferent people obeyed it, but all who had a political life struggled against it. The army disappeared, and the Empire toppled without combat, without opposition, by a push from the crowd. Its chiefs fled to foreign countries, and no one tried to defend it.[19]

19. Ibid., p. 248.

Objective history or not, the praetorian theme of republican historiography remained intact.

Jean Maurain

In University circles, Jean Maurain was a true insider. The son of a *normalien* who became Dean of the Faculté des Sciences at Paris, Maurain was thoroughly familiar with the world of French higher education and its relationship to the politics of the Third Republic. A precocious student, he entered the Ecole Normale in 1921 and three years later received his degree in history. After a stint in the army, Maurain prepared for his doctorate at Paris and not surprisingly chose for his advisor an old family friend, Charles Seignobos.

Despite their difference in age, master and student became fast friends and frequently vacationed together at Seignobos's cottage in Brittany.[20] Seignobos later referred to Maurain as brilliant, and as probably the best student he had ever taught. The relationship was no doubt cemented by the fact that Maurain, although sympathetic to socialism, shared Seignobos's traditional vision of politics and history, all of which prompted the master to remark that Maurain "was not seduced by any of those absolute formulae so full of attraction for young men and so popular with his generation."[21] Seignobos had found a kindred spirit.

Maurain was the first professional to write a monographic study of the Empire—his dissertation, *La Politique ecclésiastique du second Empire*. The work was a masterpiece of erudition and immediately established the author's reputation. After a brief period teaching in provincial lycées, Maurain in 1933 received a position at the Faculté des Lettres at Clermont-Ferrand; as the Minister of Public Instruction noted in a memorandum, the appointment practically imposed itself given the candidate's obvious capabilities, professional support, and family connections.[22]

20. These sojourns are described in Camille Marbo (Madame Emile Borel), *A travers deux siècles*, pp. 175–183.
21. Charles Seignobos, Emile Borel, and Jules Jeanneney, *Jean Maurain*, p. 6.
22. Archives Nationales, Ministry of Education, Dossier Jean Maurain, F17 23625.

Maurain, at his new post for less than five weeks, took a leave of absence when the President of the Senate, Jules Jeanneney, called him into the government of republican defense which followed in the wake of the Stavisky riots.[23] Maurain became secretary to the Senate, and perhaps considered the possibility of patterning his career after that of Alfred Rambaud who had joined an active political life with that of a professional historian. Or perhaps, as his friends claimed, Maurain wished to gain a better understanding of politics in order to comprehend history. Whatever the case, while secretary, he continued his studies and in 1936 published a biography of Jules Baroche.[24] The following year he was named professor of modern history at the Faculté des Lettres at Lille, a post he held until his untimely death in a skiing accident in early 1939.

According to Seignobos, Maurain epitomized the perfect historian, possessing the skills and attitudes necessary for detailed research and prudent observations. Given the assumptions of empirical history, the judgment was merited. Maurain's work on ecclesiastical policy and his biography of Baroche both rested upon new source material, and he was the first to use in any extensive fashion the records of the ministries of Justice and Religious Affairs. On the other hand, the inspiration of his work was fundamentally orthodox and unoriginal; both books investigated in detail issues raised by Seignobos in the *Histoire contemporaine,* and Maurain shared his master's republican distrust of Bonapartist politics.

Maurain's was a tragically short career—he was only thirty-six years old at the time of his death—yet, it was also brilliant within the limited sphere of established historical scholarship and conventional republican politics that marked the Third Republic. Maurain had already written two major monographs, had experienced the world of contemporary politics, and had seemed destined for the Sorbonne. Jules Jeanneney properly commented upon the marriage of two worlds when he told his fellow senators: "The profound consternation and affliction experienced by his friends and colleagues in

---

23. Maurain's family connections also gave him access to the leadership of the Socialist Party, and while Secretary to the Senate, he acted as a liaison between Jeanneney and Léon Blum.

24. Jean Maurain, *Un Bourgeois français au XIXe siècle.*

the University at the tragic death of Jean Maurain . . . have not been surpassed by the feelings experienced in our parliamentary milieu."[25]

———————•◦•———————

Maurain's choice of title—*La Politique ecclésiastique du second Empire*—was somewhat misleading as it did not reveal the true extent of the dissertation. The work investigated more than the Empire's policies. It included the regime's relationship with the national Church, the papacy, and the various forces of French clericalism. Like Seignobos, Maurain argued that the Empire's political evolution was ultimately determined by the events of 1859–1860. The *Politique* provided a study of the forces Maurain held responsible for shaking loose the authoritarian Empire, and his analysis has thus far proven definitive. Other authors concerned with Church-state relations during the Bonapartist regime have for the most part merely followed his lead.[26] No doubt many a would-be revisionist has felt intimidated by Maurain's thoroughness. With nearly 1,000 pages and innumerable footnotes, the *Politique* was, indeed, intensive.

Maurain thought the Empire never resolved the dilemmas raised by the unrealistic expectations of its Emperor. Napoleon III hoped to overcome the disagreements inherited from the Great Revolution, including those which concerned the Church's role in the community. The Emperor was not an ultramontane, Gallican, clerical, or anticlerical, and he hoped his program would provide the Church with a national task: that of acting as a dike against further revolutionary disorder. The clergy would defend the right flank of both the regime and society. The government in turn would protect religion

---

25. Seignobos, Borel, and Jeanneney, *Jean Maurain*, pp. 17–18.
26. This includes: A. Latreille, J. R. Palanque, E. Delaruelle, and R. Rémond, *La Période contemporaine;* R. Aubert, *Le Pontificat de Pie IX;* and A. Dansette, *Religious History of France,* I. An exception, of course, is A. Debidour whose *Histoire des rapports de l'église et de l'état en France de 1789 à 1870* predates Maurain's work. Debidour's effort, however, is less a history of Church-state relations than an anticlerical attack against the Church's involvement in politics.

against revolutionary threats, a guarantee reassuring enough that the Church would make peace with the positive inheritance of '89.

The Bonapartist program involved a loose Church-state partnership designed to foster national harmony. In point of fact, the strategy led to a situation that merely accentuated the government's ambiguous character. The theory of national unity proved bogus when actually applied, and whether he realized it or not, Louis Napoleon struck a bargain with the clergy to destroy the republicans and neutralize the conservatives. In the first case, a theoretical consensus gave way to a defense of order executed through a general repression of the left. Conservatives, meanwhile, were divided because of their dislike of republicanism and their attachment to clericalism. When the Church joined the Bonapartist cause, traditional conservatives lost an important ally and were accordingly rendered ineffectual. For Maurain, the Empire came into being as a result of Napoleon III's agreement with the Church and its supporters.

Maurain argued that the national dispute concerning the role of the Church was, in the long run, not open to compromise, and, given the direction of modern history, could only be settled with the Church's defeat. The Empire's relations with the clericals, then, were part of a larger development, the nature of which indicated that Napoleon III had made a bad bargain. To make matters worse, the regime and the Church, insofar as principles were concerned, remained in fundamental disagreement. The Empire, progressive in outlook, accepted the principles of '89 and rested upon a democratic inspiration. The two allies were therefore at opposite poles on the major issues of the nineteenth century, and their partnership accordingly proved precarious. Even more important, Pio Nino began exhibiting an aggressiveness that frequently placed the government in an impossible situation. While demanding an interpretation of the Concordat completely favorable to the wishes of his office, Pius at the same time implemented a thoroughgoing policy of ultramontanism within the Church. Papal centralization, however, endangered the Concordat which allowed for a working relationship between Church and state. In Maurain's estimation the pope proved an unreasonable partner, intent as he was upon destroying the autonomy of the French Church and removing the previous levers of religious authority exercised by the secular government. Pius wanted his bishops and the government too.

The Empire and the Church nonetheless managed to cooperate during the early 1850s. Among Catholic groups, only the so-called liberals were hostile to the regime, and their isolation from the papacy, most bishops, and the lower clergy guaranteed their ineffectualness outside the Academy. The Empire purchased widespread Catholic support by proving amenable to clerical demands, a policy which was decisive, but founded upon a vast miscalculation. Napoleon III seemed unaware of the real purpose of the Organic Articles, the proper and strict enforcement of which would have restricted papal control over the French hierarchy and thus guaranteed the national Church's semi-independent character. Yet, the government frequently winked at outright violations—e.g., the papal nuncio's direct dealing with the bishops—and interpreted the Articles so liberally as to make them ineffective. The government in a similar fashion refused to aid Gallican bishops in their struggle against the papacy. Indeed, Fortoul, as Minister of Religious Affairs, for the most part nominated ultramontanes for episcopal vacancies. This merely weakened the government's position, since a regime that lost control of the bishops soon lost the very essence of Gallicanism.

While the French Church was subject to increased papal control, the clergy strengthened its institutional and social powers within France. Again, government deference was responsible. Legislation granted easier authorization for female orders, the clergy received higher salaries, and nonauthorized male congregations were tolerated. The Church in general held a privileged position, retaining the freedoms of 1848 (i.e., freedom of the press, assembly, and speech) which other groups had lost. Most important insofar as clericals were concerned, the Falloux Law remained intact and guaranteed the Church a large role in education. Some clericals even had hopes for the clergy gaining control of primary schooling. All in all, then, throughout the first years of the Empire, the French Church had drawn closer to Rome and ensconced itself in a position of real power. When the alliance of 1851–1852 dissipated, Napoleon III faced an opponent whose independence and strength were partially of his own making.

On the other hand, despite a willingness to administer existing laws in a fashion beneficial to the clergy, the government never abandoned its legal powers. To the contrary, it hedged its bet on the future and did so with good reason. In 1851–1852, Napoleon and his advisors rightly or wrongly thought their regime needed clerical support. Within three years, when the government seemed well established, they began to show concern over the high cost of their previous concessions. Furthermore, the regime was not truly compatible with the clergy's newly won strength. The government, according to Maurain, "was too authoritarian not to try to restrain—after having broken all other oppositions and suppressed public liberties—the privileges which assured the Church great independence and enormous influence."[27]

By 1854, government policy experienced a subtle but noticeable shift in emphasis. Although the change in policy hardly endangered Church-state relations, it proved prophetic. Fortoul expressed dismay over Church advances in secondary education, and in 1854 modifications in the Falloux Law decreased Church influence in the University. Two years later, the pace quickened with the death of Fortoul who was replaced by Rouland. The new minister reversed the policy of nominating ultramontane bishops, and he imposed state inspection upon Church schools over the protests of the congregations. The government, meantime, began allowing the *Siècle* freer expression of its anticlericalism. Even before 1860, then, the Empire had set about to mitigate the more extreme character of its ecclesiastical policies.

Maurain devoted the remaining two-thirds of the *Politique* to the developments that followed 1859–1860. A floundering Empire was apparently more interesting than a stable one, or perhaps Maurain preferred the dynamics of political change. In any case, he described

27. Jean Maurain, *La Politique ecclésiastique du second Empire de 1852 à 1869*, p. 82.

the Roman question as the issue that unveiled the contradictions of Bonapartism and destroyed the supports of the authoritarian system. Maurain commented that:

> For the first time in ten years, the political life of France was no longer dominated by the imperial government, but by the conflict between the partisans of the Church—attached to the old public law of monarchial Europe—and the anticlerical democrats—defenders of the right of peoples to dispose of themselves. The conflict, raised by the Roman question seemed so irreducible, so profound and enduring, that the dynastic question became secondary. The republicans and democratic bonapartists such as Prince Napoleon and Pietri rejoined the left; the Legitimists like La Rochejacquelein, the independents like Plichon and some imperialists like Lemercier united with the right.[28]

Most significantly, the Italian affair reestablished the old Party of Order which then whittled away the government majority. Clerical forces in 1859 immediately coalesced in their antagonism to government policy; even liberal Catholics found a respectable place in the chorus. Events were first set in motion in December of 1859 by La Guéronnière's officially inspired pamphlet, *Le Pape et le congrès,* which argued that except for Rome, the papacy should abandon its temporal holdings. The dispute was then transferred to the Legislative Body by clerical deputies such as Keller and Plichon, a move that endangered the government's position since a sizable number of majority deputies were sympathetic toward the Church. The hullabaloo threatened to unglue the system so carefully built during the 1850s, and clerical defections, which increased throughout the 1860s revitalized the liberal conservative opposition. Previously reduced to intransigent Legitimists and Orleanist chiefs, it now began to include rallied Legitimists and clericals of every persuasion. Keller and Thiers reflected the situation. Keller, an official deputy, called for a policy both Catholic and liberal, while Thiers argued that because the Pope had joined the camp of liberty, the papacy deserved the full support of the government.

Unsettled by the clerical offense, the government first responded by flexing its muscles; for example, Veuillot's *Univers* was sup-

28. Ibid., pp. 494–495.

pressed and troublesome priests were placed under prefectoral surveillance. This merely exacerbated the situation, and raised government fears about the Church's political powers. The Empire thereupon forged a new ecclesiastical policy, the foundations of which had been laid as early as 1856. Rather than settling the problem, however, the policy led to a ten-year running battle with the papacy and its French supporters.

The new policy largely involved an intensification of Rouland's previous efforts, and the minister outlined a program that included the following points: no further toleration of unauthorized male congregations; extension of state education at both the primary and secondary levels; absolute enforcement of the Organic Articles; and henceforth, the nomination of Gallican bishops. It proved a difficult policy to implement. Ultramontanism had made such heavy inroads into the French Church that the government met resistance from many bishops when it tried to enforce the full measure of the Articles. Furthermore, sympathy for Pius's predicament weakened the Gallicanism of bishops not inclined toward ultramontanism. Attempts to buttress state education, meanwhile, came under predictable attack, and particularly so when Duruy took charge of Public Instruction. As for the nomination of bishops, Pius took the unprecedented step of refusing to confirm Gallican nominees. Throughout this infighting, the clergy and its sympathizers criticized the government for waging war against religion.

As Maurain traced out in detail the Empire's dispute with the clericals, he emphasized that the regime steadily lost ground in the legislature. The 1863 elections were indicative. Alone, clericals carried no great electoral weight, but official candidates were chary about losing Church support which was now associated with a rejuvenated Party of Order. Government candidates, therefore, frequently proved more responsive to conservative than to administrative pressures. The Empire's alternatives only numbered two: either trim its sails and run with the conservative tide or renovate the membership of the Legislative Body and opt for the left. Since the latter involved too massive an undertaking, the regime really had no choice. By 1866, further defections from the majority and grow-

ing independence on the part of deputies who remained loyal
threatened the government's control of the legislature.

> The Legislative Body, in proportion to its increasing influence, pro-
> nounced more and more clearly against a conflict with the Church . . .
> In fact, the clerical independents exercised an increasing influence upon
> the Legislative Body, because the deputies elected as official candidates
> and who shared most of their [the clericals'] opinions, became more
> willing to follow their example rather than docilely obeying the
> government.[29]

These developments both guaranteed liberalization and determined its direction. "The evolution of the Empire toward liberalization," Maurain added, "took place not in accord with the democratic
anticlericals, as Prince Napoleon would have desired, but in collaboration with the independent clericals . . . "[30] Finally, by 1867,
the government did lose control. The second Roman expedition, to
repel Garibaldi's invasion, led in December to a wild legislative
session during which the majority extracted from Rouher a pledge
that the government would never abandon Rome. December, 1867,
dated the reemergence of a liberal politics.

Throughout his discussion of the 1860s, Maurain reiterated that
the general public remained fairly indifferent to the dilemmas of
Pius or the demands of the clericals.[31] Indeed, the failure to elicit a
popular response in 1860, according to Maurain, caused the clergy
to look for support from the clericals in the Legislative Body. Without explicitly saying as much, Maurain seemed to imply that the
Emperor overestimated the dangers of breaking with the Church.
Or perhaps Maurain was only hinting that Napoleon III had become
entangled in his own system. The author observed that, although
public interest was slight, the Legislative Body distorted and mag-
nified the issue because of its clerical bent. The government, in

29. Ibid., p. 739.
30. Ibid., p. 736.
31. The American scholar, Lynn Case, on the other hand, has argued that Maurain
underestimated public concern, although Case admits that the public became less
interested with the passage of time. See Case's *French Opinion on War and Diplomacy during the Second Empire*, pp. 102–109, 137–139, 159–164.

short, paid a high carrying charge for its choice of candidates in 1852.

On the other hand, by Maurain's own admission, the Italian question was no tempest in the clerical teapot. Republicans immediately employed the Roman question as a wedge for squeezing back into the political arena. The Italian affair became omnipresent, according to Maurain, and divided the community between clericals and anti-clericals. The split then assumed the more general political expression of left versus right. By 1869 a politicized France reexperienced the conditions of 1848 and had to choose between the republicans and the Party of Order. "This division," Maurain continued, "that the imperial government had tried to represent as being suppressed, once again became one of the principle elements and perhaps the fundamental principle of French political life."[32]

While describing the government's difficulties, Maurain had to admit the reality of liberalization. By ending his narrative with 1869, however, he failed to confront the product of liberal evolution. The *Politique* left the reader with no clear picture of where the story had led. Maurain dropped the whole matter just when the dynamics of change apparently brought a political transformation. Perhaps he thought the liberal experiment undeserving of serious attention. He later wrote in *Du libéralisme à l'impérialisme, 1860–1870:* "The liberal evolution of the Second Empire had only given negative results; it had destroyed the authoritarian regime, permitted the rebirth of political life and the reconstitution of parties. But it had not brought the implementation of a true parliamentary regime. The war of 1870 came to show the frightening weakness of the bastard system to which Ollivier had lent himself . . ."[33] Yet Maurain's observations in the *Politique* indicated that in its search for political support, the Empire had made the obvious and necessary choice. Napoleon III surrendered to a liberal conservatism which, by

32. *La Politique,* p. 952.
33. *Du libéralisme à l'impérialisme* was a collaborative effort on the part of Jean Maurain, Henri Hauser, and Pierre Benaerts. The quoted passage, from page 26 of the first edition (1939), was dropped from the second edition (1952), revised by F. L'Huillier.

Maurain's own admission, remained in control of French politics after 1870. Maurain further acknowledged that the Legislative Body that emerged from the elections of 1869 was thoroughly committed to a liberal politics.

Nothing in the *Politique* indicated that a liberal Empire would prove exceptionally weak. For one thing, conservative alternatives were limited, and for this reason clerical opposition in the Legislative Body never became irreconcilable. To the very end, conservative fear of the left prevented the Party of Order from reaching a permanent accommodation with the republicans; the Empire never faced a united opposition. By 1869, growing radicalism merely increased clerical fears, and the Party of Order accordingly showed less interest in a Liberal Union than a *Union dynastique*, all of which made Ollivier's liberal Empire possible. Finally, by ignoring 1870, Maurain avoided the fact that 1869 was not identical to 1849. A great deal had happened in twenty years, not the least of which was the Party of Order's acceptance of political democracy. If Ollivier was correct, 1870 provided a liberal-democratic consensus the likes of which were impossible in 1849.

In any event, Maurain only described the developments that made liberalization possible, or mandatory. He analyzed the defeat of authoritarianism with infinite detail, but the new order that emerged from defeat was ignored. The *Politique* therefore seemed incomplete. As far as he went, however, Maurain proved extremely informative—perhaps overly so. Despite the merits of erudition, the Empire's relationship with clerical forces could have been scutinized in something less than 960-odd pages of text. The *Politique* suffered on two counts: a republican's apparent ambivalence toward the liberal Empire and a professional's excessive concern for detailed erudition.

Maurain's study of Jules Baroche, while somewhat transcending the narrow limits of traditional history, elaborated upon still another theme suggested by Seignobos. Maurain recognized that Baroche's political career had served the interests of the bourgeoisie and that a common class consideration linked the Second Empire with the Third Republic. Heady stuff from a Seignobos pupil, the theory not only established *Baroche* as a model for future historians, but indicated that Maurain had somewhat widened his vision.[34] Seignobos's influence upon Maurain, however, was still real. In the *Histoire contemporaine* Seignobos had argued that the Empire's personnel impressed a conservative character upon the regime. Maurain obviously agreed and employed Baroche as an example. The minister's career revealed the attitudes that led to conservative support of the Empire, allowed the untroubled operation of the government during the 1850s, and then imposed political change throughout the following decade. Maurain's two studies therefore analyzed the same political development from slightly differing perspectives. The *Politique* approached the matter through the impact of the clerical party whereas *Baroche* described the career of a leading government figure who first embodied the success of authoritarianism and then confronted the difficulties of a renewed opposition.

Baroche epitomized the bourgeois who made good, climbed to the upper reaches of Paris middle-class society, and proved significant because he was so very typical. Descended from Parisian shopkeepers and wine merchants originally from Burgundy, Baroche attended law school and established a practice in the 1820s. Through diligence, thorough preparation, real speaking talent, and a good

34. Works obviously influenced by Maurain on this count are Robert Schnerb, *Rouher et le second Empire*, to be discussed in the following chapter; Noel Blayau, *Billault, ministre de Napoléon III*; and Paul Raphael and Maurice Gontard, *Un Ministre de l'Instruction publique sous l'Empire autoritaire.*

Blayau argues that although Billault participated in what might be called the Empire's government of bourgeois defense, he came to the task with a progressivism similar to that of Napoleon III, all of which set him apart from his fellow ministers. Whatever the case, Blayau indicates that Billault was not a true insider of the regime until shortly before his death in 1863, and that he played no significant role in establishing policy.

The case of Fortoul is somewhat different. Opportunistic and ambitious, Fortoul moved in republican and Saint-Simonian circles prior to 1848, and later became the Empire's first Minister of Education. Also an outsider in the Council of Ministers, he experienced continual frustration in his attempt to impose a regimen of order and reform upon the University. Fortoul, according to Raphael and Gontard, managed to alienate practically everyone, but at least saved the University from the more destructive plans being hatched by conservatives.

marriage, he soon made his mark. By the time of the July Monarchy, Baroche was a leading member of the Paris bar, working with and opposite such people as Dupin, Berryer, and Délangle.

During the 1840s Baroche decided to crown a successful legal career by entering politics. As a liberal he identified with the Orleanist center-left, and following his election in 1847, sat with the dynastic opposition. Baroche soon became one of Barrot's lieutenants and played a major role in the agitation that helped to ignite the February Revolution. Ironically, the destruction of the July Monarchy could not have been farther from his original intentions. From the beginning, Baroche's opposition never went beyond parliamentary legalities and support for limited suffrage extension. The Revolution a fait accompli, he nevertheless rallied to the Republic, and was elected to the Constituent Assembly in which he became a major opponent of social reform. Although Baroche accepted the new regime, the June Days frightened him, and he soon began doubting the ability of republicans to maintain an orderly society. Like many liberals of the time, fear caused Baroche to minimize his concern about the niceties of parliamentary government, and he played an active role in the Party of Order's alliance with Louis Napoleon. A member of the rue de Poitiers, a gathering of the burgraves, Baroche accordingly lent his services to the ministry of Odilon Barrot, and assumed the post of *procureur général* of Paris.

The situation grew more complicated once the combined liberal-Bonapartist offensive weakened the left. Louis Napoleon began exhibiting signs of independence, the first result of which was the dismissal of Barrot in October of 1849. This seemed to throw into question the rue de Poitiers' alliance with the President. Baroche, however, disassociated himself from Barrot and retained his post; he clearly believed the President to be necessary for continued stability. Such insights, of course, have their own reward; in March of 1850 Baroche received the Ministry of Interior and became the government's leading spokesman before the Legislative Assembly. According to Maurain, he thereby assumed the particularly important role of mediator between Louis Napoleon and the forces of conservatism, all of which reduced the chances of a conservative denial of the executive. Thiers, for instance, welcomed Baroche's appointment and thought it a guarantee of Napoleon's good behavior. And indeed, Baroche continued the crusade against the left and even succeeded in selling the President the burgraves' plan to restrict suffrage with the so-called May Law of 1850.

Baroche's success in repressing the republican party raised further difficulties. As their common enemy declined in strength, the President and the burgraves moved farther apart. This presented conservatives with a situation that ultimately destroyed their political cohesiveness, and Baroche was both victim and agent of the dilemma. Convinced that a strong executive remained mandatory, Baroche defended the President before the Assembly while laboring to keep Louis Napoleon on a conservative path. At the same time, he tried to convince both parties of the benefits of continuing their cooperation. A choice proved unavoidable as the burgraves and Louis Napoleon parted company; when the struggle ended in a coup d'état, Baroche predictably joined the Prince and lent his full support to the new regime.

Maurain continually reaffirmed that Baroche's enemies were mistaken when they accused him of mere opportunism. Despite his political journey from the Orleanist center-left to republicanism, to the rue de Poitiers, and finally to Bonapartism, Baroche remained consistent and never deviated from his basic political convictions. Maurain described the situation as follows:

> Baroche had changed much less from the political point of view than one might believe, and ambition had not been the principle cause of his evolution. Bourgeois, he had always found necessary and normal that the bourgeoisie retain the government and dominate society. As long as he had not seen that the preponderance of the bourgeoisie could be threatened, he had taken part in its internal struggles and fought Guizot, but he had always distrusted mass movements . . . Not being fastened by any dynastic devotion, he had sincerely accepted the Republic . . . However, since the socialist menace appeared, he became conscious of the profoundly conservative elements which had always been with him. He affirmed himself a man of order and authority. He remained such all his life. In the struggle that he undertook since 1848

> against revolutionary tendencies, he was guided not by ambition . . .
> but by his devotion to the interests of his class, and to what he believed
> to be good for the whole society.[35]

Insofar as Baroche was concerned, politics remained functional, and his views were shared by many so-called repentant liberals in 1851. A proper politics meant a guarantee for the bourgeoisie, and given this criterion, parliamentarianism seemed inadequate. There remained, however, the Bonapartist alternative with its emphasis upon a strong executive.

Next to the Emperor, Baroche was the regime's most influential figure during the authoritarian period insofar as internal affairs were concerned. Appointed president of the Council of State, he saw his role as mediator between Napoleon and the conservatives. The task was immense, demanding that Baroche act as the liaison between the executive and the legislature. He therefore supervised the labors of the Council and necessarily assumed responsibility for all legislation. Fortunately, Baroche was a good speaker with an affable manner; he proved adept in handling the Legislative Body and was particularly successful in smoothing over differences between the two powers.

There was, however, another side of the story. To the very end, Baroche and the Emperor remained in a kind of fundamental disagreement. The councilor saw the regime as a government primarily devoted to furthering and protecting bourgeois interests. Napoleon saw the matter differently. Maurain argued that the Emperor never ceased to be a man of '48, at odds with the narrowness of the bourgeoisie. Unlike Baroche, Napoleon III remained committed to a vague socialism and vast designs, the logic of which always escaped the councilor.

> Napoleon III dreamed of an Empire where the sovereign, strong in
> his personal power, would rest his support upon the people and would
> work for its happiness in directing not only political life, but the economy
> of the country. Baroche desired an Empire where the power, authori-
> tarian in politics, but liberal in economic matters, would maintain and
> consolidate the hegemony of the bourgeoisie—a task that the July Mon-

35. Maurain, *Un Bourgeois français*, pp. 40–41.

archy had not been able to fulfill. Napoleon III had a romantic conception of the Empire, which Persigny, who shared it, understood was profoundly opposed to the bourgeois conception of Baroche.[36]

Agents such as Duruy and Haussmann best reflected the Emperor's attitudes, and predictably Baroche never appreciated the prefect of the Seine. The Council of State's president attacked Haussmann's *caisse de la boulangerie* as an affront to correct economic principles, tried to obstruct the rebuilding of Paris, and defended Haussmann with obvious reluctance before the legislature. Baroche, in fact, waged something of a guerrilla war against the Emperor's most imaginative and humanitarian designs. He likewise disapproved of the Empire's foreign policy over which he exercised no influence. Furthermore, had Baroche had his way, universal suffrage would have remained suppressed in 1851. On only one question did he share Napoleon's vision: the lowering of tariffs, and Baroche played a role of some importance in the treaty of 1860. Yet, the Emperor and his advisor reached an accord on this matter almost in spite of themselves. Baroche adhered to free trade on the basis of economic principle; the Emperor hoped to improve the living standard of the poor.

Baroche worked in close harmony with Rouher and Fould. Personal friends who agreed on the merits of authoritarianism, "the three" or "the trio," as they were called, largely directed the internal politics of the 1850s. Napoleon's foreign policy, however, destroyed the basis of authoritarianism and brought a new politics, forcing Baroche to confront a less malleable Legislative Body. Indeed, he bore the brunt of the conservative opposition, and perhaps fatigued by his already immense labors, seemed inadequate for the task. Napoleon responded to the situation with liberalization, which marked a decline in Baroche's position. The liberalization, among other things, allowed the Senate and Legislative Body to formulate

36. *Ibid.*, pp. 506–507. The idea that imperial ministers stamped a conservative imprint upon the regime was outlined earlier in biographical form in the not terribly useful study by Joseph Durieux, *Le Ministre Pierre Magne*. What the neo-Orleanist Durieux considered to be a sign of civic responsibility, the republican Maurian viewed as a subversion of the Emperor's progressive impulse.

an address to the throne, during the discussion of which government agents would answer questions concerning policy. Baroche lost his position as the government's sole spokesman before the legislature, a task he now had to share with Magne and Billault.

Baroche, according to Maurain, was so thoroughly entangled with the early Empire, that any dismantling of authoritarianism worked to his disadvantage. By 1863 Baroche moved further into the secondary realm; leaving the Council of State, he took the ministries of Justice and Religious Affairs, a position he held until 1869. Baroche nevertheless retained an important voice in government councils, and continually opposed liberalization. Naturally, the "three" had tried to prevent the reforms of 1860. They saw liberal politics as a threat to both themselves and the regime they served. When Billault's death in 1863 placed Rouher in a commanding position, Baroche immediately joined him in resisting further liberalization. Indeed, Rouher and Baroche effectively fought the influence of Walewski and aborted the Emperor's plans for reform in 1864, 1865, and 1866.

Maurain argued that Baroche failed to comprehend the demands of the new politics. The minister hoped to retain an authoritarianism no longer feasible. To escape political isolation, the regime had only one choice: regain widespread conservative support through a policy of liberalization. Baroche's obtuseness concerning this problem was particularly striking given his position as Minister of Religious Affairs where he continually faced the clerical opposition. A thoroughgoing Gallican, Baroche found Pius's obscurantism and ultramontanism unbearable, and he responded by following Rouland's policies, all of which added to the government's grief. More astute than his advisors, Napoleon in 1867 simply announced further reform in a public letter. The Emperor miscalculated, however, by not introducing new personnel, a failure which gutted the proposal's effect since the liberal opposition mistrusted Baroche and his allies. Political pressure therefore continued to increase both within and without the Legislature—so much so that the elections of 1869 forced a complete reevaluation of government policy. Baroche and his friend Rouher resigned in 1869.

The liberal Empire saw Baroche retire to the regime's pasture for old workhorses—the Senate. According to Maurain, the ex-minister made no attempt to disrupt the new order. Indeed, Baroche stopped visiting the Tuileries in order to squelch rumors that he was fomenting a fronde against Ollivier. Baroche actually accepted the 1870 ministry and its political implications. On the other hand, Maurain, without offering any evidence, alluded to Baroche's hope that the massive plebiscitary victory would lead to an authoritarian counter-offensive. Yet, the author also admitted that the peace-minded Baroche never favored the war of 1870, a struggle from which the more intransigent authoritarians hoped to extract a victory over both Bismarck and Ollivier. In any case, 1870 brought Baroche's political demise and his death. September 4 forced the ex-minister into exile. He died while on Jersey, broken by the news of the death of his son who was killed defending Paris against the Prussians.

Even by Maurain's own admission, however, Baroche's career had not been in vain, despite the disaster of 1870. He lent himself to authoritarianism because of his commitment to a politics of bourgeois preeminence. It was a choice made by many conservative-liberals as a result of the 1848 Revolution, and Baroche commanded an important enough position to shape the internal politics of the Empire. Amongst other things, he helped to hold the regime on a conservative course despite its utopian Emperor. Baroche "had been one of the representatives of the French bourgeoisie in the councils of a sovereign who knew the bourgeoisie poorly and did not love it, but who protected it because he had need of its support."[37] Baroche and Thiers, Maurain continued, resembled one another, and ultimately served the same cause under different banners. Thiers's strategy of bourgeois defense was abandoned in 1851–1852 for that of Baroche, but when the Empire experienced hard times, Thiers gradually won the day over Baroche. The latter, Maurain concluded, had "his place in the line of politicians who, throughout the economic upheavals and revolutions of the nineteenth century, have in France served and defended the bourgeois social order."[38]

37. Ibid., p. 507.
38. Ibid., p. 508.

In contrast to earlier republican historians who saw the Empire as a gap in France's political evolution, Maurain recognized that dissimilar regimes could serve similar purposes. Perhaps he had learned something from his brief foray into French political life during the period of the Popular Front. Maurain's success, in any event, arose from his emphasis upon continuity. By any standard, *Baroche* was good history; its author had succeeded in finding a place for the Empire in French political development and had made the commonplace relevant.

Albert Thomas

While the radicalism of Charles Seignobos represented with few exceptions the political orthodoxy of the Third Republic, Albert Thomas's commitments were toward the left, but still moderate, side of the republican spectrum. The late nineteenth century marked the emergence of an organized working-class movement and a socialist party, and herein lay great historiographical possibilities, either through the use of Marxian categories or some other means of integrating social and political themes.

In giving life to these possibilities Marxism proved influential, but less so than one might expect, largely because France possessed her own indigenous political traditions. For one thing, the socialist party remained historically affiliated with the democratic movement, as was demonstrated by Jaurès's decision to join the Dreyfusards in their defense of the Republic and by the socialist willingness to pursue the Radical red herring of anticlericalism. Gallic socialism also showed a healthy respect for political democracy, all of which had ramifications in a community with a large peasant and shopkeeper population. As Jaurès often noted, French socialists owed as much to Michelet as Marx, and they seldom exhibited the latter's animosity toward the peasantry. Until the crisis engendered by World War I, the Section Française de l'Internationale Ouvrière, at least insofar as the leadership was concerned, was not a revolutionary organization, but, rather, the most advanced expression of a democratic impulse very much at home within the limited confines of the Third Republic.

To complicate matters, French workers, the theoretical base of the party, were frequently suspicious of politicians and political action. They saw the union or *syndicat* as a tool for radically reorganizing society outside the channel of regular politics. The aims of the labor movement, therefore, did not altogether coincide with those of the socialist party, but instead contained a strong current of what French commentators have called *ouvriérisme*—an emphasis upon the integrity and independence of working-class organizations and particularly trade unions.

The attitudes associated with the French left had their effect upon socialist historiography at the turn of the century. Socialist historians confronted an obvious problem when analyzing the party and its relationship to French society. Their efforts involved an attempt to mask the weakness of a party that was not altogether aligned with its theoretical constituency and that was forced to ally itself with other republican groups noteworthy for their social conservatism. Given their acceptance of Marianne and the added impact of syndicalism, socialist historians, when dealing with the very recent past, did not so easily follow the Marxian pattern of relating politics to an economic substructure. They usually retreated into a republican narrative painted in red, or else emphasized the aspirations of the workers and the emergence of working-class institutions. How the two themes might be joined remained the choice of the individual historian; in the case of Albert Thomas's treatment of the Second Empire, the results indicated the author's loyal adherence to the republican tradition of the SFIO and to the party's claim of being at one with the French labor movement. As a result, Thomas craftily avoided in the history of the Second Empire the problems that bedeviled socialists throughout the Third Republic.

The son of a baker, and born in the village of Champigny-sur-Marne near Paris, Thomas rose to prominence through the opportunities made possible by the republican educational system.[39] He

39. There are numerous printed sources of information concerning Thomas. Of particular importance are B. W. Schaper, *Albert Thomas;* Robert Lafrance, ed.,

entered the Ecole Normale in 1899 and studied history. Like so many *normaliens*, he felt the influence of Charles Andler and Lucien Herr, and his republicanism soon included a commitment to socialism. After graduation, Thomas was torn between political activism and a University career; at first he chose the latter but did not relinquish his interest in politics, for he began researching a thesis on the political thought of Babeuf. Yet, within two years, Thomas had abandoned scholarship for socialist journalism and politics. In 1904 he helped to found *Humanité*, and six years later he was a member of the Assembly and Jaurès's right-hand man. Unlike Jaurès, however, Thomas was deeply involved in the labor movement. Founder of the *Revue syndicaliste*, which he merged with the *Revue socialiste* when he assumed the latter's editorship in 1910, Thomas primarily saw socialism as an expression of the working class. Distrustful of Marxism, he had little interest in Marx as an historical figure or, for that matter, in the historical impact of ideology. Thomas considered working-class figures such as H. Tolain and Eugène Varlin to be of far greater importance than any philosopher-historian. Thomas's sympathies for the labor movement, however, were joined with a strong commitment to the Republic. In the words of a recent observer, Thomas more than anyone "represented the new generation of Socialist leaders, educated in republican schools, drawn to the SFIO by Jaurès's democratic Socialism, and inclined to favor reformism."[40] A republican faith accounted for Thomas's continual affirmation of reformist methods rather than revolution. Democracy, he thought, would allow the workers to enlarge their power within the community, and in the process reorganize society around syndicalist principles. The Republic provided a framework for the posi-

---

Albert Thomas vivant; and Madeleine Rebérioux and Patrick Fridenson, "Albert Thomas: pivot du réformisme français." An important unpublished source is Martin Fine, "Toward Corporatism: The Movement for Capital-Labor Collaboration in France, 1914–1936." See also the following obituary notices: Lucien Febvre, "Albert Thomas," *Annales d'histoire économique et sociale* 4 (1932), 380–384; Georges Lefebvre, "Albert Thomas," *Annales historiques de la Révolution française* 9 (1932), 378–379. There is also a fine article in the *Encyclopedia Brittanica,* 1960 edition, XXII, 144–145. For Thomas's career in the I.L.O., Edward Phelan's *Yes and Albert Thomas.*

40. Robert Wohl, *French Communism in the Making, 1914–1924,* p. 56.

tive efforts of both the Section Française de l'Internationale Ouvrière and the Confédération Générale du Travail.

Although a supporter of working-class unity and a staunch internationalist—he broke with Andler in 1913 when the latter clashed with Jaurès over the dangers of what Andler called "German imperialism"—Thomas nevertheless remained an ardent patriot. Like Michelet, he identified the revolutionary tradition with France, and in 1914 Thomas rallied to the nation's defense. With Jules Guesde, he became the symbol of socialist adherence to the *union sacrée*, and assumed the ministry of Munitions. In 1917 Thomas undertook a special mission to Russia in order to press the Kerensky government to continue the war effort. He predictably perceived the Bolshevik Revolution as an affront to democratic principles, and in the National Assembly argued for intervention, claiming that Europe's choice lay with either Lenin or Wilson. As the socialist movement divided over the disputes emerging from World War I and the question of the Third International, Thomas withdrew from French political life and returned to his first love, the labor movement. By 1920 Thomas had found a new public career with the International Labor Organization, of which he became the director, a post he held until his death in 1932.

Despite a decision to make rather than write history, Thomas nonetheless contributed to the historiography of the Second Empire. When Jaurès first planned the multivolume and collaborative *Histoire socialiste,* he chose Andler to write the volume on Napoleon III's regime, but when Andler's health proved inadequate for the task, Jaurès turned to his young lieutenant, Albert Thomas. Although highly idiosyncratic, practically devoid of Marxian influences, and displaying the author's dual commitment to republicanism and to the labor movement, Thomas's *Le Second Empire* suited the editor's general design. Jaurès wanted a series written by competent scholars who employed "scientific methods" of research while approaching the material from a socialist perspective. Whatever its didactic purposes, *Le Second Empire* established Thomas's reputation as an historian of the Bonapartist experiment. When the editors of *The Cambridge Modern History* began searching for a contributor on the

Empire, their choice fell upon the *normalien* who had demonstrated a familiarity with the proper method. For his own part, Thomas recognized that *The Cambridge Modern History* was not socialist history. His two essays were accordingly political narratives, and proved that Thomas could equal the unrivaled dullness of his fellow contributors.[41] Fortunately, the *Histoire socialiste* was less restricted by the demands of empirical history, and for that reason *Le Second Empire* proved more interesting.

A thoroughgoing republican, Thomas made no attempt to veil his dislike of the Empire. Although he conceded that Napoleon III was sincere, well meaning, and idealistic, Thomas echoed his republican predecessors to the effect that Bonapartism was the worst imaginable form of reaction. Beyond this, he said very little about the regime aside from calling it a conservative settlement supported by the upper classes, the Church, the army, and certain Orleanist administrators and politicians. He also repeated the praetorian theme, and thought the Empire the product of Louis Napoleon's personal ambition, an ambition opposed to history's progressive direction.

Le Second Empire, however, did not primarily concern Napoleon III or his government. It was instead devoted to analyzing the emergence of certain forces that made the Empire impossible. Thomas's use of sources revealed what his volume was all about. For political matters, he relied upon Tchernoff's *Le Parti républicain au coup d'état et sous le second Empire* and Delord's *Histoire du second Empire*. To these Thomas added his own research, relying heavily upon the *procureur général* reports concerning worker attitudes, and the private papers of working-class leaders such as Benoît Malon and Albert Richard. *Le Second Empire* was a venture in the writing of republican-socialist history, with particular attention paid to social considerations and the working-class movement.

The 1850s unfortunately presented a problem: the decade witnessed no working-class activism, political or otherwise. To make

41. Albert Thomas, "Napoleon III and the Period of Personal Government (1852–1859)"; and "The Liberal Empire (1859–1870)," in the same volume.

matters worse, by Thomas's own admission the workers passively accepted the coup d'état because of the Second Republic's repudiation of social reform. In the workers' eyes, republicanism for the moment seemed irrelevant, all of which made the 1850s unsuited for the main theme of Le Second Empire. Rather than writing a shorter book and concentrating upon the 1860s alone, Thomas instead approached the Empire's first decade in terms of republican political history. The result was a mere rehash of previous republican writers. Appropriate criticisms were made of Bonapartist institutions, and Thomas affirmed the viability of republicanism by noting the Empire's inability to destroy the movement. The role of the workers in all this, however, remained vague. Despite his earlier observations about working-class passivity toward the coup, Thomas argued that the workers nevertheless remained loyal to republicanism. Whatever the case, Thomas failed to enlarge upon the matter; he affirmed the working-class link with republicanism, dated it from the July Monarchy, and then discussed the republican party as if the issue were closed. Lacking material for socialist history, Thomas absorbed, and thereby lost, the workers in a political category.

A republican commitment also prevented Thomas from granting any relevance to the regime's social programs during the 1850s. He dismissed Bonapartist social policy as a series of half measures, and argued that the government was thwarted by its authoritarian character. For one thing, a despotic government naturally distrusted the workers, and placed them under a restrictive and paternalistic surveillance.[42] The working class, as a result, was entangled in a web of bureaucratic controls. Mutual aid societies, for instance, received official recognition only on the condition their officers were chosen by the government. As for the Empire's public works' programs, Thomas was no less critical, arguing that they provided employment only within the confines of an exploitative economy. Thomas therefore dismissed the 1850s as a vast loss for the working class, and did so by ignoring the impact of Saint-Simonian doctrines within official

42. Albert Thomas, Le Second Empire, pp. 66–70. This point is reiterated in Pierre-Léon Fournier, Le Second Empire et la législation ouvrière, a doctoral dissertation in law which was greatly influenced by Thomas.

circles. No mention was made of the fact that the government pursued an economic policy designed to enlarge productivity, lower prices, increase competition, and reduce unemployment through private investment. Instead of granting the regime its due, Thomas accused the Empire of allowing the bourgeoisie a clear field for economic exploitation, the results of which were industrialization.[43] Thomas, in fact, denied the Empire's contribution with the comment that "*coups d'état* do not have the power to raise brusquely from the ground industries and railroads; and forms of government do not influence the general economy as much as some wish to believe."[44]

More concerned with why the regime fell than why it endured, Thomas naturally showed greater interest in the 1860s than in the preceding decade. The regime stumbled, he argued, because the Italian affair antagonized conservative supporters. Weakened, the Empire proved unable to maintain the oppressiveness of the previous decade, all of which allowed the republicans to reenter the political arena. They were then joined by the workers whose growing class awareness involved a politics of revolutionary republicanism.

Thomas naturally emphasized the role of the workers, and particularly what he called their growing self-awareness or class consciousness. The most significant manifestation of this development, he argued, was the recognition of the importance of organization. To take one example, a worker delegation attended the 1862 Exposition and discovered that unions provided the English working class

43. These conclusions were somewhat at variance with Thomas's later hopes for an improved political economy after the Great War. Influenced by the economic controls of 1914–1918 and the productivity of American industry, Thomas during the 1920s organized the I.L.O. to lobby for an efficient and humane capitalism designed to raise productivity and lower unemployment. To further this cause, Thomas collaborated with French industrialists and bankers who perceived him as a responsible labor leader sympathetic to the practical dimensions of social reform. By this time, while retaining his republicanism, Thomas desired a capitalism sharing certain features with the political economy of the Second Empire. Thomas, however, by 1920 had left the history of the Empire behind, and his evaluation of the regime was naturally marked by a prewar character. As we shall see in the next chapter, Thomas's later views about a functional capitalism were part of a larger development that ultimately led to a revision in the historiography of the Empire. On Thomas's attitudes during the 1920s, see Martin Fine, "Toward Corporatism."

44. Thomas, *Le Second Empire*, p. 167.

with higher wages and shorter hours. Unionization soon became the symbol for the workers' determination to protect their interests against the *patrons*. Progress was slow, but by 1863–1864, a group of workers in Paris had laid the rudimentary foundations of a union movement and helped to establish the International. These same workers, moreover, exhibited a new sense of independence, as indicated by the elections of 1863, when they put forth their own candidates in order to bring attention to the social question. Even more importantly, the candidates paved the way for two statements of purpose that represented milestones in the emergence of a French labor movement. The first—the so-called "Manifesto of the Sixty"—appeared in the *Opinion nationale* and affirmed the workers' need to express demands separately from those of the bourgeoisie. The second, Tolain's pamphlet, *Quelques Vérités sur les élections de Paris*, emphasized the necessity of abandoning the utopian idealism of '48 for more practical matters—the establishment of unions and credit associations. In modern terminology, there was a growing sense of and demand for "worker power."

While applauding the concept of working-class integrity or separateness, Thomas the republican nevertheless insisted that the workers were inseparable from republicanism. Indeed, he went one better and made the republican party the political arm of the workers. Whereas he had absorbed the working class into the republicanism of the previous decade, he now reversed the formula for the 1860s, and simply set the moderate and larger wing of the party aside. Thomas's ploy was fairly direct. He distinguished between two republicanisms. The first was illegitimate, nonrevolutionary, bourgeois, and showed no real concern for the social question. The second was a true republicanism—revolutionary vis-à-vis the Empire, socially oriented, and the product of the workers and their allies. It was the workers' revolutionary attitude that rescued the republican cause from the debilitating effects of those who could not see beyond the political issues. Thomas therefore observed that, "the real cause for the republican renewal after 1863 was the opposition of the workers."[45]

45. Ibid., p. 154.

By asserting the indivisibility of the working-class movement and revolutionary republicanism, Thomas set the stage for a narrative largely based upon wishful thinking. He argued that a wave of revolution, led by workers and joined by students and various radicals associated with Blanqui, gathered momentum throughout the middle years of the 1860s. By 1868 the Empire was in its death throes, with the only remaining question being whether the successor government would be socialistic. The International, under the astute leadership of Malon and Varlin, meanwhile, assumed the role of channeling working-class activism, and therefore provided the possibility of society's reorganization. Thomas in particular underscored the importance of the series of strikes that swept France during the years 1869–1870, and called them a manifestation of a revolutionary impulse that was both political and social.

Thomas, however, deceived both himself and the readers of the *Histoire socialiste*. By his own admission the left, divided in the face of working-class radicalism, and moderate republicans, including Gambetta, were soon scurrying for conservative cover. Despite Thomas's faith in the near demise of the liberal Empire, the revolutionary threat merely consolidated the regime and Ollivier's experiment. The revolutionaries, working class and otherwise, had little support within the community, and the socialists had even less. A case in point was the 1869 elections; republicans may have experienced success, particularly with working-class voters, but few socialist candidates emerged victorious. Matters became worse with the passage of time; the plebiscite represented a clear defeat for all republicans, both revolutionary and nonrevolutionary. Thomas, ever adroit, nevertheless chalked up the referendum as a Bonapartist defeat and a left-wing victory. He alluded to an opposition which, on the eve of a revolutionary victory, began dividing as a prelude to the struggle for power in the postrevolutionary period. Factions therefore went their separate ways and failed to coordinate their policies. The small *no* vote was a manifestation of revolutionary power. With the plebiscite thus transformed from an historical defeat into an historian's victory, Thomas concluded by hinting that the Franco-

Prussian war aborted the nearly victorious revolutionary-socialist movement.

Whatever criticism Thomas deserved for refusing to acknowledge the difficulties confronted by the revolutionaries, there was an even more serious flaw in his analysis of the 1860s. To support the dubious contention that revolutionary republicanism and the working-class movement were identical, Thomas refused to draw necessary distinctions. *Le Second Empire*, as a result, represented a massive confusion of issues. For Thomas, a major issue was the emergence, in the wake of industrialization, of a proletarian consciousness leading to an organized labor movement. He had to admit, however, that this new awareness originated in Paris, a city where industry remained primarily decentralized and where workers were artisans. Furthermore, the workers who manifested this consciousness were an elite consisting of artisans—a large number of whom were drawn from the printing trades—unconnected with the heavy and concentrated industries developing in the suburbs.[46] Thomas avoided these complexities by simply treating the elite as though it were typical of both the Parisian working class and all French workers. In point of fact, it was typical of neither. Equally important, the elite's relationship with the general working-class population has never been adequately disentangled. Thomas skirted the issue by referring to the elite as "workers who were most conscious." Since all workers were theoretically in the process of becoming conscious, the reader could only assume that any difference was a matter of degree.[47]

46. Ibid., pp. 171–172. Jacques Rougerie has reaffirmed the overwhelmingly predominant role played by artisans and workers drawn from traditional trades in forming the International; see his "Sur l'histoire de la première Internationale." Conditions surrounding the working-class movement in Lyon, where industry remained artisanal, were similar, but not identical. Indeed, worker awareness appears to have been more advanced and extreme in Lyon than Paris. See Sreten Maritch, *Histoire du mouvement social sous le second Empire à Lyon;* Maurice Moissonnier, "La Section lyonnaise de l'Internationale et l'opposition ouvrière à la fin du second Empire"; and Jacques Rougerie, "La Première Internationale à Lyon, 1865–1870."

47. Thomas, *Le Second Empire*, pp. 193–194. Thomas certainly must have known the issue was more complicated. Emile Levasseur had already drawn attention to the difficulties of grasping the relationship between the working class and its elite. See Levasseur's *Histoire des classes ouvrières et de l'industrie en France de 1789 à 1870,* II, 787–788.

In his attempt to minimize the differences separating the elite and the mass of workers, Thomas implied that the former shared the latter's republican commitments. The elite, however, was distinctly Proudhonian, and exuded a distrust for political partisanship. Rather than engaging in republican politics, its members hoped to organize institutions such as the International in order to protect worker interests. The 1863 elections provided an expression of independence from the republican party. For this very reason the republican press launched a wholesale attack upon the idea of working-class candidacies, claiming that they represented a reactionary affront to the principles of 1789 which abolished the legal status of class. The party, moreover, had other reasons, apart from the challenge to republican legal fictions, for distrusting members of the working-class elite. Some, like Tolain, were politically nonpartisan and primarily concerned with extending the workers' civil liberties, while others were openly sympathetic to a government headed by Napoleon III. Little wonder that as late as 1877 Jules Ferry was still arguing that the 1863 candidacies sprang from a Bonapartist plot.

In point of fact, the Paris elite owed the Empire a great deal. During the early 1860s, the Emperor indicated a willingness to cooperate with its members through the offices of his cousin, Prince Napoleon. With ties on the left, the Prince employed the revolutionary journalist and future Communard Armand Lévy as an intermediary. The response was real and sizable, to the point that contemporaries spoke of a Palais Royal contingent within the working class. According to a recent observer, these workers who were drawn from the elite, believed "that the Second Empire had more to offer the working class than other regimes . . . Many veterans of 1848, moreover, still recalled the 'betrayal' of the February Revolution."[48] The Palais Royal group, including Tolain, was instrumental in starting the working-class movement in Paris. A tenuous affiliation with

48. David Kulstein, "Bonapartist Workers during the Second Empire," p. 229. See also his article entitled, "The Attitude of French Workers towards the Second Empire," and his book, *Napoleon III and the Working Class: A Study of Government Propaganda under the Second Empire.*

the regime allowed its members relatively free expression, and they published pamphlets concerning the social question, and reminded the Empire of its duties toward the workers. Prince Napoleon also convinced his friend Guéroult to open the columns of the *Opinion nationale* to the workers, and the journal was ultimately responsible for organizing the 1862 Exposition delegation from which the International sprang. Republicans quite naturally believed the whole movement to be a government plot, and their accusations became even more virulent with the 1863 working-class candidacies.

Republicanism of course drew much support from the workers; but such support came from the general working-class population of Paris and not the elite. Most Parisian workers placed political considerations before the social question, as indicated by the small membership of the International and the paltry number of votes— 323 and 11—received by the worker candidates. There were even cases of workers requesting the International to disband since the organization might antagonize bourgeois republicans. Fundamental to Thomas's refusal to acknowledge these facts or their implications was an unwillingness to accept the complexities of the 1860s. A transition period insofar as the working class was concerned, the decade necessarily involved numerous contradictions and much diversity. Thomas, however, insisted upon portraying the 1860s as being dominated by a revolutionary wave involving a unified working class. The reality was in fact less a wave than a series of eddies and cross currents. To take one example, Thomas refused to acknowledge the strength of Bonapartist sympathies within the International. He merely pointed out that Tolain, like so many Proudhonians, unfortunately proved too unaware of the importance of the political struggle. He then implied that the Paris Section's shift toward political activism was both natural and expected. Thomas, however, failed to indicate that Tolain and his colleagues made the move partially for tactical reasons, in order to capture a larger following. What Thomas described as a leadership role was a case of would-be leaders trying to catch their hoped-for followers. The Paris Section's entry into republican politics was something of a surrender.

Even Varlin, who assumed control in 1868 as a result of government action against the International, was a republican who placed the social question above political action.

With one important exception, the situation in Paris resembled that in Lyon, which had its own Section of the International and which was the only other French city with an articulate working-class elite of any size. The Lyonnais Section, however, showed even greater resistance than its Parisian counterpart to the revolutionaries. Albert Richard, the former's leading figure, was sympathetic toward the Emperor, and he became more so after 1870. A close associate of Bakunin and one of the pioneers of the International in France, Richard argued that political revolution would lead to a republic necessarily opposed to socialism and working-class needs.

Because of his preconceptions, Thomas often failed to investigate the most meaningful problems. Rather than searching for the reasons behind the continued republican faith of the mass of workers after the events of 1848 and 1851, Thomas merely stated the fact. Rather than investigating the link between the elite and the workers in general, he treated it as a one-to-one relationship, thereby affirming the republican credentials of the elite. Finally, Thomas gave Paris most of his attention, and treated the provinces as appendages of the capital. Thomas introduced the provinces primarily when it proved convenient to do so—when a series of strikes swept across the country in 1869–1870. Having already established to his own satisfaction that the Paris movement was both social and political, he assumed the same held true for the provincial strikes. In actual fact, the strikes seemed to have resulted from economic considerations and working conditions. This was true even in Lyon where the workers were politicized.[49] Fernand L'Huillier's study of provincial

49. Maritch, *Histoire du mouvement social*, p. 219. For a nearby department, however, Pierre Léon argues in "Les Grèves de 1867–1870 dans le département de l'Isère," that confusion reigned supreme given an immature working-class consciousness. Some strikes were politically motivated, with the workers participating in an opposition that included bourgeois republicans opposed to any use of the strike, political or economic. At other times strikers acted from economic considerations and viewed the government as an ally against their employers. Thomas's treatment of political factors underlying the 1869–1870 wave of strikes raises a major historical problem not yet disentangled. Following in the footsteps of François Simiand,

labor unrest during the last years of the Empire has shown that most of these clashes never became politically oriented because of the government's adroitness and conciliatory attitude.[50] The government honestly tried to be fair and frequently supported the workers' cause against the *patrons;* this was particularly true on the question of hours, the most explosive issue. In some cases, such as in Alsace, the Empire even engendered a widespread Bonapartist sentiment on the part of the strikers. The bloody conflict at Creusot, which involved a firm owned by a family closely allied with the regime and which quickly assumed antigovernment overtones, was not typical.

L'Huillier's observations have raised another and more fundamental point. An unwillingness to grant the Empire any positive social content whatsoever allowed Thomas to obscure the character of the regime. Whatever the merits of republicanism, the Empire provided a *césarisme social.* Born of the 1848 failure, the regime was partially an attempt to deal with the social question, and its program did gather some measure of working-class support. Thomas, however, simply ignored the observation by Emile Levasseur that no preceding government had done so much for the workers. It was both appropriate and revealing that the Manifesto of the Sixty, the first major expression of modern French working-class consciousness, appeared in a semiofficial newspaper. The Empire labored to maintain a high employment rate, it legalized strikes, tolerated the organization of permanent union committees, reformed the councils of *prud'hommes,* abolished the legal precedence of the *patron's* word over that of the worker, and greatly enlarged the number of mutual aid societies. Last but not least, the International in part owed its existence to government policy. Albert Richard had a point when he argued that the working class could hardly expect more

---

Michelle Perrot, "Grèves, grévistes et conjoncture," and Jean Bouvier, "Mouvement ouvrier et conjoncture économique," have recently suggested that periods of labor unrest result less from politics than rises in prices. Whatever the case, the last years of the Empire were marked by rapidly rising prices. Finally, Edward Shorter and Charles Tilly have suggested that the 1869–1870 strikes were political in inspiration, but were meant to influence local conditions rather than to challenge the regime; see their *Strikes in France, 1830–1968,* pp. 110–112.

50. Fernand L'Huillier, *La Lutte ouvrière à la fin du second Empire.* L'Huillier's general study is substantiated by A. Fortin's more limited analysis, "Les Conflits sociaux dans les houillères du Pas-de-Calais sous le second Empire."

from republicanism. A new republic, after all, was apt to mean that Jules Simon would become the expert in residence on working-class affairs, and his suggestions on ending poverty hardly went beyond the idea of emptying the cabarets.

There was, in any event, some indication that the government's restrained approach to the strikes of 1869–1870 actually began to win some degree of working-class support. Whether or not the regime's hopes for a working-class *ralliement* were overly sanguine—and they probably were—they revealed a whole side of the issue ignored by Thomas for the sake of a socialist politics dedicated to republicanism. Rather than a history, *Le Second Empire* was a declaration of faith revealing the author's belief that French workers had found a political solution in a Third Republic. The assumption was even questionable in 1907, and when applied to the 1860s, it merely distorted the confused realities of the Second Empire.[51]

51. The complexities of the nineteenth-century working-class movement and its politics are just now being addressed; see in particular the valuable study by Bernard Moss, *The Origins of the French Labor Movement.*

Chapter V

The New Historians

The Great War of 1914 and its aftermath destroyed the world of the Third Republic. Stanley Hoffmann has perceptively described that world as a stalemate society, geared to a timid and almost Malthusian bourgeois vision which emphasized economic restraint and accepted only a very limited social mobility—and that primarily through the republican educational system. The Republic's major social priority was to protect already acquired positions rather than to enlarge the possibilities for economic opportunity, a condition that accommodated the peasantry while ignoring the needs of the proletariat. Given these conditions, the impact of a democratic politics was both limited and negative. The government acted as a caretaker guaranteeing the status quo and proved unwilling to intervene in society for fear of disturbing vested interests. Appropriate to its limited task, the regime possessed a weak executive and never discovered a formula for strong leadership. The Republic was a political system that sprang from a society held together by a general, but narrow, bourgeois consensus, and it remained viable only as long as conditions remained stable and there were no great pressures. In Hoffmann's words, "the only world for which French politics was made was the golden age of the Third Republic," and that age did not survive World War I.[1]

1. Stanley Hoffmann, "Paradoxes of the French Political Community," p. 21.

The 1920s provided an incubation period for the political fevers that struck throughout the following decade. Although one of the victors, France was bled white by a war which, for some, called into question the merits of a system that led to such a bloody horror. Further, the nature of the peace indicated certain difficulties, as the conclusive impact of American intervention raised the possibility that a traditional power like France would be reduced in stature and have fewer options on the international level. There was the added effect of revolutionary Russia and a Communist party with its special appeal to the working class. Finally, matters were complicated by the French desire for security which had driven Clemenceau to press for a peace dependent upon outside guarantees. When these guarantees failed to materialize, the Republic's leaders, from the French point of view, compromised the settlement's integrity, all of which served to anger a right committed to a hard line against Germany.

The 1930s were a turning point for the Third Republic. A decade of incipient civil war, extended crises and political polarization, it compounded the difficulties of the 1920s with the final collapse of Versailles, the rise of Nazi Germany, the onslaught of depression, and a new working-class militancy. These developments literally shattered the republican consensus, scrambled traditional loyalties, and thereby led to a reign of near absolute confusion. With the world wracked by economic difficulties and apparently dividing between fascist and communist camps, France seemed to collapse in a maelstrom not of her own making. Leaders from both sides of the political spectrum fumbled for answers, and ultimately underwent dramatic, if not traumatic, attitudinal shifts. The left, now resting its case on antifascism, abandoned its earlier flirtation with pacifism and accommodation with Germany. The right, on the other hand, whose support of the Republic had always been contingent upon a guarantee of the social order, found its raison d'être in anti-Marxism, began spawning antiparliamentary leagues, and turned its traditional animosity for Germany against the Soviet Union.

The confusion of the 1930s gave birth to a host of reviews with such upbeat titles as *Mouvements, Esprit, Homme nouveau, Ordre nouveau, Terre nouvelle,* and *Plans.* Literary watering holes for politicized intellectuals and disenchanted outsiders, the journals were filled with frequent references to Péguy and Proudhon, the first as a spiritual inspiration for national action and the second as a Gallic alternative to Marx. Whatever their many differences, the journals' editors belonged to a subculture and shared a common set of antipathies. They filled their reviews with columns attacking capitalism, rationalism, materialism, parliamentarianism, Alainism (meaning individualism), and editorialized to the effect that France must overcome her traditional political divisions if she was to escape the general European crisis.[2] By raising first principles about politics and social philosophy, the reviews put everything up for grabs. They also provided suggestions for a third way, by which was meant a unique French answer to communism and fascism which would provide for greater internal unity. These and similar suggestions proved so bountiful that the number three was nearly squared. Perhaps the most influential of these programs, because it was the most ambitious, was that associated with Emmanuel Mounier's *Esprit.*[3] Under the rubric of personalism, Mounier threw together a grab bag of vague, social Catholic ideas meant to resolve the dilemmas of the modern world. Personalism called for a spiritualized, but pluralistic, society responsive to individual needs. Mounier argued that a society so organized would negate both capitalistic materialism and republican individualism, and thereby arrest the two false responses to modernity, communistic collectivism and fascist statism.

Mounier, however, held no monopoly on the search for a middle way. Even Georges Izard, his major collaborator in establishing

2. On the world of the reviews, see J. L. Loubet de Bayle, *Les Non-conformistes des années 30,* and Jean Touchard, "L'Esprit des années 1930." For the general attempt at revaluation during the 1930s, see Roy Pierce, *Contemporary French Political Thought,* and H. Stuart Hughes, *The Obstructed Path.*
3. There is an ever increasing plethora of material on Mounier and *Esprit.* See Emmanuel Mounier, *Mounier et sa génération;* Michel Winock, *Histoire politique de la revue "Esprit," 1930–1950;* Joseph Amato, *Mounier and Maritain;* William Rauch, *Politics and Belief in Contemporary France;* Donald Wolf, "Emmanuel Mounier: A Catholic of the Left"; David Lewis, "Emmanuel Mounier and the Politics of Moral Revolution"; John Hellman, "The Opening to the Left in French Catholicism: The Role of the Personalists"; and M. H. Kelly, "The Fate of Emmanuel Mounier." Mounier's most useful statement, *Le Personalisme,* has recently been republished in the Que sais-je? series.

Esprit, from the beginning held a different conception of what they hoped to accomplish. As a result, their plan included not only a review, but a political movement which Izard promptly christened the Troisième Force. For Izard their enterprise entailed both theoretical speculation and political activism. Mounier, too much the disciple of Péguy, argued that politics would sacrifice their idealism on the altar of immediate affairs. He also felt some unease over Izard's affinity for the left and his attraction for the ideas of Gaston Bergery, an important neo-Jacobin political figure whom Mounier insisted upon viewing as a neo-Bolshevik. By 1933 the founders of *Esprit* and the Troisième Force parted company, the review becoming Mounier's exclusive property while Izard took charge of the movement. Within a year, the Troisième Force predictably merged with Bergery's Front Social which provided the original inspiration for the Popular Front. With this alliance, Izard joined the political fray with a passionate antifascist trying to organize like-minded people to establish a mass movement leading to a government of public safety. Bergery's proposal for a third way looked to the left and called for a purified republic able to rejuvenate the community by incorporating the workers into a national struggle against fascism.

Ideas for a French alternative were not limited to the reviews or the left. During the late 1920s some rather daring recommendations were heard from André Tardieu on the republican right.[4] Every inch a notable of the regime, Tardieu was a highly respected observer of diplomatic affairs who maintained close ties with the military and had assumed the role of Clemenceau's political heir. As he watched the collapse of the Versailles peace, Tardieu attributed France's difficulties to a multiparty parliamentary politics which prevented the implementation of a firm national policy. He watched with fear the apparent unity of fascist Italy, and believed that Frenchmen had lost their sense of dedication to the *patrie.* Tardieu, drawing upon his knowledge of the United States, recommended the establishment of a strong executive and two parties,

---

4. On Tardieu, see A. Aubert et al., *André Tardieu;* Rudolf Binion, *Defeated Leaders;* and Monique Clague, "Vision and Myopia in the New Politics of André Tardieu."

one of which would join moderates and conservatives in a single anti-Marxist bloc. He hoped that a politically unified bourgeoisie, with the support of a government works program, would prove less Malthusian and more American, and thereby modernize the economy and mitigate working-class hostility. Tardieu's was an appeal for a new, conservative (though by French standards, innovative) politics patterned after an aggressive American capitalism. When Tardieu became prime minister in 1929–1930 and tried to implement his ideas, he was quickly hamstrung by an opposition which accused him of harboring Bonapartist ambitions. Angry, Tardieu retired from both politics and Paris; like Ollivier, whose politics resembled his own, he withdrew to the Midi and launched a literary campaign against republican institutions until he was silenced by a stroke in 1939. During his own time Tardieu's third way proved a dead end, but many of his ideas reappeared with the fall of the Republic.

Tardieu's appeal for a more productive capitalism drew him to an ideology which was a response to the interwar years, and which transcended traditional politics. As a result of the rediscovery of Saint-Simonism and the belief, at least during the 1920s, that the United States provided a model for economic renewal, France witnessed the emergence of an ideology best described as technocratic.[5] Many-sided, it cut across both the left and the right, and represented a fundamental challenge to the so-called stalemate society. This technocratic impulse made its greatest appeal to those who were disenchanted with the political and economic status quo. For some, technocratic reform would provide necessary economic strength for a firm foreign policy, while others emphasized the possibility of blunting the impact of Marxism. Practically all proponents of the idea, however, agreed that it demanded a new politics—if not a strong executive, then at the very least a state guided by economic and managerial experts.

Tardieu's particular link with the technocratic movement was

---

5. See Philippe Bauchard, *Les Technocrates et le pouvoir;* Charles Maier, "Between Taylorism and Technocracy: European Ideologies and the Vision of Industrial Productivity"; and Richard Kuisel, "Technocrats and Public Economic Policy."

through the Redressement Français of Ernest Mercier.[6] Of rightist political persuasion, Mercier was a *polytechnicien* who was the organizing force behind France's electrical system. The Redressement, which was most influential during the late 1920s, called for a stronger executive to lead the Republic, and demanded a greater role for "apolitical experts" who would not cater to the whims of the various parties. The idea theoretically involved a repudiation of politics. In actual fact, it was an attempt to save caplitalism from the old politics by way of a new one. A disinterested elite would modernize the economy, raise productivity, and thereby establish that French capitalism was functional.

Other suggestions for technocratic innovation were less obviously inspired by conservative sentiments. During the 1930s, for example, the X-Crise group, concerned with the effects of depression, brought together engineers and *polytechniciens* who recommended *dirigisme* as a solution for economic catastrophe. Protean and somewhat diffuse, the technocratic impulse also merged with experiments in socialist planning during the Popular Front, all of which joined technocracy with the quest for social justice. In any event, the idea of an *économie dirigée* represented still another suggested escape from the difficulties of the interwar period; as such, it was a third way with striking parallels to the Saint-Simonian alternatives presented by Napoleon III in an earlier period of economic and social crisis.

By 1940, after ten years of internal dissension and economic difficulties capped by military catastrophe, the Republic was totally discredited. Even men closely associated with the regime called for fundamental change in the face of new conditions. The field, suddenly abandoned by the republicans, was filled with the dissidents of the 1930s, and the various intellectual currents of the period came together in both Vichy and the Resistance. Indeed, the two antagonists that struggled for France's destiny until 1944 were brothers under the skin, and although Vichy looked to the right and the Resistance to the left, they both repudiated the republican past

6. See Richard Kuisel, *Ernest Mercier, French Technocrat.*

and shared common watchwords. The ensuing confusion engendered by a German victory explained how Bergery, the intellectual father of the Popular Front, could join Pétain, or how so many others, like Mounier, after accepting Vichy, found their way into the Resistance.

As for Vichy's National Revolution, it was a hodgepodge of ideas designed to provide an alternative to both fascism and communism.[7] To counter the Alainist individualism of the Republic, the regime looked to the Church and employed the watchwords *patrie* and *famille*. It also searched for national reconciliation by placing the community under the auspices of a statism guided by a paternalistic leader. In the political realm, Marshal Pétain's decrees became law; France finally had a strong executive and, it should be added, no assembly.

The National Revolution of course involved numerous ideological hopes. Some supporters were influenced by Mounier, others were Proudhonian corporatists or Maurrasian nationalists, and still others called for a return to the virtues of a rural and agrarian society. Antimodernism, however, did not exhaust the reality of Vichy. The regime recruited professional experts, and in one case this had profound ramifications.[8] When it overhauled the economic and financial administration, the government introduced men of a technocratic bent who were particularly attuned to France's needs, since a severe shortage of goods and services necessitated rationing. Further, France had been absorbed into Germany's sphere of influence and her economy organized accordingly.[9] This, like rationing, called for planning and led Vichy to form organizational committees which directed industry and established production goals. The impact was significant, with the technocrats organizing an *économie dirigée*. Despite its retrograde symbols and vocabulary, Vichy had the effect of instigating economic modernization by means of statist intervention.

If Vichy broke the pattern of the Third Republic, the Resistance did no less. So diverse that a *mystique* was necessary to hold it

7. On Vichy, see Robert Paxton's excellent study, *Vichy France.*
8. See Richard Kuisel, "The Legend of the Vichy Synarchy."
9. See Alan S. Milward, *The New Order and the French Economy.*

together, the Resistance drew inspiration from Mounier, the Communists, old-fashioned nationalists, proponents of a new politics, and those who desired social integration. When the Resistance took charge in 1944, there was nevertheless some continuity with the preceeding regime as the Fourth Republic, and later its successor, discovered the value of economic planning. Once Communist solutions were discarded, the neo-Saint-Simonian mix of capitalism and socialism seemed to represent the best method for achieving social justice and internal pacification. Indeed, *dirigisme* provided common ground for the non-Communist heirs of the Resistance: "The Left saw [economic] rejuvenation as the means of improving the lot of the masses, while the Gaullists envisioned it as a prerequisite of France's return to the ranks of the great powers."[10]

In the postwar consciousness, the Third Republic's governing principle of education was replaced by that of productivity. Perhaps even more intriguing, at least for the political historian, is that *dirigisme* was accompanied by the reemergence of a powerful executive acting in conjunction with administrative experts. The stalemate society and its politics were relegated to the past, and the present-day agreement, while owing much to the American example, has obviously drawn upon native traditions associated with the Second Empire. The interwar crisis of the 1920s and 1930s has led Frenchmen to retrace at least some of the steps taken during the 1850s and the 1860s.

The change in attitudes associated with the interwar years did not leave French historians untouched. On the contrary, they mirrored the shifts and frequently participated in the disputes that marked the period. The currents of thought which questioned the stalemate society and the Third Republic were paralleled by both a challenge to the old history that remained so much a product of the old politics, and a quest for a new approach that repudiated traditional narrative history (*histoire événementielle*) with its focus upon political matters. Man, so the dissidents' argument ran, was far more than a creature living within the confines of a state.

The historiographical shift partially followed from a series of

10. Kuisel, "Technocrats and Public Economic Policy," p. 81.

logical responses to events disruptive of previous assumptions. The horror of World War I, for instance, called into question for many the legitimacy of the traditional state system. Political history was therefore naturally suspect to those who refused to join the idea of humanity with an agent of long-term, mechanized violence. There was also the impact of revolutionary Marxism's success in Russia and its ensuing relationship to a domestic Communistic party and working-class alienation. Proletarian militancy did not mix easily into the world of the Third Republic, and Marxism, reinforced by the prestige of victory in the east, provided a marvelous intellectual tool for discrediting republican politics, or for that matter, any politics. Finally, the depression of the 1930s underscored the importance of economics, something that the practitioners of the old history had virtually ignored.

The shift in historiographical emphasis has been directly associated with several sources: the neo-Marxian approach of Albert Mathiez and Georges Lefebvre, the work of Henri Berr, and the collaborative efforts of Lucien Febvre and Marc Bloch.[11] These men fought a guerrilla war against the University establishment erected during the late nineteenth century, and they ultimately won. Mathiez, a student of the politically orthodox Aulard, was first influenced by Jaurès's volumes on the Great Revolution in the *Histoire socialiste* which treated the upheaval as a case study in class warfare. It was nevertheless the events of World War I and the Russian Revolution that definitively redirected Mathiez toward Marxism. Of equal importance, Mathiez converted the French Revolution into a field of study dominated by a leftist scholarship practiced by those who engaged in a history of Marxian social analysis. Further, Mathiez's very success allowed Lefebvre by the late 1930s to ensconce himself in Paris, the center of the University system, and to exert tremendous influence by the very magnitude of his erudition.

Far more innovative was Henri Berr, who remained outside the

---

11. Useful statements concerning the "new history" are: Louis Girard, "Les Problèmes français"; Jean Glénisson, "L'Historiographie française contemporaine"; and Michel François, "Historical Study in France."

establishment and organized the *Revue de synthèse* as a counter-periodical to the *Revue historique* even before World War I. Berr, something of a positivist, argued that historians should specialize less and generalize more, set aside their obsession with politics, and grasp the larger view of man emerging from the social sciences. He also drew together like-minded people, including Febvre and Bloch, and was viewed as a troublesome maverick by the orthodox professionals. Such independence frequently carried stiff penalties in the world of the University, and Berr was even denied an advancement from the lycée Henri IV to the Collège de France.

In contrast, the younger Febvre and Bloch were more effective and have been credited with the renewal of French historical writing. Professional historians and good friends, the two in 1929 began publishing their now famous journal, the *Annales,* to lead an attack against narrative political history.[12] Febvre seems to have feared that if historians failed to comprehend the social sciences, their discipline would simply disappear. In some respects, Febvre launched an offensive action meant to capture the social sciences for history, and justified his undertaking by alluding to the work of Jules Michelet and Emile Durkheim.[13] In the first case, Febvre appealed to a model long held in disrepute by professionals: that of an historian prepared to draw daring generalizations from his material. As for the sociology of Durkheim, an emphasis upon the importance of a community's shared values and ideas provided a theory well suited for historians hesitant to embrace Marxism.[14] Febvre and Bloch believed that individuals must be perceived as members of collective social groups sharing common attitudes. Both agreed that

12. For a scathing attack by Lucien Febvre against Seignobos, see the former's "Entre l'histoire à thèse et l'histoire-manuel." The article is also reproduced in *Combats pour l'histoire,* a collection of Febvre's best essays and reviews.

13. William Keylor in his *Academy and Community,* pp. 163–207, argues that some historians, and particularly Seignobos, had shown an interest in Durkheim's sociology since the Dreyfus Affair. Even so, the interest was more theoretical than real, as Seignobos wanted sociologists to think historically while he continued to write history in the traditional fashion.

14. As we shall see, Durkheim's ideas paralleled those of Marx while also providing an alternative. While waging a common battle against traditionalists, the practitioners of neo-Marxian social analysis on the one hand and the practitioners of the *Annales* approach on the other were somewhat at odds.

histoire événementielle should be abandoned for a discipline involving *mentalité, structure* and *conjoncture;* a true history was total and concerned society's numerous manifestations of which politics was only one, and the two friends tried to grasp society's wholeness by showing the interrelationship between institutions, ideas, religion, political life, and economic structure.

The proponents of a new history ultimately experienced real success. The work of Mathiez and Lefebvre now stands in a hallowed tradition, and since World War II the *Annales* has become the new establishment, publishing its own books and distributing government largesse for various research projects designed for a total history.[15] One result of these developments has been the emergence of economic history. Whenever the traditionalists considered economics, they did so as an aside, treating it as a service discipline. Virtually no attention was given to acquainting students with statistical methods or the problems of determining national income. Indeed, before World War II economic history was the preserve of the law schools, where students wrote dissertations about administrative controls and legal regulations, or of journalists, retired *fonctionnaires,* and a few idiosyncratic specialists such as Emile Levasseur and Marcel Marion. The belated recognition of the importance of economic matters, however, did not merely follow from the new historians. The precedent they established was in tune with the difficulties of the interwar years, and later with France's post-World War II concern with *dirigisme* and economic productivity. New attitudes were accompanied by the appearance of historians less concerned with defending republican politics than with investigating the dynamics of industrialization, and particularly economic productivity. More interested in social than political history, they focused their attention upon the nature of industrialization,

---

15. On the *Annales* as establishment, see the reflective essay of Febvre's and Bloch's heir, Fernand Braudel, "Personal Testimony." An iconclastic, but admiring, treatment is J. H. Hexter, "Fernand Braudel and the Monde Braudellien." Also of value are Georg Iggers, *New Directions in European Historiography,* pp. 43–79; Maurice Aymard, "The *Annales* and French Historiography"; and Traian Stoianovich, *French Historical Method.* On Febvre, H. D. Mann, *Lucien Febvre,* is useful.

paying special attention to the role of transportation, entrepreneurial attitudes, and credit facilities. Not surprisingly, those
who were or became historians of the Second Empire and participated in the original search for new ways and a new history during
the interwar years necessarily brought to their work considerations
quite different from those of their predecessors. Further, they were
frequently outsiders at odds with certain features of the Third
Republic, and had they been otherwise, their contributions might
very well have been of another sort. Despite their many differences,
they shared a common historiographical assumption that the Empire
was historically meaningful because it succeeded in laying the basis
for a modern industrial society. They also showed little interest in
attacking the politics of Bonapartism, and at times they even betrayed a clear sympathy for the Saint-Simonian concept of a directed
economy. Their effect, as we shall see, is still very much alive,[16] To
the point, the historiography of the Empire has been nothing less
than transformed by the crises and the final dissolution of the
so-called stalemate society.

Marcel Blanchard

Marcel Blanchard, who identified with a family tradition of government service dating from the First Empire, had little in common
with the Alainism associated with the Republic. Instead, he viewed
the state as a means for achieving both progress and order, and
believed that an enlightened regime could guide the community in

---

16. It should be noted that American scholars have written much in a similar vein
about the Empire. Charles Kindleberger reflected their attitude when he wrote: "Not
until 1944 and 1945 with the Monnet Plan did positive governmental intervention for
growth assume the proportions of the Second Empire. The deep current of Saint-
Simonian thought, with its emphasis upon economic expansion, surfaced again in an
atmosphere altered by two doctrines—socialist planning, on the one hand, and
Keynesian pinning of responsibility for full employment and growth on the government, on the other." The quoted passage is from Charles Kindleberger, *Economic
Growth in France and Britain, 1851–1950*, p. 188. For other American writers, see in
particular Arthur Dunham, *The Anglo-French Treaty of Commerce of 1860;* David
Landes, *Bankers and Pashas;* David Pinkney, *Napoleon III and the Rebuilding of
Paris;* and Rondo E. Cameron, *France and the Economic Development of Europe,
1800–1914.*

establishing its priorities. Patriotic and by temperament a man of action, Blanchard was naturally drawn to the army, but a severe case of nearsightedness precluded a military career. After completing his studies at Grenoble and Lyon in 1909, he became a teacher in a provincial lycée. Called to the army in World War I, he served with valor as a company commander and was twice wounded, the second time so seriously that he lost an arm and an eye. Discharged with a Croix de Guerre and membership in the Legion of Honor, Blanchard then returned to teaching, took his doctorate at Grenoble in 1919, and became professor of modern history at Montpellier.

Throughout his life Blanchard maintained close ties with the military. Active in the veterans' movement during the interwar period, he became history examiner of the admissions board for St. Cyr in 1924, and by 1935 its president. With a clear sense of duty, Blanchard in 1940 rallied to Marshal Pétain, under whose government he first served as rector at Grenoble, and later as professor of colonial history at the Sorbonne. For Blanchard, the end of World War II was followed by an early retirement. The army, however, held loyalty in high regard, and retained Blanchard's appointment at the Ecole Supérieure de l'Intendance, where he remained until 1954. His death eleven years later went virtually unnoticed by the historical profession; the army nevertheless remained appreciative, and Blanchard was buried with full military honors.

In the world of professional historians, Blanchard was somewhat atypical. He received a Catholic secondary education and pursued his higher studies in the provinces. While most of his colleagues viewed Paris as an object of conquest and a model for imitation, Blanchard remained a true provincial, retaining close ties with his family and its native locale. His work, as a result, was marked by a personal and even idiosyncratic character not at all in harmony with the official school. His thesis, essentially a study in economic history, followed from an interest in the Blanchards' long participation in the Alpine carrying trade.[17] The work nevertheless transcended merely regional considerations and Lucien Febvre praised its author

17. Marcel Blanchard, *Les Routes des Alpes occidentales à l'époque napoléonienne, 1796–1815.*

for tracing the effects of geography in determining trade routes. In subsequent studies, given his awareness of the social and economic changes brought by the PLM line to Montélimar, a small town on the Rhone where he spent much of his childhood, Blanchard directed his attention to the history of railroads. To the very end, personal reflection upon a familial and provincial experience played a primary role in Blanchard's approach to history. It was not the kind of work produced by Sorbonnists, and it won Blanchard a place as an occasional contributor to the *Annales*.

While aiding the quest for a new history, Blanchard actively participated in the search for a new politics. A thoroughgoing nationalist, he believed that only an industrialized and economically powerful France could maintain the position won at Versailles. In opposition to the timid political economy of the Third Republic which fostered class division and national disunity, Blanchard argued that France had to recapture the Saint-Simonian impulse for economic planning. Favorable toward the technocratic idea, he joined the Redressement Français and became president of its chapter at Montpellier.[18] He also held in great esteem André Tardieu who shared Blanchard's concern for economic, military, and political renovation. In sum, Blanchard's history mirrored his politics, and both were very much a part of the French response to interwar difficulties.

Because of his interest in the relationship between transportation and economic development, Blanchard was naturally drawn to the regime of Napoleon III, and one suspects that he believed the Third Republic could have used a good dose of the Second Empire. He scattered throughout numerous provincial journals a host of articles filled with praise for imperial railway policy.[19] His *Le Second Empire*, which appeared after the war, provided a summation and revealed the author's technocratic bent. The general tone of these studies revealed the author's assumption that economic rather than

18. Professor Richard Kuisel of the State University of New York at Stony Brook first brought Blanchard's membership in the Redressement to my attention.

19. The most complete list is provided in the bibliography of Henri Sée, *Histoire économique de la France*, II, 373–374.

political developments shape the character of a community. Blanchard argued that traditional historians failed to recognize that railroads literally revolutionized French society, and with Montélimar in mind, he wrote:

> In France the construction and development of the railroads have . . . provoked and accompanied industrial development: the extension of mining, the renovation and rise of metallurgy, the transformation of the old textile industries . . . Yes, our grandfathers watched, between 1850 and 1880, this profound transformation—far more serious and heavily charged for the future than any revolution of a political order, without excepting 1789 and 1848. Our grandfathers . . . watched the end of the old, rural, agrarian, and stable France—the France of antique, small villages, drowsy and discreet along the length of the great highways . . .[20]

An admirer of the Saint-Simonians, Blanchard published the journal of Michel Chevalier[21] and lauded the sect for producing a host of figures, such as the Pereires, Talabot, Arlès-Dufour, and particularly Enfantin, who understood the demands of industrialization and provided the entrepreneurial leadership for the new economy. Further, he repeated Enfantin's scathing attacks on the July Monarchy's failure to overcome the local rivalries and parliamentary indecisions that impeded the task of railroad construction. Like the Saint-Simonians, Blanchard remained noticeably insensitive to the Empire's strong-arm tactics. While discussing police surveillance during the 1860s, he once wrote that, "it is superfluous to add that there is in these lines no intended hostility or polemic in respect to these methods of the Second Empire's administration; such procedures can exist anytime and under any regime.[22] Blanchard shared the Saint-Simonian assumption that authoritarianism could frequently serve useful purposes, all of which guaranteed that he would treat the Empire in a manner quite different from that of more traditional historians.

20. Marcel Blanchard, "La Politique ferroviaire du second Empire."
21. Contained in the *Revue des deux mondes*, November 1932, and the *Revue historique* 171 (1933).
22. Marcel Blanchard, "Une Enquête administrative dans l'Isère en 1859." p. 73.

Le Second Empire provided a precise and masterful sketch in a little more than two hundred pages. Something of an essay posing as a general history, the small volume contained the basic arguments associated with a productivist point of view. On the other hand, Blanchard never ignored the Empire's politics. *Le Second Empire* was structured according to the regime's political evolution, and was divided into four parts roughly covering the years 1852–1859, 1859–1863, 1863–1869, and 1870.

Le Second Empire blazed no new trails in the area of political history; Blanchard followed earlier writers such as Maurain, and then provided his own mixture of general conclusions. While recognizing the personal quality of the regime, he commented upon the Emperor's natural goodness, middling intelligence, and naïveté. The latter quality, he argued, was reflected in the Bonapartist plan to overcome the community's political divisions. From the beginning, the regime was caught between the demands of a utopian Emperor and the demands of the Empire's conservative supporters; Napoleon III engaged in a precarious balancing act in which he necessarily represented a major source of disequilibrium.

The regime's weakness became fully evident when the Emperor embarked upon an adventurous foreign policy. The year 1859 marked the beginning of a one-man subversion of the established European order, and Napoleon III proved unequal to his own conspiracy. He became little more than an apprentice sorcerer unable to control his own creation. As such, Italy determined the regime's destinies, all of which led Blanchard to devote one whole section constituting one-fifth of the book—and entitled "Les Années tournantes"—to the character and ramifications of the Italian war. The latter, he argued, dislocated conservative support, and irretrievably damaged the Empire. During the 1860s, Napoleon III therefore confronted a situation demanding liberalization and a surrender to the political forces theoretically destroyed in 1851. Meanwhile, the same foreign policy that imposed liberalization led to a series of developments catastrophic for France's position within the European community, particularly since the Emperor lacked an adequate military force.

Unlike traditional historians who devoted the bulk of their attention to the dynamics of political change during the 1860s, Blanchard gave equal weight to the preceding decade. Such an approach placed in perspective a period of political quiet when the regime neutralized the various parties. Freed of parliamentary encumbrances, the Empire, he asserted, began a massive transformation of French society. The coup d'état established the style of a whole decade during which the Emperor tried to renew French society and improve the lot of the poor through a policy of stimulating industrial productivity. It was a conscious attempt to copy the English pattern of economic development, and in Blanchard's mind, the *grande pensée* of the regime was not Mexico, but the Bonapartist plan "to organize the national prosperity and the industrial equipment of the French nation."[23] The first decade of the Empire, in short, could not be fairly judged according to the narrow dictates of political historiography. As indicated in the famous Bordeaux declaration of 1852, the government was dedicated to goals outside the range of orthodox politics.

According to Blanchard, the mid-point of the nineteenth century separated modern France from that of the *ancien régime*. Before the Empire, traditional modes of transportation preserved a community in which provinces represented the largest regional markets, and where the economy was agrarian and highly decentralized. These conditions, in turn, naturally shaped the character and quality of the whole social structure. With most towns and villages isolated from the outside world, a national life remained virtually nonexistent, while local affairs were under the surveillance and control of the notables and clergy. The July Monarchy, as the political manifestation of this society, was a government concerned with little more than providing justice and maintaining a foreign policy. Its personnel lacked the ideological wherewithall to assume a dynamic role in stimulating social change through economic development.

23. Marcel Blanchard, *Le Second Empire*, pp. 20–21, 59.

As a case in point, administrative views concerning the budget remained tied to the demands of the Parisian *haute banque,* a collection of financiers who imposed their unimaginativeness upon the economy under the guise of fiscal responsibility. As a result, the government passively presided over the economy's undercapitalization, a situation that impeded industrial growth and helped to ignite the crisis of 1848.

In contrast, the Empire deliberately fostered industrialization and thereby brought about a new period of social development. Although Blanchard acknowledged that external conditions, such as the influx of gold from California and Australia, aided government policy, he emphasized the regime's effective utilization of a favorable situation. By accelerating the pace, the Second Empire qualitatively changed the character of economic development during the 1850s. Blanchard attributed this success to Napoleon III's wise decision to employ the Saint-Simonians. The Emperor, who justified his caesarism in terms of increasing the community's material well-being, allowed them to implement their theories, with the result that Saint-Simonism and Bonapartism virtually became indistinguishable. Even the Orleanist personnel of the Empire underwent the effects of the productivist doctrine. In Blanchard's words, they were "invigorated" to the point of administering a government economic policy completely at odds with their previous training.

The government's partnership with the Saint-Simonians led to the implementation of two basic policies: construction of a national railroad network and the development of a banking system adequate for capitalizing a modern economy. The two policies were in fact inseparable. Railroads and industrialization went hand in hand. Without a broader and more speculative system of banking and investment, construction of the main railway lines had little chance of rapid completion. This accounted for the importance of Emile and Isaac Pereire, whose Crédit Mobilier neutralized the *haute banque's* restrictive control over the economy. Opposition to the Mobilier on the part of the *haute banque* was therefore predictable, and became part of a larger and more general resistance to Napoleon III. The Pereires represented the economic side of an authoritarian democracy which threatened the vested interests of a more traditional society, and just as Bonapartism's democratic qualities excited mistrust on the part of the conservatives, the Mobilier's commitment to economic dynamism did likewise. There was, in short, a parallel between the machinations of the Party of Order and the *haute banque,* and Blanchard's sympathies were obviously on the side of the authoritarians.

In discussing the remainder of the government's policies, Blanchard commended the transformation of Paris and observed that only the Empire had possessed the courage and will necessary for such an undertaking. On the other hand, he said surprisingly little about the 1860 trade treaty, aside from noting its political effects. As for railroad construction, Blanchard emphasized the Empire's sense of political strength and permanence. Self-confidence allowed the regime to escape the "mediocre and fragmentary" results of the July Monarchy. The latter, because it lacked faith in its own future, feared the rise of huge, powerful rail companies, and therefore studiously ignored the Saint-Simonian formula of profitable, consolidated lines providing regional service. More bold and enterprising, the Empire instigated a program of mergers, entered into partnership with the new lines, and guaranteed their interest payments—policies which allowed the companies to extend their operations while attracting capital from previously untapped small investors. The result was an updated economy organized around a national railway system that brought France into the modern world.

Blanchard was both brief and to the point. Whatever the virtues of the *ancien régime,* the Empire allowed Frenchmen to escape the restrictiveness necessarily associated with more traditional societies. By fostering industrial development, the Empire speeded the process of democratization. In Blanchard's words:

> The fact remains, however, that by the technical means accorded to individual conceptions, the means to acquire wealth and influence were multiplied for all who were audacious and enterprising. The social structure became more mobile, and there was a constant fluctuation of social values which is properly democratic. This was indeed what the Emperor and his advisors wished.[24]

24. Ibid., p. 73.

Despite a willingness to admit the political shortcomings of Bonapartism, Blanchard clearly believed that the Empire experienced its
own kind of success. He attributed the regime's failures and gains
to a common source: the utopian imaginativeness of Napoleon III.
The question then became one of priorities, and Blanchard apparently thought the benefits France received from the Empire out-
weighed the liabilities. If nothing else, *Le Second Empire* reflected
the technocratic and Saint-Simonian belief that an inspired authoritarianism had its own justification.

Robert Schnerb

Robert Schnerb was a casualty in the struggle for a new history,
and the events surrounding his *carrière manquée* are hardly a credit
to the University.[25] In the early 1930s and by means of neo-Marxian
analysis, Schnerb developed a pioneering approach that weighed
the economic and social impact of government fiscal policies. In
spite of his new methodology and in part because of it, Schnerb was
virtually blackballed from teaching at the level of *enseignement
supérieur,* and his work was ignored by the historical establishment.
Schnerb's plight did not go unnoticed, but his defenders were not
well enough established in the 1930s to aid him in any significant
fashion. By the time they had arrived, it was simply too late. Only
toward the very end of his career and after his death did Schnerb
begin to receive his due. One can only speculate as to what might
have been his scholarly accomplishments had he received the
academic support allocated to others.

Schnerb, who was both prickly and independent, studied at Dijon
where he worked with Febvre and Mathiez, the latter becoming
his adviser. The relationship between master and student proved

25. For published works on Schnerb, see Madeleine Schnerb, *Mémoires pour deux;*
and Madeleine Schnerb, ed., *Robert Schnerb,* which also contains a near complete
bibliography of Schnerb's work compiled by Albert Soboul. Finally, see Albert
Troux, "Robert Schnerb," *L'Information historique* 5 (1962), 184; Jacques Godechot,
"Robert Schnerb," *Annales historiques de la Révolution française* 171 (1963), 129–
135; and Pierre Léon, "Robert Schnerb," *Annales (Economies-Sociétés-Civilisations)*
18 (1963), 825–832.

stormy, in part because Schnerb reacted against Mathiez's more
doctrinaire qualities. Like most young leftists, however, the student
shared his teacher's fascination for the Revolution. Mathiez unfortunately died in 1932, just before the completion of Schnerb's dissertation, *Les Contributions directes à l'époque de la Révolution dans le
département du Puy-de-Dôme*. Philippe Sagnac assumed direction
of the thesis and convened a jury without consulting Schnerb as
to its membership. The jury, weighted with traditionalists, included
a frequent target of Mathiez's combative pen. To make matters
worse, the University demanded discretion and a certain respect
for elders from those who were ambitious enough to seek entry into
its highest levels. Schnerb and his wife, both lycée professors who
supported the new history, had written book reviews critical of
several established traditional historians, one of whom now sat on
the board. Finally, Schnerb refused or failed to follow proper eti-
quette by calling upon all jury members. To the point, Schnerb
confronted a hostile board, and Sagnac, who knew or cared little
about economic matters, proved unable to protect his adopted
student. Although the dissertation passed, it received only honorable
mention, and Schnerb's reputation suffered accordingly.[26] Given the
small number of positions available in higher education, he received
no appointment and was forced to return to the lycée at Clermont-
Ferrand. Worse still, Schnerb was to discover that gerontocratic
bureaucracies are blessed with long memories and that his career
was permanently compromised.

The higher reaches of the University constituted a small, tight-
knit, subculture where advancement frequently depended upon
both professional merit and criteria of another sort. That Schnerb
was a provincial Jew of Marxian sympathies probably did not help
his cause. Mathiez's death, moreover, left Schnerb without a patron

---

26. The thesis nevertheless received strong praise from Lucien Febvre in the
Annales; like-minded reviewers were Ernest Labrousse in the *Revue d'histoire
économique et sociale* 4 (1933), 61–65, and Georges Lefebvre in the *Annales historiques de la Révolution française* 10 (1933), 470–476. Febvre later repeated his
earlier praise in *Pour un histoire à part entière*, pp. 393–397. Finally, Jean Bouvier
has recently written that French historians have yet to understand properly the importance of the approach utilized by Schnerb in his thesis; see Jean Bouvier and
Jacques Wolff, eds., *Deux Siècles de fiscalité française*, p. 227.

in a system where "old boy" ties and family connections counted for much; as an added complication, Schnerb did not study at the Ecole Normale, from which the educational elite sprang and where they had shared common experiences.[27] Finally, he remained tempermentally unsuited for establishing his own connections by cultivating those in authority; certainly proud, but a bit shy and sensing himself an outsider, he retreated into his studies and earned a reputation for stubborn aloofness.

Ignored by the University throughout the prewar years, Schnerb became the bitter witness of other peoples' advancement. While young professors, some less capable, joined the scramble for the available seats in higher education, Schnerb watched from his lycée while others, including Jean Maurain, held his coveted prize: the chair of modern history at Clermont-Ferrand. Schnerb did not, however, fall into despairing inactivity. After the Stavisky riots in 1934, he briefly worked with Gaston Bergery and organized the local chapter of the Comité de Vigilance des Intellectuels contre le Fascisme. This foray into politics proved to be both unique and brief. Although a leftist and worried about the direction of French politics, he remained an intensely private individual who was primarily a scholar. Schnerb therefore continued to pursue his work in economic history, and wrote numerous articles concerning the mid-nineteenth century.[28] Febvre, meanwhile, remained a loyal supporter, vainly lobbying for his ex-student and publishing his articles in the *Annales*. Schnerb, however, did not become an *Annaliste* in the full sense of the word, partially because of his neo-Marxism. As a result, he joined with another Mathiez student, Albert Troux, in establishing the *Information historique*, a journal in which Schnerb wrote reviews of recent works in related fields. The articles had barely established his reputation as a wide-ranging generalist able to synthesize disparate but related works into a common theme when World War II suddenly destroyed what he had thus far salvaged from the disappointment of 1933.

27. The importance of patronage and other such matters is described by Terry Clark, *Prophets and Patrons*, pp. 66–92.

28. During this period, Schnerb wrote an important, though now dated, bibliographical article: "Napoleon III and the Second French Empire."

The year 1940 brought catastrophe. Vichy's ugly discrimination against Jews forced Schnerb from his teaching post, whereupon he temporarily retreated to his property just outside Clermont.[29] Wisely fearing the worst, he later fled with his family into the mountains where he remained until the end of the war. Liberation, however, proved no unmixed blessing, as Schnerb and his wife were to discover that both sides of their families had been virtually wiped out by the Nazis. The University, on the other hand, made some attempt to right previous wrongs by offering several positions in higher education, but even this soured when no post was made available at the Faculté des Lettres at Clermont. Schnerb, so distraught by the war that he nearly changed his name, simply refused to abandon the country house which had once served as a refuge, and he even rejected an offer from an old admirer, Ernest Labrousse, to join the prestigious Ecole Pratique des Hautes Etudes. Angered by the troubles that had plagued his thirty-year career, Schnerb remained at the lycée in Clermont, took an early retirement in 1960, and died two years later.

The postwar period nonetheless brought Schnerb a degree of success and recognition. He and Troux resurrected the *Information historique,* and Schnerb, contributing articles to numerous journals and even projecting a massive history of taxation, soon established his reputation as a prolific scholar. His most politically revealing work was a brief study of Ledru-Rollin, in which Schnerb criticized the radical leader for believing in the reconcilability of labor and capital.[30] Indeed, he blamed precisely this attitude for the failure of 1848. As an historian, however, Schnerb usually took a more dispassionate view, and hesitated to judge particular political issues. In his greatest work, *Le XIXe siècle* (a volume in the *Histoire générale des civilisations* series), he emphasized the relationship between economics and social history. The book's subtitle, *L'Apogée de l'expansion européenne,* revealed the essence of Schnerb's message. Europe, guided by the bourgeoisie and economically or-

29. The Jewish lycée teacher mentioned by Professor Danton in Marcel Orphul's "Le Chagrin et la pitié" is none other than Schnerb.
30. Robert Schnerb, *Ledru-Rollin.*

ganized according to the precepts of capitalism, experienced a transformation involving industrialization and the harnessing of a previously unimagined source of power. *Le XIXe siècle*, drawing together economic and social developments into a grand synthesis, provided a marvelous example of the new history at its best. Political considerations, in contrast, were virtually ignored, and when a notable of the old school complained that the book mentioned Palmerston only twice, Schnerb noted with his usual testiness that the English leader was in fact mentioned three times.

Schnerb was no great admirer of Bonapartism, and once attributed its emergence to the failure of reactionary bourgeois governments to maintain stability.[31] He nevertheless retained a particular interest in the Second Empire, because of the regime's contribution to economic development. With the prompting of Febvre, he undertook a biographical study of Rouher, an Auvergnat who maintained his original ties with Clermont-Ferrand and nearby Riom.[32] The biography, crowned by the Académie Française, analyzed the role of a major participant in the Bonapartist experiment, and provided an excellent example of how the new historians strove to enlarge their discipline beyond the boundaries of mere politics. Schnerb underlined one of the Empire's major achievements while once again establishing that he was indeed a very talented historian.

━━━━━━►◄►◄━━━━━

It was from Maurain's *Baroche* that Schnerb drew inspiration for a study of Rouher, who was the government's leading spokesman during the 1860s and a figure who became totally identified with the politics of authoritarianism. The two biographies, however, were not altogether similar because, unlike his close friend Baroche, Rouher left behind few personal papers of historical importance.[33] He had little interest in personal fame, and government records

31. Robert Schnerb, "Marx et Proudhon devant le coup d'état du 2 décembre," *Revue socialiste* 2 (1947), 526–536. The article is reproduced in Madeleine Schnerb, ed., *Robert Schnerb*, pp. 161–173.
32. Robert Schnerb, *Rouher et le second Empire*.
33. Those that are available are the Papiers de Cerçay, seized by the Germans in 1870 and returned to France in 1919.

failed to reveal his exact contribution in the Empire's councils. Because of scarce documentation, it proved extremely difficult to determine the extent of Rouher's influence. Schnerb, as opposed to Maurain who was able to work with far greater resources, had to draw conclusions of a provisional sort.

Rouher belonged to an old bourgeois, Auvergnat family with a long tradition of producing lawyers and middling government administrators. He properly took his legal studies during the early years of the July Monarchy, and upon graduation, established a practice at Riom. Contemporaries thought him a perfect example of native virtues—hardworking, methodical, and disciplined. Because of these qualities, Rouher quickly made his mark as a provincial lawyer; in the courtroom he was aggressive, well-prepared, and a powerful speaker who overwhelmed his opponents with the combined force of logic and rhetorical skill. Continual success at the bar allowed him, with the help of Morny and Guizot, to become the government's candidate for the Chamber of Deputies during the 1846 elections. His defeat by the incumbent, a Legitimist, cast some doubt upon his political future within the confines of Orleanism. The destruction of the monarchy reopened Rouher's opportunities: 1848 marked the real beginning of his remarkable career.

During the Second Republic, Rouher followed a path parallel to that of Baroche. He set aside his Orleanism, rallied to the new regime, and entered the Constituent Assembly as a defender of a strong republic capable of maintaining order against further revolution. Like Baroche, he was frightened by the June Days, and concluded that France needed a powerful executive. After voting for Cavaignac, Rouher joined the burgraves at the rue de Poitiers, supported the Barrot ministry, and threw his weight behind the new President, Louis Napoleon. However, he soon faced the dilemma confronting all conservatives. The President and the majority of the newly convened Legislative Assembly, to which Rouher belonged, began to part company. When Louis Napoleon dismissed Barrot, Rouher made the most decisive move of his career. The President needed conservatives willing to man the new ministry despite his growing dispute with the leaders of the Party of Order. More concerned with guaranteeing security than with parliamentary liberties, Rouher joined Baroche and Fould, thus forming the ministry's nucleus.

None of the three, however, wanted a break between the executive and the Assembly. They hoped to mediate between the two and follow a policy meant to assuage conservative sensibilities. As Minister of Justice, Rouher brought the full measure of the law to bear against the republicans, supported Baroche's pet project, the May Law, and quickly established his reputation as a powerful speaker particularly skillful at intimidating and baiting the left. In one case, he threw the republican deputies into a rage by calling the February Revolution a "veritable catastrophe." Rouher was not, however, spared the second choice confronting conservatives, and he rallied to the coup d'état, reassuming the Ministry of Justice. He played a large part in writing the 1852 constitution, thus indicating his conversion to Bonapartist political principles. The minister, according to Schnerb, had "perfectly assimilated the constitutional thought of Bonapartism, and, deliberately turning his back on preceding methods of government, prepared to take an eminent place in the midst of the personnel charged with the task of applying the new institutions."[34]

After a brief resignation over the expropriation of Orleanist family property, Rouher returned to the government as the number two figure of the Council of State, and by 1855 he assumed the ministry of Public Works. Throughout the 1850s, however, it was Baroche rather than Rouher who held the center of the political stage. Only with the declining strength of Baroche and Billault's unexpected death did Rouher become Napoleon III's leading advisor and spokesman before the Legislative Body. The year 1863 therefore opened the period contemporaries humorously, and with some exaggeration, called the "Rouhernement." In any event, Rouher assumed a heavy burden just as political life underwent a renewal and the legislature began to provide a forum for the growing attacks against Bonapartist policies. He engaged Thiers in a running five-year rhe-

34. Schnerb, *Rouher et le second Empire*, p. 56.

torical duel, and according to Schnerb, proved his opponent's match.

On the other hand, Schnerb argued that Rouher's career during the 1860s epitomized the regime's greatest political failing: an inability to move rapidly enough from authoritarianism into liberalization. Schnerb compared Rouher's role to that of Guizot almost twenty years earlier. Both men, he commented, "defended the prerogatives of the monarch to the point of precipitating the ruin of the regimes of their choice."[35] The 1860s called for flexibility, but Rouher maintained his attachment to the principles of 1851–1852. His continual reaffirmation of such principles was his only response to the community's renewed political awareness, and he led a continual rearguard action against liberalization. Yet, Rouher ironically suffered the consequence of his own authoritarian commitment. When, for example, Napoleon III decided to liberalize the press laws and the rules governing public meetings, the minister had no choice but to resign or adhere to the Emperor's wishes. He chose the latter, thereby assuming the awkward task of guiding measures, to which he was opposed, through the Legislative Body. Such malleability, however, failed to endear Rouher with the opposition. As the living symbol of a personal politics, he bore the brunt of criticism from the republicans and the *tiers parti*. The very logic of liberalization demanded his resignation, and the long-overdue political transformation of 1869–1870 brought his replacement by Emile Ollivier.

According to Schnerb, Rouher learned nothing from the obvious lessons of the Empire's last decade. Although he never plotted against Ollivier's government, Rouher had little faith in the liberal experiment. From his new position as president of the Senate, he patiently awaited the return to authoritarian principles. War, however, prevented the issue from being joined and, at the same time, forced Rouher into exile. The 1870s, on the other hand, merely underscored Rouher's persistence. Ever loyal to past methods, he assumed leadership of the Bonapartist contingent in the National Assembly, and led the party's attack against the Republic. With the Prince Imperial's death in 1879, Rouher retired from politics in

35. Ibid., p. 159.

1881, and died three years later. Insofar as political matters were concerned, Rouher had devoted his life to a lost cause.

Schnerb, on the other hand, recognized that the Empire involved more than politics, and herein lay the real significance of Rouher's contribution. There were, in fact, two Rouhers: the Minister of Public Works and the Minister of State, and each reflected a particular side of the Bonapartist program. Schnerb granted the Minister of Public Works the favorable appraisal he denied the Minister of State, a distinction that revealed the author's attitude toward the Empire. Schnerb, for example, pointed out that like Baroche, Rouher was a thoroughgoing bourgeois politician with an Orleanist past. At first, Rouher saw the Empire as only the most effective means of social defense. He joined the Bonapartist cause without the slightest sympathy for the social programs of Louis Napoleon. On the Council of State he supported Baroche in sabotaging Napoleon III's more utopian proposals, and he played a major role in guaranteeing the regime's conservative political character. Yet, Rouher's attitudes underwent a change during the period he served on the Council. Although he certainly never became a socialist, Rouher did acquire an interest in the economic function of credit and the general problem of industrial expansion. He also played an important role in establishing the Crédit Foncier, and soon proved to be an enthusiastic supporter of railroad construction. Rouher was perhaps influenced by Saint-Simonians such as Chevalier, who served on the Council. In any case, his later views were virtually indistinguishable from the pragmatic Saint-Simonism associated with the Bonapartist regime. Indeed, Rouher made his reputation during the 1850s as the government's leading spokesman for a policy of stimulating economic productivity. It was, according to Schnerb, a policy meant to increase the effectiveness of capitalism by overcoming traditional attitudes towards banking, the role of the market place, and the nature of profits. Rouher became convinced of "the enlivening virtue of a liberal capitalism prepared to impel humanity into well-being under the tutelage of a kind of enlightened despotism."[36] As opposed

36. Ibid., p. 92.

to Baroche, who never escaped his Orleanist past, Rouher was beginning to feel the effect of the Bonapartist vision.

By the mid-1850s, Rouher had become the government expert in economic affairs. In 1855 he assumed the Ministry of Public Works, and as the new minister, he was responsible for implementing Bonapartist political economy. Rouher coordinated government projects in road and port improvements, acted as the regime's liaison with the private sector on such matters as railway concessions, and was ultimately responsible for the rail conventions of 1859. On the other hand, despite his conversion to productivism, Rouher never accepted the full measure of Bonapartist economics. The financial orthodoxy of both Fould and Baroche no doubt had its effect, and Rouher remained skeptical of the more extravagant methods employed by Haussmann and the Pereires.

Rouher personally thought that his greatest contribution involved the establishment of freer trade. Like Chevalier, with whom he worked in negotiating the 1860 trade treaty with England, Rouher believed that enlightened economic policy and political authoritarianism were inseparable. In the Legislative Body, he argued that with nearly ten years of rapid economic development, France could successfully compete on an international level, while freer trade would open up foreign markets and stimulate producers to employ more efficient methods. Schnerb, for his own part, sympathized with Rouher's argument, and granted that the treaty laid the basis for an economic revolution. Insofar as it challenged conservative economic interests and lowered prices, the 1860 treaty had a democratic impact. Schnerb also underlined its unpopularity with the bourgeoisie, and pointed out that the future of free trade depended upon the continuation of an authoritarianism originally responsible for its very implementation. Furthermore, Schnerb thought the treaty no less responsible than the Italian imbroglio for disrupting the government's political base. By destroying the French market as a special preserve for domestic producers, it challenged a major conservative principle. Committed to an economy of limited, high, and assured profits rather than an economy of increased productivity, the Party of Order never accepted the idea that government policy should grant consumers a parity equal to that of producers.

Schnerb's *Rouher* added a perspective largely ignored by Maurain's *Baroche*. Maurain portrayed a situation in which Napoleon III surrendered control of the regime to his major advisors. The latter, so the argument ran, were largely drawn from the ranks of ex-Orleanists, and they managed to pervert the democratic and progressive character of Bonapartism. In spite of himself, Napoleon III became the servant of political reaction. This argument, of course, was not altogether untrue, as the "trio" labored to keep Napoleon III on the political straight and narrow. Yet, and as Schnerb clearly indicated, Napoleon III was no fool, nor was he powerless. Rouher was valued for his loyalty, and whatever the differences separating Emperor and Minister, the latter could usually be counted upon to defend and execute Napoleon's final decision. Such malleability, in fact, led the opposition to charge that Rouher lacked scruples and would serve any cause whatsoever in order to preserve his position. The charge, according to Schnerb, missed the point. Rouher believed in the merits of authoritarianism, and thought he could best serve the good cause by effectively serving Napoleon III. He accordingly adopted the general attitudes of the Emperor. Energetic, and an articulate defender of the regime's policies, he thereby came to symbolize both the virtues and shortcomings of Bonapartism. In Chevalier's words, he was nothing less than the "Atlas" of the regime, and it was Rouher that Marcel Blanchard particularly had in mind when he observed that the Empire "invigorated" its Orleanist servitors. Schnerb's message was clear. To have transformed a one-time protégé of Guizot into an ardent supporter of Saint-Simonian productivism was no small accomplishment. Like Blanchard, Schnerb had to grant that Bonapartism had its own successes.

Georges Duveau

Georges Duveau provides a marked contrast to the austere dedication of Marcel Blanchard or the angry aloofness of Robert Schnerb.[37] Extroverted and sentimental to the point of being maud-

37. The best printed sources on Duveau are André Canivez, "La Pensée de

lin, Duveau attracted a host of friends and admirers throughout his continually evolving career. He nevertheless remained something of an outsider, a critic of the Third Republic, and until the very end of his life, at odds with the character of modern society and the direction of French history. That he finally perceived *planification* and *dirigisme* as possible means of escape from history's previous failures represents a minor tribute to the Saint-Simonian vision.

A member of the generation that reached maturity during World War I, the young Duveau exhibited a serious mistrust for established society, and believed that art provided an artificial world of self-expression more real than life itself. While a student of philosophy at the Sorbonne in the early 1920s, he was primarily interested in matters outside the University. Self-indulgent, a bit precious, and greatly influenced by Maurice Barrès, Duveau soon established a reputation in avant-garde circles; at the age of 18 he assumed the editorship of the journal, the *Oeuf dur,* and was a visible figure in Montparnasse's café society.

Duveau, the young dandy, however, was a far cry from the mature Duveau who became an impassioned supporter of a socialist vision that was both utopian and nationalistic.[38] Influenced by Péguy, he turned his enthusiasm from the self to the community. The result was that Duveau, like Michelet, became convinced that France's strength lay in her common people. The problem, then, became one of overcoming French disunity, and by the end of the decade Duveau had surrendered himself to a political and social engagement dedicated to national reconciliation.

Duveau argued that Frenchmen could at once transcend their difficulties and differences if they would again take up the task of 1848. He directly attributed the problems of the 1930s to the failure of the mid-century revolution when France missed the opportunity to establish a society founded upon fraternity. Bourgeois fear of social reform brought repression, with the result that capitalism's

---

Georges Duveau"; Edouard Dolléans, "Georges Duveau, sociologue et historien"; Marguerite Grepon, ed., "Georges Duveau"; and Gabriel Le Bras, "Georges Duveau."

38. Duveau chronicled the beginning of his change of heart in the autobiographical *Testament romantique,* a book meant to be the *Sentimental Education* of the 1920s.

quest for gain disrupted the community and allowed Marxism to capture the impulse for social reconstruction. Indeed, he attributed Marxism's preeminence to a kind of historical accident, to which a Marxist might reply that Duveau had learned nothing from history. Whatever the case, the twentieth-century results were obvious: a divided France unable to meet the twin political threats of the modern world, communism and fascism. With these issues in mind, Duveau, although not himself a Catholic, in 1932 played a major role in organizing *Esprit* and the Troisième Force, and he quickly emerged as the movement's leading public speaker. His sympathies, however, lay with political activism and he remained with the Troisième Force when it broke with *Esprit* and joined Bergery's Force Populaire.[39]

Duveau's primary concern was to find an alternative to Marx. As a socialist he had no difficulty in defining his opposition to capitalism or the right. Marking out a position on the left proved more troublesome, however, since Marxism left so little room for its competitors. As a result, Duveau fabricated a rather questionable distinction. Marxism he labeled a typically Germanic ideology, and worse, a socially disruptive oversimplification of a complex reality. Later, he pursued the point by trying to discriminate between French and German political traditions. The first, he argued, took its inspiration from the eighteenth century, the Great Revolution, and the utopian socialists. As such, the French experience was an attempt to impose an abstract justice upon a recalcitrant history; it represented nothing less than a noble effort to overcome history. In contrast, the German tradition sprang from the likes of Hegel and Marx who made justice a function of history, and thereby sanctioned too easily history's violence. Duveau's argument was obviously flawed. The question concerned ends and means, and, in particular, the role of violence. Whatever the merit of national comparisons, the French Revolution from which Duveau partially drew his inspiration was not, despite

39. Duveau remained politically involved throughout the 1930s; a good statement concerning his politics at the end of the decade is Georges Izard, André Deléage, and Georges Duveau, *La Bataille de France,* which argues that unless France reintegrated the working class into the community, she would remain paralyzed in the face of German fascism.

its Promethean character, a pacifist's affair. As a result, Duveau was
forced to focus his attention upon the utopian socialists and then to
decry their failure in 1848.[40]

As sympathizers with or spokesmen for a Catholic socialism, the
men of *Esprit* owed much to a conservative nineteenth-century intellectual tradition emanating from the values of a preindustrial and
agrarian society. Viewed by their critics as antimodernists, they considered Marxism to be a symptom of, and not a remedy for, the
human alienation and spiritual depravation of capitalist society.
When they spoke of the disorder of the established system, their
words implied something very different from those of Marx who
believed that justice would ultimately emerge from social conflict.
Indeed, Duveau and his colleagues were interested in what brought
men together, not what separated them into warring classes, and
thus they found both Marxism and capitalism indefensible.

The demand for both justice and national unity accounted for
Duveau's parallel interest in Durkheimian sociology, a body of
thought which provided an apparent alternative to Marxism. Had he
not come into contact in 1931 with Célestin Bouglé, the successor of
Durkheim and the director of the Ecole Normale, Duveau would
probably have made a political career with the S.F.I.O. As it was,
Bouglé brought Duveau into the Centre de Documentation Sociale
at the Ecole Normale, oversaw his work toward the doctorate, and
directed his career into the University.

The importance of Durkheim rested in his belief that societies
function as much according to attitudes as to economic considerations. This being the case, it would then become possible to avoid
certain difficulties proclaimed as inevitable by the Marxists. Although politically liberal, Durkheim was fearful of the direction of
modern history and worried that secularization and individualism
might dissolve the bonds necessary for an ordered society. To the
point, individuals, for their own good and society's continued ex-

---

40. See Georges Duveau, *Sociologie de l'utopie*, particularly the essay entitled,
"Utopie et planification," pp. 22–39. Duveau's anti-Marxism proved intense enough to
lead him to wish the 48ers had unleashed a general European war. Had they done so,
he argued, they would have saved their revolution and prevented the unfortunate
ascendancy of Marxism. So much for ends and means. See "L'Europe et le socialisme."

istence, must be contained and constrained—or incorporated if you prefer—by common institutions, collective ideas, and shared beliefs. Sociologists, as defined by Durkheim, became healers who discovered the collective norms that provide social integration and solidarity.

For Durkheim, disorder represented a form of social pathology, and he was particularly concerned about the difficulties posed by working-class alienation. Since he was unwilling to challenge the class structure and assumed the necessity for the division of labor, Durkheim showed understandable interest in the utopian socialists, especially Saint-Simon and Proudhon. Bouglé naturally shared his master's interest, and when Duveau joined the Centre de Documentation Sociale, he became a member of what was nothing less than a center of Proudhonian studies, with Bouglé presiding over meetings devoted to the idea that Proudhon's corporatist theories could provide the order and structure so lacking in modern industrial society.[41]

After the fall of France in 1940, Duveau withdrew to the provinces where he played a minor role in the Resistance and completed his dissertation, *La Vie ouvrière en France sous le second Empire*. A work of monumental proportions, it immediately established his reputation as a leading scholar, and he soon received the chair of sociology at Strasbourg. The very massiveness of the study, however, nearly overwhelmed its author. The breadth of the original design, an all encompassing study of the workers during the Empire, quickly forced Duveau to lower his sights to a more manageable subject: the material and psychological conditions of the working class. His secondary thesis involved a subject originally planned for incorporation into the *La Vie ouvrière*—a study of the working-class elite's views on education.[42] A projected but never completed third volume was to consider the workers' political and social attitudes, and thereby complete a triptych in *histoire sociale*.

---

41. It was at these gatherings that Bouglé and his colleagues decided to edit Proudhon's works, a task to which Duveau made important contributions. P. J. Proudhon, *La Révolution sociale démontrée par le coup d'état*, and P. J. Proudhon, *Contradictions politiques*.

42. Georges Duveau, *La Pensée ouvrière sur l'éducation pendant la seconde République et le second Empire*.

Because Duveau treated sociology and history as one, *La Vie ouvrière* escaped the limits of traditional disciplines, and provided a study in *structure* and *mentalité*, all of which won the appreciative applause of Febvre who called the book a scholarly *édifice*. The work, however, was exceedingly passionate and personal in tone, leading some to conclude that Duveau wrote in equal measure from the head and the heart. An amorphous and diffuse, even undisciplined, quality also marked *La Vie ouvrière*. Fearful of what he called the oversimplification of Marxism which attributed human consciousness to economic considerations, Duveau struggled to preserve the poetic texture of history. To do otherwise, he argued, was to ignore the many-sided character of human nature. Something of a romantic, Duveau felt his way through the material with empathy. Fascinated with reality's complexity, he wrote less to distinguish the important from the unimportant than to describe reality's infinite manifestations. The result was a literary mosaic, the design of which frequently threatened to escape its author.

It should be noted that *La Vie ouvrière* represented a way station in Duveau's evolution toward an acceptance of modern society. Written during the Occupation when Duveau's earlier fears seemed more than ever justified, the work exuded a profound pessimism about France's past and future. Duveau leveled harsh words against industrial capitalism and drew upon the criticisms of social Catholicism, Proudhonian socialism, and Durkheimian sociology. *La Vie ouvrière*, as a result, treated the Empire as a period of destructive capitalist expansion. Later, however, after having witnessed the successes of the postwar period, Duveau became more hopeful. By the time of his death in 1958, he was convinced that *dirigisme* and *planification* would make it possible for France once again to capture the utopian impulse of 1848—a theme which pervaded his posthumously published *Sociologie de l'utopie*. Similarly, the later Duveau somewhat shifted his attention insofar as utopian socialism was concerned. He became less obsessed with Proudhon's criticisms and more sympathetic toward Saint-Simon's affirmations, and he praised the prophet of an industrial society for comprehending not only the need for technocratic planning, but also the necessity for infusing the modern world with humane and religious principles.

Duveau also set about to rehabilitate Napoleon III, although he had never shown any animosity toward the Bonapartes—either Napoleon I or Napoleon III—and had even made several kind references to the nephew in *La Vie ouvrière*. He now treated the Bonapartes as agents of the French utopian quest to impose justice upon history, and he affirmed that Louis Napoleon had rightly been called a Saint-Simon on horseback, searching for a third way between reaction and revolution.[43] The implication was clear: the spirit of 1848 had not completely perished in the June Days, but had survived into the Second Empire and had been revived after 1944. The technocratic and utopian aims of Saint-Simonism had allowed Duveau to fight his way to a partial acceptance of both past and present while he avoided the trauma of Marxian conflict.

For Duveau, when he wrote *La Vie ouvrière*, the major issue confronting French society was that of social change within the context of industrialization, and its effects upon the workers. As a result, two hundred and some odd pages of *La Vie ouvrière* were devoted to an analysis of industrial affairs. Filled with statistics and regional comparisons, the analysis was meant to describe the economic *cadre* or framework in which the working class was formed. Duveau approached the Empire not as a regime, but as a period characterized by economic developments that were generally destructive, and which the community failed to control, either before or after 1870. In spite of Duveau's lack of interest in the regime itself—indeed, he never even considered the Bonapartist economic program—*La Vie ouvrière* nevertheless represented an important contribution to the historiography of the Second Empire.

Duveau's use of sources reflected his relative indifference to the political question. He relied heavily upon government and private archives concerning the economy and working conditions. He also used contemporary accounts of working-class life, and he paid particular attention to members of the working-class elite: A. Bazin,

---

43. See in particular Duveau's article on Napoleon III, "Qui est cet homme?"

A. Corbon, E. Fribourg, A. Perdiguier, and Denis Poulot. Duveau, however, showed little love for the Empire, which he identified with capitalism. Yet, *La Vie ouvrière* in sparse but explicit references betrayed a real sympathy for Napoleon III. Duveau noted that during the 1840s Louis Napoleon had shown an awareness and concern for the social question and had championed numerous reforms which represented a program attractive to the workers who, for this reason, greeted the coup d'état with open sympathy. Dreams of a socialist Empire nevertheless came to naught, as Napoleon III reigned over a government controlled by social conservatives who prevented the initiation of any meaningful program. Despite the failure of it all, Duveau granted that the Emperor had remained popular with the workers, who frequently used dynastic loyalty in order to express their independence from the *patrons*. Empire and Emperor were somewhat divorced, at least in Duveau's mind. Napoleon III escaped censure while his regime was treated as an abysmal failure, responsible for the ills of industrial capitalism.

Duveau believed that the French economy was highly complex, so much so that he thought it unique. In spite of increased urbanization and economic concentration, factories neither destroyed the small workshop nor succeeded in replacing artisanal modes of production. The factory system was merely superimposed upon the traditional economy, and the resulting hybrid system, a strange mixture of the old and new, provided both industrial growth and stability. The working-class population, for instance, failed to increase and industrial decentralization remained a major feature of the economy; in 1872 France still had only three workers for every *patron*. Furthermore, a marked shift toward new productive forces remained geographically limited to the North, Northeast, Northwest, and to the departments of the Seine, Loire, Rhône, and Saône-et-Loire.

Duveau utilized a mass of detail to describe the complexities of the situation. After struggling through a jungle of facts and figures, Duveau concluded that there were four distinct groups of workers that emerged from the economic *cadre*, or framework. The first inhabited the major urban centers such as Paris, Lyon, and Marseille.

These cities provided a "multicolored" life that absorbed the worker's attention and interest. "In Lyon as in Paris," Duveau wrote, "the milieu forged by the city was more powerful than that forged by the workshop or factory."[44] A second category of workers developed in villages and towns dominated by a large industry. Creusot provided one example of this genre, and contemporaries rightly called it an industrial colony. Life presented a rather drab spectacle, and the workers, usually drawn from the peasantry, were docile unless angered, whereupon they were prone to violence. Urban centers of middling importance, such as Orléans, produced a third working-class category. Cities of this sort usually contained few factories, and industry remained diverse and decentralized. While more simple than in Paris, life had its rewards and civic distractions. Finally, the workers in the countryside who retained their peasant character completed the list. Duveau's description of this group betrayed his belief that preindustrial society held certain advantages:

> To say that the villager has an internal life less rich and has a more limited human experience than the town dweller would be foolishness. To argue the contrary would be closer to the truth. Compare, for example, a weaver from the Amiénoise countryside and a weaver from Lille. The latter is far more riveted to his task than the former. The one works the fields for a good part of the year; he directs a family upon which he imposes a strict division of labor; he multiplies his efforts in different directions and delicate responsibilities weigh upon him. The other lives in an obscure cellar. While the second is crouched, the eye dull, before his pot of beer, the first leads his horses to work, breathes the wind that stirs the Picard plain, and even morally experiences a larger universe.[45]

On the question of the physical and material conditions of the working class, Duveau described a situation of abject misery. Matters were even worse than might have been expected because the Empire experienced several economic crises with heavy unemployment and high bread prices. The treaty of 1860 added to the problem since the *patrons* were impelled to lower wages and move

---

44. Georges Duveau, *La Vie ouvrière en France sous le second Empire*, p. 226.
45. Ibid., pp. 228–229.

toward further concentration. In the cities, meanwhile, rents continued to rise because of urban renewal. Duveau therefore concluded that the workers in no way benefited from industrialization's increased productivity—just the contrary. He argued, for example, that urbanization and factory conditions physically debilitated the working class. On the issue of wages, Duveau was no less grim. In spite of the difficulties in computation and the conclusions of Levasseur and François Simiand, he argued that real wages failed to rise. The material condition of the working class, in short, either remained stable or declined; Duveau found no indication of an improvement over the previous decades.

Duveau's observations deserve some comment. Convinced that industrial capitalism enlarged its field of operation, Duveau treated social misery as being necessarily more acute in both a qualitative and a quantitative sense. René Villermé's 1836 study of working-class conditions, however, catalogued the same ills as had Duveau for the 1850s and 1860s. Whatever the merits of criticizing the costs and shortcomings of industrialization, *La Vie ouvrière* may have provided a rather lopsided approach. By arguing that the workers were debilitated by industrialization and its accompanying urbanism, Duveau stood in a celebrated French tradition. Adolphe Blanqui in 1848 had employed the same observation to argue for a government policy of retarding industrial development. Even before Blanqui's study, the economist Eugène Buret had concluded that since the majority of French hospitals were located in cities, urban workers were less healthy than their rural counterparts. Levasseur, however, had since argued that the question was not so easily resolved. For one thing, purely agrarian departments tallied the highest rejection rate, on physical grounds, of army recruits. As for the question of wages and living standards, Duveau found himself in disagreement with both Levasseur and Simiand. The latter, although chary about drawing conclusions given the paucity of information, cautiously suggested that wages more than compensated for the problem of rising prices.[46] Levasseur proved even more direct.

---

46. Simiand's conclusions are presented in *Le Salaire, l'évolution sociale et la monnaie,* I, 383–506.

Convinced that industrialization brought greater wealth to everyone, although he admitted that the bourgeoisie raked off the greatest
share, Levasseur argued that real wages dropped only where industrialization remained nonexistent. He also concluded that working-class material conditions generally improved, except possibly in
housing, and that wages acquired greater purchasing power.
Workers, he argued, may have continued to spend the same per-
centage of their salaries on food, but they ate more and better.[47]

Duveau obviously felt some uneasiness over the fact that his findings on real wages failed to tally with those of Levasseur. On the
other hand, he was less concerned about the question of physical
misery than the psychological impact of industrialization and its
effect upon the quality of working-class life. Duveau argued that the
factory system cast a shadow over the whole economy, and the
workers' existence thereby became "greyer." Industrial society was
noteworthy for a "depersonalization" that threatened to destroy the
sense of community. Duveau thus shifted his attention from material conditions, and La Vie ouvrière became a moral criticism of
modern society. The volume accordingly echoed Proudhon and betrayed the author's preference for the social organization associated
with the ancien régime. The latter's corporate structure provided—
so the argument ran—social integration and meaningful ties that
joined individuals into a viable community.

> Under the ancien régime a series of bonds—religious, feudal, corpo-
> rative traditions and traditions compagnonniques—united men . . .
> Capitalism destroyed one after another all of these ties . . . More and
> more, man measured the circle of his universe with his money. Most
> social relations were established by a brutal material interest which ex-
> cluded all warmth, all poetry.[48]

47. Emile Levasseur, Histoire des classes ouvrières et de l'industrie en France de
1789 à 1870, II, 721–727, 730. See also his article: "Le Mouvement des salaires."
Studies subsequent to Duveau's have confirmed Levasseur's more optimistic conclusions on the wage question. Jacques Rougerie in his "Remarques sur l'histoire des
salaires à Paris au XIXe siècle," argues that a high rate of employment during the
Empire kept the level of real wages on an upward swing. Jean Lhomme in "Le
Pouvoir d'achat de l'ouvrier français au cours d'un siècle," writes that real wages
rose during the Empire, and suggests that Duveau drew his conclusions with
"imprudence."
48. Duveau, La Vie ouvrière, pp. 414–415.

The dissolution of traditional ties represented only the indirect destructiveness of modernity. Capitalism also caused serious social divisions that led to a class struggle, and France thereby became a community divided against itself. Duveau reserved his harshest criticism for the role of industrial concentration in fostering these animosities. By their very size and the nature of mechanization, factories established an unbridgeable gulf between the *patron* and the workers. Depersonalization of the employer-employee relationship replaced the bonds of a traditional trust. The problem of wages likewise proved disruptive. Whatever the direction of real wages, the worker never received anything approximating a fair share of society's increased productivity. While his own living standard remained at best stable, the worker observed the rapidly rising wealth of the bourgeoisie. The obvious disparity, in Duveau's words, led to a "psychological real wage": the worker became convinced that his own economic status was dropping in a relative, if not absolute, sense. Finally, industrial development separated the two classes in yet another fashion. The worker felt entrapped in a factory system both massive and rigid. Mobility upwards, Duveau argued, proved increasingly difficult and became well-nigh impossible by the 1860s. Given the demands of capitalization and the division of labor, the days when a laborer could patiently employ skill and thrift to open his own shop were gone. The frustrating limitations of the situation bred working-class despair and anger, both of which ultimately ignited a class war.[49]

The shift in housing patterns was a physical manifestation of growing class divisions. Heavy industries, by locating on the outskirts of the cities, spawned suburbs with a predominantly working-class population. To make matters worse, the Empire's urban renewal programs reinforced the movement toward geographic separation of the classes. The remodeling of cities, particularly Paris, destroyed lower-class housing at the city center, raised rents, and forced workers into the suburbs. Whereas old Paris was typified by

49. Ibid., pp. 415–416. Pierre Pierrard, in a more limited study patterned after Duveau's work, also emphasizes these points in "social psychology." See his *La Vie ouvrière à Lille sous le second Empire.*

a housing pattern that integrated the upper and lower classes into the same buildings and neighborhoods, something completely different arose in the wake of Haussmann's wreckers. The city center became increasingly bourgeois, and was surrounded by a ring of suburbs consisting of alienated workers.

Modern industrial society also demoralized the workers, partially because they were overwhelmed by sheer physical misery. Duveau, however, largely blamed the demoralization on the factory's role in "atomizing" the working class and reducing it to a mass of "uncadred" and unskilled laborers. The victims of social processes over which they had no control, the workers lost their traditional system of values and sense of social responsibility. The results were nearly catastrophic, particularly for the family, the institutional bulwark of working-class morality. According to Duveau, the family's near disintegration reflected the moral brutalization of working-class life. He thereupon noted with alarm the workers' high rate of illegitimate births, the popularity of "licentious dance halls," the growing problem of pornographic literature, and the problem of drunkenness and alcoholism. Finally, Duveau linked the question of morals to that of aesthetics. He claimed that although industrialization divided the classes, it nevertheless gave rise to a common vulgarization of taste. Mass production destroyed the traditional and distinctive styles of class expression—e.g., in clothing and household furnishings—and thereby reduced the life of the two social groups to a common banality. In the process, the worker lost his previous high-minded simplicity.

Duveau's conclusions concerning industrialization's psychological impact are difficult to judge. They were, however, the result of an extreme and possibly false comparison involving Duveau's idealization of an artisan economy and his somber portrayal of modernity. Duveau, moreover, frequently blamed industrial capitalism for developments predating industrialization. Alcoholism and drunkenness, for instance, were serious problems long before the Second Empire. Although Duveau argued that the "encadred" worker drank less, he also had to admit that artisans drank more than factory workers. There was also the disconcerting fact that the more the worker

earned, the more he drank. Despite Duveau's affirmation that artisans had better morals and a stronger family system than their
cousins in the factory, Levasseur had long before indicated that the
illegitimacy rate, at least during the July Monarchy, was the same
for both groups. The argument of declining morality, in fact, seems
dubious. The workers of the July Monarchy, who were exposed to
less industrialization, exhibited the same rate of moral turpitude, in
comparison to other classes, as their counterparts during the Second
Empire. Villermé's study catalogued the same "social irresponsi-
bility" mentioned by Duveau. The well-known study by Louis
Chevalier reveals that in Paris the problem reached such a state that
observers could no longer distinguish between the workers and the
criminal element.[50] Duveau even undercut his argument and the
thesis of increased brutalization when he at one point acknowledged
that working-class morality actually seemed to improve during the
Empire. If such were true, *La Vie ouvrière* needed serious revision.

Duveau's approach to the problems of social integration and increased separation between the classes also raised certain questions.
Duveau attributed great importance to industrial concentration and
the corresponding lack of mobility upwards. The factory system,
however, was never imposed upon the French economy in any full
measure. With a worker-*patron* ratio of three to one, France still
remained a community of *ateliers,* all of which made Duveau's emphasis upon the factory somewhat disingenuous. Proletarianization
occurred, but many workers still continued to save their francs,
master skills, and open their own shops. Louis Chevalier, a specialist
in the demography of Paris, has shown that the city remained
primarily artisan in character and provided a high level of integration and mobility. The suburbs, with their burgeoning heavy industry, tapped the mass of unskilled workers emigrating from the
provinces. Once established, despite miserable conditions, these
workers moved upwards and toward the center of the city. The rate
of upward mobility was also heightened because Parisian industry
actually became more decentralized, in spite of the emergence of

50. Louis Chevalier, *Classes laborieuses et classes dangereuses à Paris pendant la
première moitié du XIXe siècle.*

heavy industry. Duveau's observations concerning housing likewise seemed exaggerated. Cities had traditionally contained working-class quarters or ghettos. Although life in Paris's *grande banlieue* proved considerably more bleak than life in the faubourg Saint-Antoine, separation through housing patterns hardly originated in the 1850s. Furthermore, sizable working-class contingents still lived in each of Paris's arrondissements. Haussmannization, finally, did not drive masses of workers into the suburbs; the suburbs primarily absorbed provincial immigrants. When urban renewal forced a worker to move, he generally went to the adjoining neighborhood and thereby remained close to his *atelier*.[51]

La Vie ouvrière was a product of the interwar period, the work of a pessimist at odds with his times. It reflected Duveau's empassioned involvement in the events which led to the catastrophe of 1940. As a result, *La Vie ouvrière* seemed a bit contrived and not altogether convincing despite its expression of legitimate fears. On the other hand, the work made an important contribution to the historiography of the Second Empire. An example of the new history, it followed from Duveau's belief that the Bonapartist regime was an integral part of the fatal development begun in 1848 when industrial capitalism began to rip apart the community's social fabric. The Empire therefore assumed a natural position within France's apparently aberrant historical pattern; instead of changing or overcoming historical patterns, the Empire had become their accomplice, and was judged accordingly.

Before his death, however, Duveau underwent a change in attitude which altered his assessment of the regime. Although occupying a period of industrial growth, the Empire also became a source of social reconstruction. The interwar tone of pessimism found in *La Vie ouvrière* was replaced with a postwar hope that France had finally discovered a third way in the Saint-Simonian vision of utopian technocracy. Napoleon III therefore emerged as a ruler of remarkable foresight, and while referring to him as being both

---

51. Louis Chevalier, *La Formation de la population parisienne au XIXe siècle*, pp. 77–80, 122, 223–234, 237–267.

progressive and wise, Duveau criticized France for not granting the Emperor the means for implementing his grand design for a third force.[52] If one views French history as a series of attempts to impose justice upon a reluctant reality, the Second Empire receives yet another set of historical credentials.

At Present

The assessments made by Blanchard, Schnerb, and the later Duveau are now typical of French historians, and the emphasis remains upon economic and social considerations. Politics, however, has not been ignored, although the tone of historians has changed from that found in the work of earlier professionals. The postwar emergence of a presidential regime has apparently removed some of the animosity toward Bonapartism's powerful executive. An important expression of this new attitude is the work of Pierre Guiral, a social and political historian at the Université de Provence and something of a maverick, given his belief in the importance of literature as source material. Guiral has written a dissertation on Prévost-Paradol, a major Orleanist opponent of the Empire who finally rallied to the reforms of 1869. By means of a biographical study, Guiral has pointed out the weakness of an elitist and liberal opposition in the face of a democratic caesarism.[53]

The vast majority of present-day professionals, however, has treated the Empire rather differently. Interest in economic history has led to a concern for the dynamics of productivity and industrial development, and some historians have paid special attention to the impact of transportation, urban renewal, entrepreneurial attitudes, and credit facilities.[54]

52. Duveau, "Qui est cet homme?"

53. Pierre Guiral, *Prévost-Paradol*. Guiral is also the editor of a new edition of Ollivier's *Histoire et philosophie d'une guerre, 1870*, in the preface of which he calls Ollivier a "noble spirit." As for the liberal Empire, Guiral believes that it was solidly established, but fell victim to a war that no regime could have survived. In an interview on September 21, 1972, he told the author that the Empire's definitive establishment of universal suffrage was one of the great achievements of the nineteenth century.

54. For works dealing with the imperial period, see in particular: Jean Bouvier,

The most general and recent expression of this revised historiography is the work of Alain Plessis of the Université de Paris VIII.[55] Drawing upon recent scholarship, Plessis emphasizes both the political and economic contributions of the Empire. Further, he alludes to the similarity between the plebiscitary tradition of Bonapartism and the referendums that have marked the Fifth Republic. He also argues that Napoleon III experienced real success in confronting the major dilemma of modern politics: how to bring the general population into the political process, traditionally a preserve of the leisured and wealthy classes, and at the same time find a politics that mediates between the contradictory demands of capital and labor. The Emperor, according to Plessis, discovered the very modern answer of a political economy designed to guarantee expanding productivity.

The revisionism of University historians has not been ignored outside professional circles. The late Adrien Dansette, who stood in the hallowed tradition of lettered gentlemen and was a skilled observer of the Empire, in 1961 brought out the first tome of a projected six-volume history of the regime. A modern general study designed to replace La Gorce, the work treats its subject from the perspective of Ollivier while adding the technocratic affirmations of recent professionals.[56]

The historian whose work perhaps most clearly reflects new attitudes toward the Empire is Louis Girard. A student of Charles Pouthas and admittedly influenced by Marcel Blanchard, Girard was, until his recent retirement, professor of modern history at the Sorbonne.[57] The nature of Girard's work indicates the success of the *Annales* school in transforming the professional establishment. A

Le Crédit Lyonnais de 1863 à 1882; Claude Fohlen, L'Industrie textile au temps du second Empire; Louis Girard, La Politique des travaux publics du second Empire; Jeanne Gaillard, Paris, la ville (1852–1870); and three works by Bertrand Gille: La Banque en France au XIXe siècle; Histoire de la maison Rothschild, 1848–1870; and La Sidérurgie française au XIXe siècle.

55. Alain Plessis, De la fête impériale au mur des fédérés, 1852–1870.

56. Dansette completed three volumes of the work before his death in 1976. They are: Louis Napoléon à la conquête du pouvoir; Du 2 décembre au 4 septembre; and Naissance de la France moderne. Dansette referred to economic development as the Empire's major contribution, emphasized the importance of Saint-Simonian doctrines, and treated Louis Napoleon as a Keynesian.

57. Generally traditional in his scholarship, Pouthas, who died in 1974, followed

prolific author, Girard has either written or collaborated in the writing of numerous works concerning electoral geography, institutional history, and traditional political matters.[58] It was, however, his doctoral dissertation, *La Politique des travaux publics du second Empire*, that established Girard's reputation both as a scholar and as an historian of the Empire.

Girard has commented rather extensively in a recent essay on the ramifications of his work.[59] While acknowledging that traditional historians focused upon a meaningful problem—the struggle to reconcile liberty and democracy—he also argued that politics presented a mere "summit" beneath which lay more fundamental considerations: the community's economic and ideological evolution. Political historians were therefore peculiarly unsuited to comprehend the Empire's greatest contributions, and their work studiously ignored the importance of urbanization and railroad construction. The twentieth century, according to Girard, has brought a gradual shift in attitudes particularly evident since the Second World War, and he has attributed much of the sudden interest in economic history to the French government's conversion to the principles of *dirigisme*.

There is, on the other hand, a great concern for nuance in Girard's approach to the Empire. While praising the scholarly work of Blanchard, he has shown impatience toward those who constituted the regime's political opposition, and has suggested that Bonapartism provided a meaningful alternative to the confusion of 1848. Nevertheless, he has also argued that political instability so clearly marked the Empire that liberalization led to a weak compromise easily disrupted by the events of 1870. The strength of Bonapartism obviously rested in economic policy and not politics, despite Napoleon III's attempt to join them in a Saint-Simonian political economy.

Seignobos in the chair of modern history at the Sorbonne and played a significant role in directing students toward the economic and social history of the Empire. Although Pouthas did little original work on the regime, he summarized his views in the *Histoire politique du second Empire*, a collection of mimeographed class lectures. See also his *Démocraties et capitalisme, 1848–1860*, first published in 1941 and scheduled to be rewritten by Pierre Guiral under the title of *Démocratie, réaction et capitalisme*.

58. He has, for instance, edited *Les Elections de 1869*, collaborated with A. Prost and Rémi Gossez on *Les Conseillers généraux en 1870*, and written *La Garde nationale* and *La Ile République*.

59. Girard, "Les Problèmes français."

Girard has argued in *La Politique des travaux publics* that before 1851 France failed to meet the challenge posed by the revolutionary changes in transportation. Railroads promised to establish the framework for an economy geared to steam power and mass production. A national rail system would bind the domestic economy into a single unit, which in turn would become an integral part of a European and world market. France needed an organized policy that would provide for the rapid building of a rail network with particular emphasis upon the Le Havre–Paris–Marseille axis. The July Monarchy, however, proved unequal to the task. Although government leaders moved wisely with the law of 1842, which provided government support of mainline construction and mapped out the most important lines, the results were at best fragmentary. The program fell victim to political intrigues, but even more important, banking and investment facilities were inadequate for the capital demands. During the 1840s credit was seriously overstrained, to the point of causing the financial crisis that ignited the 1848 Revolution. Unfortunately, the Second Republic proved even less effective than the July Monarchy. With the collapse of the private sector, the government should have employed the budget to propel the economy forward. Instead, the Republic foundered because of the abortive National Workshops; following the June rebellion, conservatives gained control of the regime and imposed a policy of budgetary retrenchment which merely worsened the situation. Insofar as economic policy was concerned, France had moved from one failure to another.

Unlike most political figures, Louis Napoleon understood that the situation demanded a thoroughgoing public works policy on the part of the government. He also recognized the alternatives in implementing a meaningful program: direct state intervention and/or government encouragement of the dynamic forces within the private sector. As a result, some form of political authoritarianism was necessary in order to overcome the traditionalism of the *haute banque* and the cautious politics of parliamentarianism. The *haute banque*, for instance, was partially responsible for the economy's undercapitalization because of the bankers' commitment to preindustrial methods. Centered in Paris, French banking was devoted to floating government loans and meeting the short-term needs of well-established merchants. The situation victimized the provinces, which were largely ignored, and merchant banking in no way met the needs of industrial development. Indeed, the *haute banque* primarily limited itself to discounting ninety-day, three-signature notes. French bankers were also imbued with a rigid sense of personal financial responsibility, which led to a marked distrust of the joint stock company with its limited liability. They therefore disliked corporate banking structures, and in general shied away from investing in the so-called *sociétés anonymes*. Such attitudes, of course, only impeded the development of the one institution absolutely necessary for an economy of large-scale production. To compound the problem, traditional political leaders showed no inclination to offset undercapitalization by means of the government budget. Girard, in another context, observed that the notables of the Orleanist Chamber of Deputies were "dominated by a rather sordid routine" devoted to perpetuating an outdated economy.[60] Given the nature of parliamentary government, they exercised control over a miserly budget subject to annual legislative approval. The result was a short-sighted fiscal policy planned on a year-to-year basis rather than on the long-run demands of economic development.

Girard divided the Second Empire into three periods: 1851–1856, 1856–1859, and the 1860s. Each represented a separate stage in the government's public works program, and the first, he argued, established the raison d'être of the Empire—economic progress. Of equal importance, during the 1851–1856 period, the government stimulated the private sector and thereby attained its goals without having to tamper with the budget in any significant fashion. Eager to avoid a policy that would have forced the government to rely upon the Legislative Body, which still retained final control over expenses, Napoleon III shrewdly circumvented the problem by deliberately fostering private investment. The Emperor was aided by the fact

60. Louis Girard, "Le Règne de Louis Philippe; la Révolution de 1848; le second Empire," II, 270.

that conditions were ripe for an economic upswing. By guaranteeing stability, the coup d'état stimulated a wave of speculation until then restrained by the political difficulties of the Second Republic. "To speculate," Girard wrote, "is to look to the future, to attribute to a security not its immediate value, but what will be drawn from it perhaps ten years later. To the preceding years' psychosis of uncertainty followed in contrast an inverse infatuation. The future seemed assured."[61] There was, however, more to the Bonapartist program than merely guaranteeing political stability. Napoleon III recognized that during the immediate decade railroad construction would provide the major force for pushing the economy forward. The regime therefore had to induce both speculation and investment, all of which called for a radical restructuring of French credit. Herein lay the importance of the Saint-Simonians. They struck a bargain with the regime, and thereby implanted their program of democratizing credit. In Girard's mind, the result was an alliance between the forces of a dynamic capitalism and universal suffrage, which in turn led to a *socialisme à direction capitaliste*.

Central to the government program were the Pereires, whom Girard called *Napoléons des affaires*. The founding of the Crédit Mobilier, he continued, represented an industrial coup d'état meant to neutralize the *haute banque*'s traditional control over the economy. The Mobilier was, in fact, authorized in 1852 in response to the *haute banque*'s attempt to discipline the new government by raising the interest rate. A joint stockholding company, the Mobilier implemented the old Saint-Simonian idea of an investment bank, employing previously untapped capital. It was based upon calculated speculation and the optimistic belief that once started, the economy could be kept on an upward path. By strategically allocating its resources while balancing long-range ventures against immediately profitable ones, the Mobilier would hopefully stimulate the economy and realize a handy profit. The idea was, of course, anathema to the notables of the *haute banque*, which led Girard to call the Mobilier the financial manifestation of the regime's demo-

61. Girard, *La Politique*, p. 85.

cratic impulse.[62] Girard, on the other hand, implied that the government cleverly exploited the Pereires. The Mobilier's tremendous activity in railroad financing forced the *haute banque* and its allies to respond in kind; otherwise, the Pereires threatened to gain control of some rather important concessions. A massive struggle ensued which pitted the forces led by the Rothschilds against those of the Mobilier. As both sides competed, the government, serenely balanced between the two, assumed the role of arbitrator, and apportioned concessions. Meanwhile, the struggle fostered a bullish market and thereby incited further speculation. The result was nothing less than the near completion of the main lines. The Mobilier had harnessed speculation to the national cause while drawing new capital into the economy. In Girard's words: "The excessive role played by speculation was the price the government had to pay for the services of the Crédit Mobilier . . . Speculation was the source of credit, and the elasticity of credit was the gambit of a regime which benefited, without paying anything, from the construction of new lines . . ."[63]

The era of full-scale speculation nevertheless proved temporary, and its demise in 1856 marked the beginning of a new period in the history of the Empire. Near completion of the main and most profitable rail lines threatened to halt construction, the flywheel of the Bonapartist economy. Although urban renewal in Paris continued at full speed, Haussmann's program was hardly enough to offset the potential economic slack. The government therefore had to implement a compensatory policy, and accordingly shifted its attention to the problem of consolidating and then enlarging upon previous gains. This meant something of a decline in the influence of the Mobilier and its government supporters, particularly Persigny. With speculation ebbing, the regime hoped to bargain with those whose

62. The Legitimist Berryer expressed the view of his fellow notables when he called the Mobilier Europe's largest gambling house. Many have since commented upon the Pereires' contribution. See, for instance, Pierre Dupont-Ferrier, *Le Marché financier de Paris sous le second Empire*, a thesis in law. There is also the more traditional work of Marcel Marion, *Histoire financière de la France*, Volume V of which deals with the Empire. Marion showed some distaste for what he called the Pereires's propensity for carrying a good idea too far: V, 494–496.

63. Girard, *La Politique*, p. 138.

services would prove more useful in a less expansionistic economy. The keystone to this new policy was the 1859 or so-called Franqueville conventions. Eager for the construction of secondary rail lines, the government pressured the companies to continue building. For this reason the regime from the beginning had sponsored large, profitable companies able to absorb and thus maintain unprofitable segments. The companies, since the decline in speculation, showed no interest in constructing lines that promised future losses. And indeed, some companies were already experiencing difficulties. The conventions settled the matter by distinguishing between old and new networks. The second could only tap the profits of the first after usual dividends and interest payments had been met; any surplus from the first network would be applied to the second, and the government guaranteed the interest payments on the latter. Railroad construction thereby continued, but not on the basis of a speculator's market. In Girard's words, "the railroads were no longer a speculation, but an institution."[64] They became, moveover, an institution ultimately covered by the government budget. This, according to Girard, represented a fundamental change with important political ramifications. Previously the government had avoided the Legislative Body by manipulating credit; with the slowing down of the private sector, it now relied upon a budgetary guarantee which immediately enlarged legislative control over the regime's political economy. Napoleon III still proved imaginative enough to move from one success to another, but the 1859 conventions also threatened to damage Bonapartist authoritarianism.

The period from 1856 to 1859 represented a transition. The year 1860, however, heralded a new and more aggressive period of public works. Eager to prove his new commitment to European peace, Napoleon III reaffirmed the principles of the 1852 Bordeaux declaration concerning internal reconstruction, and tried to implement what Girard called a "program of peace" and a "new deal." Yet, conditions remained unsuited for reenacting the experience of 1851–1856. Railroad construction could no longer assume a predominant

64. Ibid., p. 206.

role, and the injection of a greater speculative spirit was not the major need. New methods were therefore necessary, and the "new deal" represented something of a potpourri. At one level, the 1860 trade treaty imposed economic modernization through the impact of international competition. Speculation, on the other hand, remained limited to the financial manipulations of urban renewal. Authorized to enlarge its clientele and deal with municipal governments, the Crédit Foncier embarked upon a program of aiding Haussmann and provincial cities willing to follow the Parisian example. The third level of the 1860s program directly involved government financing, and represented an attempt to capitalize programs unable to attract, or unsuitable for, private investment. Roads and canals received particular attention in the hope that competition would lower railroad freight charges. The government also pressured the rail companies into building a third network, and again guaranteed the interest payments of the obviously unprofitable system. The government in general tried to develop a complete framework of modern transportation, around which a new economy could form. There was also a program of land reclamation and reforestation, through which the regime tried to spread its economic benefits into the rural areas. In general, this third level of the 1860s policy adapted the principles of industrial investment to government finance: through deficit spending, Napoleon III planned to realize greater long-run revenues from the taxes provided by a wealthier community.

The 1860s program achieved some success. First, the Anglo-French trade treaty forced manufacturers to meet the pressures of foreign competition. Secondly, railroad construction continued at a rapid pace, with stipulations for the construction of a third network written into the rail convention of 1863. Haussmann, finally, managed to overcome staggering financial problems and thereby maintained his position into the last year of the regime. There were, however, real troubles throughout the 1860s, and they ultimately hindered the government program. Amongst other things, the 1860 treaty engendered political resistance; accustomed to treating the domestic market as a private preserve, French industrialists simply

refused to accept freer trade. Meanwhile, the growing power of the
Legislative Body acted as a brake upon the government policy. A
rise in the national debt in 1860–1861 spurred the *budgétaires* to
call immediately for a more orthodox fiscal program. Fould, a conservative on financial matters, echoed their demands and in 1861
succeeded in replacing Magne at the Ministry of Finances, a post
he held until 1867. Girard had nothing but harsh words for Fould,
and criticized his role in the reform of December, 1861, in which
Napoleon III surrendered the power to decree credits outside the
regular budget. The Emperor lost a major lever of control for
unilaterally instigating public works programs, and Girard commented that this reform in favor of parliamentary authority nearly
terminated the Emperor's historical role. Furthermore, the change
reflected the confused state of Fould's mind. For Girard, authoritarianism and public works were opposite sides of the Bonapartist
coin; Fould, however, favored political authoritarianism while trying
to impose an orthodox fiscal policy which strengthened parliamentarianism. To make matters worse, the Minister also labored to
undercut the Pereires and hoped to reconcile Napoleon III with the
haute banque.[65] When the Mobilier fell on hard times—given its
long-term and speculative investments, the holding company was
unable to realize profits quickly enough—Fould prevented the bank
from acquiring a broader capital base, and the whole structure
eventually toppled in 1867. To use Girard's phrase, the *haute banque*
with the aid of Fould took its revenge upon the creative finances
of Bonapartism.

Fould, in short, jeopardized the "new deal" proclaimed in 1860.
Only in the area of urban renewal did he experience a real defeat.
Haussmann, in his never-ending struggle to obtain greater funds
than a legislature dominated by rural interests was willing to grant,
proved more clever than the Minister. To uncover new sources of
capital, Haussmann was at once devious, shrewd, and unscrupulous.
An early ploy, with which Girard sympathized, was the establishment by executive decree in 1858 of the Caisse des Travaux de Paris,

---

65. Girard emphasized this point in his article, "L'Affaire du chemin de fer Cette-
Marseille (1861–1863)."

a municipal institution authorized to issue bonds; the bank, of course, merely acted as Haussmann's tool, and financed urban renewal. Both the legislature and the Emperor's more conservative advisors disliked the Caisse, and Fould took the Ministry of Finance to halt just such activities. He nevertheless failed. Still enjoying the Emperor's full support, Haussmann ignored his critics. While Napoleon III employed his power to decree an act of public utility in order to begin construction on new streets, the prefect busily devised new financial gimmicks, such as the so-called delegation bonds, and the use of funds earmarked for amortizing previous debts. The Minister's inability to contain Haussmann, however, had real political repercussions. The prefect became a symbol of an uncontrollable authoritarianism, and therefore necessarily the antithesis of liberalization. Girard, reflecting a lack of sympathy for the proponents of liberalization, commented that the Emperor and Haussmann "saw better" than the opposition, over whose protests they managed to implement "one of the greatest ideas of the century."[66]

Fould's departure from the Ministry of Finance in 1867 brought no revitalization of the government's public works program. The grève du milliard curtailed investment, and political liberalization prevented any new departures. Girard argued that Fould and liberalization destroyed the regime's raison d'être, as liberal politics and orthodox fiscal policies guaranteed the end of Bonapartist political economy. On the other hand, France was by this time so thoroughly equipped for industrialization, and thereby thrust into the modern world, that authoritarianism no longer proved necessary. By means of the Empire, France had come of age, and Girard accused Frenchemen of ungratefulness toward Napoleon III. The Emperor's adoption of the Saint-Simonian formulas concerning banking, investment, railroad mergers, and guaranteed interest rates allowed the Empire to succeed where other regimes failed. Girard also confirmed the judgment of Michel Chevalier that France's major political dilemma, the reconciliation of democracy and liberty, was ultimately dependent upon greater productivity. The

66. Girard, La Politique, pp. 338–339.

author thereby implied that Bonapartist political economy brought to fruition the democratic impulse of 1848.

Published six years after the end of the Second World War, Girard's conclusions reflected the concerns of a period when Frenchmen could both ponder the wisdom of the economic controls of Vichy and the meaning of a postwar political economy designed to provide class reconciliation and economic productivism. *Dirigisme* had obvious parallels with the Bonapartism of Napoleon III, and Girard underscored the positive contributions of the Empire. To use his own words: "The *comptes fantastiques* are forgotten and abolished; the work raised by the French of the Second Empire, under the energetic and persevering impulsion of the builders, remains—in its essentials—on the map of the country and the plan of our cities."[67]

67. Ibid., p. 402.

Conclusion

The reader of this study might well conclude that the historiography of the Empire merely reflects the fickle nature of historical judgment. Historians of the regime, after all, have clearly assessed the Empire on the basis of contemporary political issues. This situation, however, need not lead to a despairing skepticism; in fact, just the contrary is the case. Because historians are present-minded, their works become subject to historical inquiry and thereby provide yet another dimension to our understanding of the past. Never definitive, the writing of history lives in the present just as surely as it will live into the future and continue to be recreated according to contemporary considerations.

If history's history provides an understanding of the past, the historiography of the Second Empire reveals much about France since 1870. The Empire's first three major historians, for example, were participants in the struggles associated with the early Third Republic. Each wrote to defend certain political values. Delord, a member of the Assembly, extolled republicanism against Bonapartist caesarism. The Catholic monarchist La Gorce was understandably more cautious, as he viewed both the Empire and the Republic as regimes hostile to a moderate conservatism resting upon traditional elites. Ollivier, in contrast, argued that the Republic would only survive if it adopted the Bonapartist principle of a strong executive with plebiscitary powers.

Apart from Albert Thomas, who wrote from the left side of the republican spectrum and believed that the Empire was a mere prologue to a Republic leading to socialism, a later generation of historians treated the Empire rather differently. Professionals and spokesmen for a rigorous erudition meant to establish history as an "objective science," Seignobos and Maurain assumed a tone of Olympian detachment. They described the Empire as a failure attributable to the shortcomings of a naive Napoleon III who hoped to overcome France's political divisions. Their conclusions, however, were hardly the result of an objective science. The professionals owed much to the Republic which both sponsored professionalization in hopes of engendering a national consensus and placed historians in charge of a national school curriculum designed to foster loyalty to republican institutions.

Throughout the first two generations, the historiography of the Empire was dominated by historians whose clearest perception was that the regime's character was authoritarian. As a result, it was inevitable that the Empire was most frequently treated as a pause in France's political development. After 1870, the Empire seemed peripheral to what many viewed as the community's primary task: the establishment of a parliamentary and democratic government. Despite its indirect contribution to this phenomenon—Napoleon III, after all, forced liberals and republicans to forge the alliance that ultimately formed the Third Republic—the Empire's role in creating a liberal politics was understandably ignored given the configuration of French political life at the end of the nineteenth century. Those who might have granted the Empire its due on this score were, like La Gorce, ambivalent enough about the Republic not to join its virtues to those of a liberal Empire, or else they were inhibited by the national response to the humiliation of 1870. Ollivier, as a result, could only bemoan his fate and protest that public opinion refused to see things as they were.

By the 1930s, on the other hand, the political tangle which characterized the interwar period brought about a greater understanding for the dilemmas that led to the establishment of the Second Empire. Revision began in the work of Marcel Blanchard, Robert Schnerb, and Georges Duveau, three historians whose works were grounded in the difficulties of the 1930s. Although dissimilar from one another as men and historians, and while writing from altogether different perspectives, each described an Empire bearing little resemblance to the regime portrayed by their predecessors. They instead described an Empire which established the socio-economic basis for a modern France, and, at least for Blanchard and Duveau, the Empire ultimately provided a model for escaping the difficulties associated with the interwar period.

For the revisionists, Bonapartism represented something more than a political consensus imposed by executive power. It also stood for social pacification through a Saint-Simonian program of economic expansion. Whatever its political shortcomings, the Empire's formula provided an escape from the snarl of 1848. Grounded in the social theorizing of the 1840s, Bonapartism confronted the problems which destroyed the Second Republic and ultimately undermined the Third. Indeed, it was the inability of the Third Republic to continue a Saint-Simonian political economy that led to many of the difficulties identified with the period after World War I. Although the stalemate society functioned with limited success before 1914, it did not meet the challenge of international conflict, economic depression, and totalitarian ideologies.

The matter of parallels, however, reaches beyond the difficulties of 1848. The demise of the Third Republic, an event which has clearly led to the Empire's rehabilitation, in some measure resembles the fate of the July Monarchy. Like the Third Republic almost a century later, the Orleanist regime exhausted its ideological and moral resources by failing to master its own time. For the Orleanist leadership, the implications of industrial development and political democratization were met with timidity. There were nevertheless numerous alternatives to the narrow vision of Guizot and his colleagues, and the 1840s provided a gold mine of speculation as to the needs of a modern and democratic France. Bonapartism, a product of that theorizing, ultimately filled the void left by the

monarchy's fall, and Louis Napoleon certainly provided an answer
to what the cautious and unimaginative Orleanists refused to per-
ceive as a problem.

Only with the work of the so-called new historians has the Empire
been judged by a standard anywhere approaching its own, and the
conclusions of the revisionists have become the historical orthodoxy
of the post-World War II period. Some have even suggested that
contemporary successes find much of their inspiration in Bonapartist
political economy. This shift in historiographical values reflects the
apparent reshaping of French political life. Governments are now
judged largely on the basis of their success in directing and ordering
economic productivity, all of which seems to indicate that Frenchmen have put aside both the Third Republic and the issues that
dominated its early and middle years. For the moment, France lives
under a regime very different from that which spanned the period
from 1870 to 1940, and her present government is characterized by
a revitalized executive presiding over a technocratically inclined
administration committed to *dirigisme*. The professor, who many
believed personified the Third Republic, has in the process given
way to the technocrat, a figure whose function too closely resembles
that of the Saint-Simonian banker to escape the historian's notice.

With the present somewhat reminiscent of a Bonapartist past,
contemporary and recent authors have brought about a major revision of the Empire's historiography. Their scholarship may very
well aid the completion of Napoleon III's self-appointed task, that
of establishing a productivist economy. It has already brought to
fruition the prophecy of the Emperor who once claimed that his
place in history would finally be determined not by politics, but
by "the railroads in the provinces and the monuments in Paris."[1]

1. Adolphe Granier de Cassagnac, *Souvenirs du second Empire*, II, 222.

Bibliography

I. *Archival Sources*

Paris. Archives de l'Académie Française. Dossier Pierre de La Gorce.
Paris. Archives Nationales. Ministry of Education. Dossier Jean Maurain (F17 23625); Ministry of Education. Dossier Charles Seignobos (F17 23801); Ministry of Interior. Dossier *Siècle* (F18 417).

II. *Published Sources and Dissertations*

Adam, Juliette. *Mes Sentiments et nos idées avant 1870.* Paris: Lemerre, 1905.
Agulhon, Maurice. *La République au village: les populations du Var de la Révolution à la seconde République.* Paris: Plon, 1970.
———. "La Résistance au coup d'état en province: esquisse d'historiographie." *Revue d'histoire moderne et contemporaine* 21 (1974), 18–26.
Allem, Maurice. *La Vie quotidienne sous le second Empire.* Paris: Hachette, 1948.
Amann, Peter. "The Changing Outlines of 1848." *American Historical Review* 68 (1963), 938–953.
———. *Revolution and Mass Democracy: The Paris Club Movement in 1848.* Princeton: Princeton University Press, 1975.
———. "Writings on the Second French Republic." *Journal of Modern History* 34 (1962), 409–429.
Amato, Joseph. *Mounier and Maritain: A French Catholic Understanding of the Modern World.* University, Ala.: University of Alabama Press, 1975.
Amoyal, Jacques. "Les Origines socialistes et syndicalistes de la planification en France." *Mouvement social* 87 (1974), 137–169.

Anderson, R. D. *Education in France, 1848–1870.* Oxford: Clarendon Press, 1975.

Armengaud, André. *L'Opinion publique en France et la crise nationale allemande en 1866.* Dijon: Bernigaud, 1962.

Arnaud, René. *The Second Republic and Napoleon III.* Reprint. Translated by E. F. Buckley. New York: AMS Press, 1967.

Aubert, A., et al. *André Tardieu.* Paris: Hachette, 1957.

Aubert, R. *Le Pontificat de Pie IX.* Volume XXI in *Histoire de l'église,* under the direction of Augustin Fliche and Victor Martin. Paris: Bloud et Gay, 1962.

Aubry, Octave. *Le Second Empire.* Paris: Fayard, 1938.

Avenel, Henri. *Histoire de la presse française depuis 1789 jusqu'à nos jours.* Paris: Flammarion, 1900.

Aymard, Maurice. "The *Annales* and French Historiography." *Journal of European Economic History* 1 (1972), 491–511.

de Barante, A. Prosper. *Souvenirs.* Volumes VII–VIII. Edited by Claude de Barante. Paris: Calmann-Lévy, 1890–1910.

———. *La Vie politique de M. Royer-Collard.* 2 vols. Paris: Calmann-Lévy, 1861.

Barrot, Odilon. *Mémoires posthumes.* 4 vols. Paris: Charpentier, 1878.

Bastid, Paul. *Avènement du suffrage universal.* Paris: Presses Universitaires de France, 1948.

Bauchard, Philippe. *Les Technocrates et le pouvoir.* Paris: Arthaud, 1966.

Beau de Lomenie, E. *Les Responsabilités des dynasties bourgeoises.* Volume I. Paris: Denoel, 1943.

Beaujouan, G., and E. Lebée. "La Fondation du Crédit Industriel et Commercial." *Histoire des entreprises* 5–6 (1960), 5–40.

Bellessort, André. *La Société française sous Napoléon III.* Paris: Perrin, 1932.

Bellet, Roger. *Presse et journalisme sous le second Empire.* Paris: Colin, 1967.

Belouino, Paul. *Histoire d'un coup d'état.* Paris: Brunet, 1852.

Bergson, Henri. *Discours prononcés dans la séance publique tenue par l'Académie Française.* Paris: Firmin-Didot, 1918.

Berr, Henri. "Les Rapports de l'histoire et des sciences sociales d'après M. Seignobos." *Revue de synthèse historique* 4 (1902), 293–302.

Berton, Henry. *L'Evolution constitutionnelle du second Empire.* Paris: Alcan, 1900.

Bigo, Robert. *Les Banques françaises au cours du XIXe siècle.* Paris: Sirey, 1947.

Binion, Rudolf. *Defeated Leaders: The Political Fate of Caillaux, Jouvenel, and Tardieu.* New York: Columbia University Press, 1960.

Binkley, Robert. *Realism and Nationalism, 1852–1871.* The Rise of Modern Europe series, edited by William Langer. New York: Harper, 1935.

Blanc, Louis. *Révélations historiques en réponse au livre du Lord Normanby.* 2 vols. 3d ed. Paris: Lacroix, 1872.

Blanchard, Marcel. "Aux origines de nos chemins de fer: Saint-Simoniens et banquiers." *Annales d'histoire économique et sociale* 8 (1938), 97–115.

——. *Une Bataille de réseaux: Besançon, l'Est et le P.L.M.* Montpellier: privately published, 1937.

——. "Une Enquête administrative dans l'Isère en 1859." *Revue des études napoléoniennes* 16 (1919), 72–77.

——. *Essais historiques sur les premiers chemins de fer du Midi languedocien et de la vallée du Rhone.* Montpellier: Chambre de Commerce de Montpellier, 1935.

——. *Etude sur la polémique des chemins de fer dans le département de l'Isère.* Paris: Rieder, 1928.

——. "Financiers français et chemins de fer suisses sous le second Empire." *Revue d'économie politique* 51 (1937), 1591–1606.

——. *Géographie des chemins de fer.* Paris: Gallimard, 1942.

——. "Les Grandes Etapes du réseau ferroviaire français." *Revue des deux mondes* (1941), 186–194.

——. "La Politique ferroviaire du second Empire." *Annales d'histoire économique et sociale* 6 (1934), 529–546.

——. "Les Premiers Chemins de fer autour d'Orléans." *Revue d'histoire économique et sociale* 22 (1934–1935), 375–401.

——. *Premiers Projets de chemins de fer par la vallée du Rhone—Premiers liaisons ferroviaires de Lyon avec la région alpine.* Lyon: Audin, nd.

——. "Quelques Points de l'histoire des chemins de fer autour de Lyon." *Revue de géographie alpine* 20 (1932), 199–236.

——. *Les Routes des Alpes occidentales à l'époque napoléonienne, 1796–1815.* Grenoble: Allier, 1920.

——. *Le Second Empire.* 2d ed. Paris: Colin, 1956.

——. *Les Voies ferrées de l'Hérault.* Montpellier: Société Languedocienne de Géographie, 1922.

Blayau, Noel. *Billault, ministre de Napoléon III.* Paris: Klincksieck, 1972.

Bloch, Marc. *The Historian's Craft.* Translated by Peter Putnam. New York: Vintage, 1953.

Boon, Hendrik Nicolaas. *Rêve et réalité dans l'oeuvre de Napoléon III.* The Hague: Nijhoff, 1936.

Bourdieu, Pierre, and Jean Passeron. "Sociology and Philosophy in France since 1945." *Social Research* 34 (1967), 162–212.

Bourgeois, Emile, and E. Clermont. *Rome et Napoléon III.* Paris: Colin, 1907.

Bourgin, Georges. "La Législation ouvrière du second Empire." *Revue des études napoléoniennes* 4 (1913), 220–236.

Bouvier, Jean. "Aux origines du Crédit Lyonnais." *Histoire des entreprises* 5–6 (1960), 41–64.

——. *Le Crédit Lyonnais de 1863 à 1882.* 2 vols. Paris: Imprimerie Nationale, 1961.

——. "Mouvement ouvrier et conjoncture économique." *Mouvement social* 48 (1964), 3–30.

————. "Les Péreire et l'affaire de la Banque de Savoie." *Cahiers d'histoire* 5 (1960), 383–410.

Bouvier, Jean, and Jacques Wolff, eds. *Deux Siècles de fiscalité française: XIXe–XXe siècle*. Paris: Mouton, 1973.

Braudel, Fernand. "Personal Testimony." *Journal of Modern History* 44 (1973), 448–467.

de Broglie, Albert. *Eglise et l'Empire romain au quatrième siècle*. 3 vols. 3d ed. Paris: Didier, 1856.

de Broglie, Victor. *Discours prononcés dans la séance publique tenue par l'Académie Française*. Paris. Didier, 1856.

————. *Vues sur le gouvernement de France*. Paris: Lévy, 1872.

Bury, J. P. T. *Napoleon III and the Second Empire*. London: English Universities Press, 1964.

Cameron, Rondo E. *France and the Economic Development of Europe, 1800–1914*. Princeton: Princeton University Press, 1961.

Canivez, André. "La Pensée de Georges Duveau." *Bulletin de la Faculté des Lettres de Strasbourg*, 37e année, 3 (1958), 137–145.

Carbonell, Charles-Olivier. *Histoire et historiens: une mutation idéologique des historiens français, 1865–1885*. Toulouse: Privat, 1976.

————. "La Naissance de la *Revue historique:* une revue de combat (1876–1885)." *Revue historique* 518 (1976), 331–351.

Carlisle, Robert. "The Birth of Technocracy: Science, Society, and Saint-Simonians." *Journal of the History of Ideas* 35 (1974), 445–464.

————. "Saint-Simonian Radicalism: A Definition and a Direction." *French Historical Studies* 5 (1968), 430–445.

Caron, François. *Histoire de l'exploitation d'un grand réseau; la Compagnie du Chemin de Fer du Nord*. Paris: Mouton, 1973.

Case, Lynn. *French Opinion on War and Diplomacy during the Second Empire*. Philadelphia: University of Pennsylvania Press, 1954.

Chapman, Brian. *The Prefects and Provincial France*. London: Allen and Unwin, 1955.

Chapman, J. M., and Brian Chapman. *The Life and Times of Baron Haussmann*. London: Weidenfeld and Nicolson, 1957.

Chapy, M. C. *Clermont sous le second Empire*. Clermont-Ferrand: Bussac, 1972.

Charléty, Sebastien. *Histoire du Saint-Simonisme (1825–1864)*. Paris: Hartmann, 1931.

Charlton, Donald. *Positivist Thought in France during the Second Empire*. New York: Oxford University Press, 1959.

Chevalier, Louis. *Classes laborieuses et classes dangereuses à Paris pendant la première moitié du XIXe siècle*. Paris: Plon, 1955.

————. *La Formation de la population parisienne au XIXe siècle*. Paris: Presses Universitaires de France, 1950.

Chevalier, Michel. "Journal." Edited by Marcel Blanchard. *Revue des deux mondes* (1932), 171–181.

——. "Journal." Edited by Marcel Blanchard. *Revue historique* 171 (1933), 115–142.

——. *Society, Manners and Politics in the United States.* Edited and translated by T. G. Bradford and revised by John William Ward. Garden City: Anchor, 1961.

Chrétien, Paul. *Le Duc de Persigny.* Toulouse: Boisseau, 1943.

Clague, Monique. "Vision and Myopia in the New Politics of André Tardieu." *French Historical Studies* 8 (1973), 105–129.

Clapham, J. H. *The Economic Development of France and Germany, 1815–1914.* 4th ed. Cambridge: University Press, 1955.

Clark, Terry. *Prophets and Patrons: The French University and the Emergence of the Social Sciences.* Cambridge: Harvard University Press, 1973.

Clough, Shepard Bancroft. *France: A Study of National Economics, 1789–1939.* Reprint. New York: Octagon, 1964.

Collins, Irene. *The Government and the Newspaper Press in France, 1814–1881.* London: Oxford University Press, 1959.

Commission chargée de réunir, classer et publier les papiers saisis aux Tuileries. *Papiers et correspondance de la famille impériale.* 2 vols. Paris: Imprimerie Nationale, 1871.

Cornu, Auguste. *Karl Marx et la Révolution de 1848.* Paris: Presses Universitaires de France, 1948.

Coussy, J. "La Politique commerciale du second Empire et la continuité de l'évolution structurelle française." *Cahiers de l'Institut de Science Economique Appliquée* (1961), 1–47.

Crouzet, François. "The Economic History of Modern Europe." *Journal of Economic History* 31 (1971), 135–152.

Crozier, Michel. *The Bureaucratic Phenomenon.* Chicago: University of Chicago Press, 1964.

Dansette, Adrien. *Du 2 décembre au 4 septembre.* Volume II in *Histoire du second Empire.* Paris: Hachette, 1972.

——. *Louis Napoléon à la conquête du pouvoir.* Volume I in *Histoire du second Empire.* Paris: Hachette, 1961.

——. *Naissance de la France moderne.* Volume III in *Histoire du second Empire.* Paris: Hachette, 1976.

——. *Religious History of France.* 2 vols. Translated by John Dingle: London: Herder and Nelson, 1961.

Darimon, Alfred. *Histoire de douze ans (1857–1869).* Paris: Dentu, 1883.

——. *Histoire d'un parti: le tiers parti.* Paris: Dentu, 1887.

——. *Histoire d'un parti: les cinq.* Paris: Dentu, 1885.

——. *Histoire d'un parti: les irréconciliables.* Paris: Dentu, 1888.

——. *L'Opposition libérale sous l'Empire.* Paris: Dentu, 1886.

Darmon, Jean-Jacques. *Le Colportage de librairie en France sous le second Empire.* Paris: Plon, 1972.

Debidour, A. *Histoire des rapports de l'église et de l'état en France de 1789 à 1870.* Paris: Alcan, 1898.

Delord, Taxile. *Histoire de second Empire.* 6 vols. Paris: Ballière, 1867–1875.

———. *Les Troisièmes Pages du journal Le Siècle.* Paris: Poulet-Malassis, 1861.

Digeon, Claude. *La Crise allemande de la pensée française.* Paris: Presses Universitaires de France, 1959.

Dolléans, E. "Georges Duveau, sociologue et historien." *Revue socialiste* 29–33 (1949), 224–237.

———. *Histoire du mouvement ouvrier.* 2 vols. 3d ed. Paris: Colin, 1947.

———. "Vie et pensée ouvrières entre 1848 et 1871." *Revue historique* 198 (1947), 62–78.

Domenach, Jean-Marie, and Robert de Montvalon, eds. *The Catholic Avant-Garde.* Translated by Brigid Elson. New York: Holt, 1967.

Dommanget, Maurice. *Blanqui et l'opposition révolutionnaire à la fin du second Empire.* Paris: Colin, 1960.

———. *Les Idées politiques et sociales d'Auguste Blanqui.* Paris: Rivière, 1958.

Driault, Edouard. "Un Républicain napoléonien: Armand Carrel." *Revue des études napoléoniennes* 6 (1936), 34–55.

Dunham, Arthur. *The Anglo-French Treaty of Commerce of 1860.* Ann Arbor: University of Michigan Press, 1930.

Dupont-Ferrier, Pierre. *Le Marché financier de Paris sous le second Empire.* Paris: Alcan, 1925.

Duprat, Pascal. *Les Tables de proscription de Louis Bonaparte.* 2 vols. Liège: Redouté, 1852.

Duquesne, Jacques. *Les Catholiques français sous l'Occupation.* Paris: Grasset, 1966.

Durieux, Joseph. *Le Ministre Pierre Magne.* 2 vols. Paris: Champion, 1929.

Duroselle, J. -B. *Les Débuts du Catholicisme social en France (1822–1870).* Paris: Presses Universitaires de France, 1951.

———. "Michel Chevalier Saint-Simonien." *Revue historique* 215 (1956), 233–266.

Duruy, Victor. *Notes et Souvenirs.* 2 vols. Paris: Hachette, 1901.

Dutacq, François. "La Politique des grands travaux sous le second Empire: les idées et les projets de C. -M. Vaisse, préfet du Rhône." *Revue des études napoléoniennes* 18 (1929), 36–43.

Duveau, Georges. "Comment d'étudier la vie ouvrière: les méthodes d'investigation." *Revue d'histoire économique et sociale* 26 (1940–1947), 11–21.

———. "L'Esprit fasciste et la mystique de la jeunesse." *Esprit* 16 (1934), 583–588.

———. "L'Europe et le socialisme." In *Problèmes de civilisation européenne,* pp. 129–260. Strasbourg: Centre Universitaire des Hautes Etudes Européennes, 1956.

————. *De 1848 à nos jours.* Volume IV of the *Histoire du peuple français,* under the direction of L. -H. Parias. Paris: Nouvelle Librairie, n.d.

————. "Edouard Dolléans, historien du mouvement ouvrier," *Revue socialiste* 12–16 (1947), 361–364.

————. "George Sand, témoin lucide du drame sociale." In *Homage à George Sand,* pp. 5–9. Strasbourg: Faculté des Lettres de Strasbourg, 1954.

————. *1848: The Making of a Revolution.* Translated by Anne Carter. New York: Pantheon, 1967.

————. "Les Mobiles humaines en histoire." *Diogène* 22 (1958), 32–45.

————. "L'Ouvrier de quarante-huit." *Revue socialiste* 17–23 (1948), 73–79.

————. *La Pensée ouvrière sur l'éducation pendant la seconde République et le second Empire.* Paris: Domat Montchrestien, 1947.

————. "Proudhon pendant la seconde République." *Revue socialiste* 156 (1936), 29–39.

————. "Qui est cet homme?" *Miroir de l'histoire* 8 (1957), 231–236.

————. *Raspail.* Paris: Presses Universitaires de France, 1948.

————. "Les Rélations internationales dans la pensée ouvrière, 1840–1865." In *Actes du Congrès Historique du Centenaire de la Révolution de 1848,* pp. 277–283. Paris: Presses Universitaires de France, 1948.

————. *Le Siège de Paris.* Paris: Hachette, 1939.

————. *Sociologie de l'utopie et autres essais.* Paris: Presses Universitaires de France, 1961.

————. *Le Testament romantique.* Paris: Kra, 1927.

————. *La Vie ouvrière en France sous le second Empire.* 6th ed. Paris: Gallimard, 1946.

Duveau, Georges, Georges Izard, and André Deléage. *La Bataille de France.* Paris: Tisné, 1938.

Duvergier de Hauranne, Prosper. *Histoire du gouvernement parlementaire en France.* 5 vols. Paris: Lévy, 1857–1862.

Ellul, Jacques. *The Technological Society.* Translated by John Wildinson. New York: Knopf, 1969.

Elwitt, Sanford. *The Making of the Third Republic: Class and Politics in France, 1868–1884.* Baton Rouge: Louisiana State University Press, 1975.

Emerit, Marcel. *Madame Cornu et Napoléon III.* Paris: Presses Universitaires de France, 1937.

————. *Les Saint-Simoniens en Algérie.* Paris: Belles Lettres, 1941.

————. "Les Sources des idées sociales et coloniales de Napoléon III." *Revue d'Alger* 3 (1945), 426–437.

Evans, David Owen. *Social Romanticism in France.* Oxford: Clarendon Press, 1951.

de Falloux, Alfred. *Histoire de saint Pie V.* 3d ed. Paris: Sagnier et Bray, 1854.

————. *Memoirs of a Royalist.* 2 vols. Edited and translated by C. B. Pitman. London: Chapman and Hall, 1888.

Farat, Honoré. *Persigny, un ministre de Napoléon III*. Paris: Hachette, 1957.

Farmer, Paul. *France Reviews its Revolutionary Origins*. Reprint. New York: Octagon, 1963.

———. "The Second Empire in France." In Volume X of *The New Cambridge Modern History*, edited by J. P. T. Bury, pp. 442–467. Cambridge: University Press, 1960.

———. "Some Frenchmen Review 1848." *Journal of Modern History* 20 (1948), 320–325.

Febvre, Lucien. *Combats pour l'histoire*. Paris: Colin, 1953.

———. "Entre l'histoire à thèse et l'histoire-manuel." *Revue de synthèse historique* 53 (1933), 205–236.

———. "L'Ouvrier français sous le second Empire." *Annales (Economies-Sociétés-Civilisations)* 3 (1948), 214–215.

———. *Pour une histoire à part entière*. Paris: SEVPEN, 1962.

Ferry, Jules. *Comptes fantastiques d'Haussmann*. 2d ed. Paris: Chevalier, 1868.

Fine, Martin. "Toward Corporatism: The Movement for Capital-Labor Collaboration in France, 1914–1936." Ph.D. dissertation, University of Wisconsin, 1971.

Fisher, H. A. L. *Bonapartism*. Oxford: Oxford University Press, 1961.

Fohlen, Claude. *L'Industrie textile au temps du second Empire*. Paris: Plon, 1957.

———. "Sociétés anonymes et développement capitaliste sous le second Empire." *Histoire des entreprises* 7–8 (1961), 65–79.

Fortin, A. "Les Conflits sociaux dans les houillères du Pas-de-Calais sous le second Empire." *Revue du Nord* 43 (1961), 349–355.

Fournier, Pierre-Léon. *Le Second Empire et la législation ouvrière*. Paris: Sirey, 1911.

François, Michel. "Historical Study in France." In *Historical Study in the West*, pp. 33–71. New York: Appleton-Century-Crofts, 1968.

Freedman, Charles. *The Conseil d'Etat in Modern France*. New York: Columbia University Press, 1961.

Friguglietti, James. *Albert Mathiez, historien révolutionnaire*. Paris: Société des Etudes Robespierristes, 1974.

———. "Mathiez, an Historian at War." *French Historical Studies* 7 (1972), 570–586.

Gaillard, Jeanne. "Les Associations de production et la pensée politique en France, 1852–1870." *Mouvement social* 52 (1965), 59–84.

———. "Gambetta et le radicalisme entre l'élection de Belleville et celle de Marseille en 1869." *Revue historique* 519 (1976), 73–88.

———. *Paris, la ville (1852–1870)*. Paris: Champion, 1976.

Garnier-Pagès, Louis. *Histoire de la Révolution de 1848*. 11 vols. Paris: Pagnerre, 1861–1872.

Gérard, Alice. "Histoire et politique: la *Revue historique* face à l'histoire contemporaine (1885–1898)." *Revue historique* 518 (1976), 353–405.

————, ed. *Le Second Empire: innovation et réaction.* Paris: Presses Universitaires de France, 1973.

Gerbod, Paul. *La Condition universitaire en France au XIXe siècle.* Paris: Presses Universitaires de France, 1965.

Gershoy, Leo. "Three French Historians and the Revolution of 1848." *Journal of the History of Ideas* 12 (1951), 131–146.

Gervais, Jean-Francis. "Une Théorie du changement en histoire: l'oeuvre historique de Pierre de La Gorce." *Revue d'histoire moderne et contemporaine* 24 (1977), 96–109.

Geyl, Pieter. *Napoleon: For and Against.* Translated by Olive Renier. London: Jonathan Cape, 1957.

Gilbert, Felix, and Stephen Graubard, eds. *Historical Studies Today.* New York: Norton, 1972.

Gille, Bertrand. *La Banque en France au XIXe siècle.* Geneva: Droz, 1970.

————. *La Banque et le crédit en France de 1815 à 1848.* Paris: Presses Universitaires de France, 1959.

————. "La Fondation de la Société Générale." *Histoire des entreprises* 7–8 (1961), 5–64.

————. *Histoire de la maison Rothschild.* 2 vols. Geneva: Droz, 1968.

————. *La Sidérurgie française au XIXe siècle.* Geneva: Droz, 1968.

Girard, Louis. "L'Affaire du chemin de fer Cette-Marseille (1861–1863)." *Revue d'histoire moderne et contemporaine* 2 (1955), 107–125.

————. *La IIe République.* Paris: Calmann-Lévy, 1968.

————, ed. *Les Elections de 1869.* Paris: Rivière, 1960.

————. *Etude comparée des mouvements révolutionnaires en France en 1830, 1848 et 1870–1871.* Paris: CDU, n.d.

————. "Le Financement des grands travaux du second Empire." *Revue économique* 2 (1951), 343–355.

————. *La Garde nationale.* Paris: Plon, 1964.

————. "Political Liberalism in France, 1840–1875." In *French Society and Culture since the Old Regime,* edited by Evelyn Acomb and Marvin Brown, pp. 119–132. New York: Holt, 1966.

————. *La Politique des travaux publics du second Empire.* Paris: Colin, 1951.

————. *Problèmes politiques et constitutionnels du second Empire.* Paris: CDU, n.d.

————. "Les Problèmes français." In *L'Europe du XIXe et du XXe siècle,* under the direction of Max Beloff et al., pp. 515–543. Milan: Marzorati, 1959.

————. "Le Règne de Louis Philippe; la Révolution de 1848; le second Empire." In Volume II of *Histoire de France,* under the direction of Marcel Reinhard, pp. 234–320. Paris: Larousse, 1954.

————. "Révolution ou conservatisme en Europe (1856): une polémique de la presse parisienne après la guerre de Crimée." In *Mélanges Pierre Renouvin,* pp. 115–131. Paris: Presses Universitaires de France, 1966.

————. "Le Second Empire et l'unité italienne." *Atti del Convegno Internazionale sul Tema: Il Risorgimento e l'Europa* 361 (1964), 143–149.

————. "Valeur et permanence des thèmes saint-simonienes." *Cahiers de l'Institut de Science Economique Appliquée* (1970), 773–792.

Girard, Louis, A. Prost, and Rémi Gossez. *Les Conseillers généraux en 1870.* Paris: Presses Universitaires de France, 1967.

Girardet, Raoul. *La Société militaire dans la France contemporaine.* Paris: Plon, 1953.

————. *Le Nationalisme français, 1871–1919.* Paris: Colin, 1966.

Glénisson, Jean. "L'Historiographie française contemporaine: tendances et réalisations." In *La Recherche historique en France,* under the direction of the Comité Français des Sciences Historiques, pp. ix–lxiv. Paris: Centre National de la Recherche Scientifique, 1965.

Goldberg, Harvey. *The Life of Jean Jaurès.* Madison: University of Wisconsin Press, 1962.

de Goncourt, Edmond and Jules. *The Goncourt Journals.* Edited and translated by Lewis Galantière. Garden City: Doubleday, 1937.

Gonnard, Philippe. *Les Origines de la légende napoléonienne.* Paris: Calmann-Lévy, 1905.

Gontard, Maurice. "La Carrière universitaire d'Hippolyte Fortoul." In *Mélanges d'histoire: André Fugier,* pp. 119–131. Lyon: Editions des Cahiers d'Histoire, 1968.

Gooch, Brison. *The New Bonapartist Generals in the Crimean War.* The Hague: Nijhoff, 1959.

————. *The Reign of Napoleon III.* Chicago: Rand McNally, 1969.

Gooch, G. P. *History and Historians in the Nineteenth Century.* New ed. Boston: Beacon, 1959.

————. *The Second Empire.* London: Longmans, 1960.

Gossez, Rémi. *Les Ouvriers de Paris: l'organisation, 1848–1851.* Paris: Bibliothèque de la Révolution de 1848, 1967.

Granier de Cassagnac, Adolphe. *Souvenirs du second Empire.* 2 vols. Paris: Dentu, 1879–1882.

Grant, Elliot. "Victor Hugo during the Second Empire. *Smith College Studies in Modern Language* 17 (1935), 1–68.

Grepon, Marguerite, ed. "Georges Duveau." *Ariane* 56–58 (1958), 1–24.

Guedalla, Philip. *The Second Empire.* New York: G. P. Putnam, 1922.

Guérard, Albert. *French Prophets of Yesterday: A Study of Religious Thought under the Second Empire.* New York: Appleton, 1913.

————. *Napoleon III.* Cambridge: Harvard University Press, 1943.

————. *Reflections on the Napoleonic Legend.* New York: Scribners, 1924.

Guériot, P. *Napoléon III.* 2 vols. Paris: Payot, 1933.

Guest, Ivor. *Napoleon III in England.* London: British Technical and General Press, 1952.

Guillemin, Henri. *Le Coup du 2 décembre.* Paris: Gallimard, 1951.

Guiral, Pierre. "Les Evénements de 1860 et les libéraux français." *Annales de la Faculté des Lettres et Sciences Humaines d'Aix* 35 (1961), 69–91.

————. "Le Libéralisme en France (1815–1870)." In *Tendances politiques dans la vie française depuis 1789,* pp. 17–40. Paris: Hachette, 1960.

------. "La Presse de 1848 à 1871." In Volume II of *Histoire générale de la presse française*, pp. 205–382. Paris: Presses Universitaires de France, 1969.

------. *Prévost-Paradol: pensée et action d'un libéral sous le second Empire*. Paris: Presses Universitaires de France, 1955.

------. "Quelques Notes sur la politique des milieux d'affaires marseillais de 1815 à 1870." *Provence historique* 7 (1957), 115–174.

------. "Quelques Notes sur le retour de faveur de Voltaire sous le second Empire." In *Hommage au Doyen Etienne Gros*, pp. 46–62. Gap: Louis-Jean, 1959.

------. "Réflexions sur la justice du second Empire." In *La France au XIXe siècle: mélanges offerts à Charles-Hippolyte Pouthas*, pp. 109–118. Paris: Publications de la Sorbonne, 1973.

Guiral, Pierre, Yvonne Knielbiehler, et al., eds. *La Société française vue par les romanciers*. Paris: Colin, 1969.

Guizot, François. *Histoire du protectorat de Richard Cromwell et du rétablissement des Stuarts*. 2 vols. Paris: Didier, 1856.

------. *Mémoires pour servir à l'histoire de mon temps*. 8 vols. New ed. Paris: Lévy, 1872.

Halévy, Ludovic. *Carnets*. 2 vols. 7th ed. Paris: Calmann-Lévy, 1935.

Halphen, Louis. "France." In Volume I of *Histoire et historiens depuis cinquante ans*, pp. 148–166. Paris: Alcan, 1927.

------. *L'Histoire en France*. Paris: Colin, 1914.

Hamel, Ernest. *Histoire de Robespierre*. 3 vols. Paris: Lacroix, 1865–1867.

------. *Histoire de Saint-Just*. Paris: Poulet-Malassis, 1859.

------. *Histoire du second Empire*. 2 vols. 2d ed. Paris: Flammarion, 1897.

Hanotaux, Gabriel. *Contemporary France*. Volume I. Translated by John Tarver. Westminster: Archibald Constable, 1903.

------. *Histoire politique de 1804 à 1926*. Volume V of *Histoire de la nation française*, under the direction of Gabriel Hanotaux. Paris: Plon, n.d.

Hatin, E. *Bibliographie historique et critique de la presse périodique française*. Reprint. Paris: Anthropos, 1965.

Hauser, Henri, Jean Maurain, Pierre Benaerts, and Fernand L'Huillier. *Du libéralisme à l'impérialisme*. 2d ed. Volume XVII in the Peuples et civilisations series. Paris: Presses Universitaires de France, 1952.

Haussmann, Georges. *Mémoires*. 3 vols. Paris: Havard, 1890–1893.

d'Haussonville, Joseph. *L'Eglise romaine et le premier Empire*. 5 vols. Paris: Lévy, 1868–1869.

d'Hauterive, Ernest, ed. *The Second Empire and its Downfall: The Correspondence of the Emperor Napoleon III and his Cousin Prince Napoleon*. Translated by Herbert Wilson. New York: George Doran, n.d.

Hayward, J. E. S. "Solidarity: The Social History of an Idea in 19th Century France." *International Review of Social History* 4 (1959), 260–284.

Hellman, John. "The Opening to the Left in French Catholicism: The Role of the Personalists." *Journal of the History of Ideas* 34 (1973), 381–390.

Hexter, J. H. "Fernand Braudel and the Monde Braudellien." *Journal of Modern History* 44 (1972), 450–539.

Hoffmann, Stanley. "Collaborationism in France during World War II." *Journal of Modern History* 40 (1968), 375–395.

———. "Paradoxes of the French Political Community." In *In Search of France*, pp. 1–117. Cambridge: Harvard University Press, 1963.

Houston, Douglas. "Emile Ollivier and the Hohenzollern Candidacy." *French Historical Studies* 4 (1965), 125–149.

Hughes, H. Stuart. *The Obstructed Path: French Social Thought in the Years of Desperation*. New York: Harper, 1968.

Hugo, Victor. *Les Chatiments*. Paris: Hetzel, n.d.

———. *The Complete Works of Victor Hugo*. Volumes XV, XVI, and XXII. Boston: Estes and Lauriat, nd.

Hunt, Herbert. *Le Socialisme et le romantisme en France*. Oxford: Clarendon Press, 1935.

Iggers, Georg, ed. *The Doctrine of Saint-Simon: An Exposition*. Boston: Beacon, 1958.

———. *New Directions in European Historiography*. Middletown: Wesleyan University Press, 1975.

Jeanneney, Jules. *Journal politique, septembre 1939 à juillet 1942*. Edited by Jean-Noel Jeanneney. Paris: Colin, 1972.

Jéloubovskaia, E. *La Chute du second Empire et la naissance de la troisième République en France*. Translated by J. Champenois. Moscow: Editions en Langues Etrangères, 1959.

Jerrold, Blanchard. *The Life of Napoleon III*. 4 vols. London: Longmans, 1874–1882.

Johnson, Douglas. *Guizot: Aspects of French History*. Toronto: University of Toronto Press, 1963.

Kelly, M. H. "The Fate of Emmanuel Mounier: A Bibliographical Essay." *Journal of European Studies* 2 (1972), 256–267.

Kemp, Tom. *Economic Forces in French History*. London: Dobson, 1971.

Keylor, William. *Academy and Community: The Foundation of the French Historical Profession*. Cambridge: Harvard University Press, 1975.

Kindleberger, Charles. *Economic Growth in France and Britain, 1851–1950*. Cambridge: Harvard University Press, 1964.

Kriegel, Annie. *Aux origines du communisme français*. 2 vols. Paris: Mouton, 1964.

Kuisel, Richard. *Ernest Mercier, French Technocrat*. Berkeley: University of California Press, 1967.

———. "The Legend of the Vichy Synarchy." *French Historical Studies* 6 (1970), 365–398.

———. "Technocrats and Public Policy: From the Third to the Fourth Republic." *Journal of European Economic History* 2 (1973), 53–99.

Kulstein, David. "The Attitude of French Workers towards the Second Empire." *French Historical Studies* 2 (1962), 356–375.

——. "Bonapartist Workers during the Second Empire." *International Review of Social History* 9 (1964), 226–234.

——. *Napoleon III and the Working Class: A Study of Government Propaganda under the Second Empire.* Los Angeles: California State Colleges, 1969.

Laboulaye, Edouard. *Le Plébiscite du mai 1870.* Paris: Blot, 1870.

Labrousse, E., ed. *Aspects de la crise et de la dépression de l'économie française au milieu du dix-neuvième siècle.* Paris: Bibliothèque de la Révolution de 1848, 1956.

de Lacombe, Charles. *Berryer sous la République et le second Empire.* Paris: Firmin-Didot, 1895.

de Lacretelle, Pierre. *La Vie politique de Victor Hugo.* Paris: Hachette, 1928.

Lafrance, Robert, ed. *Albert Thomas vivant: études, témoignages, souvenirs.* Geneva: Société des Amis d'Albert Thomas, 1957.

de La Gorce, Agnès. *Une Vocation d'historien: Pierre de La Gorce.* Paris: Plon, 1948.

de La Gorce, Pierre. *Au temps du second Empire.* Paris: Plon, 1933.

——. *Charles X.* Paris: Plon, 1927.

——. *Discours prononcés dans la séance publique tenue par l'Académie Française.* Paris: Firmin-Didot, 1917.

——. "Gambetta." *Correspondant* (1920), 617–632.

——. "Un Grand Evêque en un grand diocèse: le cardinal Régnier, 1850–1881." *Revue des questions historiques* 119 (1934), 548–559.

——. *Histoire de la seconde République.* 2 vols. Paris: Plon, 1887.

——. *Histoire du second Empire.* 7 vols. 12th ed. Paris: Plon, 1921.

——. *Histoire religieuse de la Révolution française.* 5 vols. Paris: Plon, 1909–1923.

——. *Louis XVIII.* Paris: Plon, 1925.

——. *Louis Philippe.* Paris: Plon, 1930.

——. "M. Thiers, un bourgeois français du XIXe siècle." *Revue des deux mondes* (1934), 296–328.

——. *Napoléon III et sa politique.* 10th ed. Paris: Plon, 1933.

Landes, David. *Bankers and Pashas: International Finance and Economic Imperialism in Egypt.* Cambridge: Harvard University Press, 1958.

——. "French Entrepreneurship and Industrial Growth in the Nineteenth Century." *Journal of Economic History* 9 (1949), 45–61.

——. "Vieille Banque et banque nouvelle: la révolution financière du dix-neuvième siècle." *Revue d'histoire moderne et contemporaine* 3 (1956), 204–222.

Latreille, A., et al. *La Période contemporaine.* Volume III in *Histoire du Catholicisme en France.* Paris: Spes, 1962.

Lavisse, Ernest. *L'Enseignement historique en Sorbonne et l'éducation nationale.* Paris: no publisher, 1882.

————. *Un Ministre, Victor Duruy.* Paris: Colin, 1895.

————. "Victor Duruy." *Revue de Paris* (1894), 225–253, and (1895), 47–85.

Lebey, André. *Louis-Napoléon Bonaparte et la Révolution de 1848.* 2 vols. Paris: Juven, 1907.

Le Bras, Gabriel. "Georges Duveau." *Archives de sociologie des religions* 6 (1958), 3–6.

Lecanuet, Edouard. *Montalembert d'après ses papiers et sa correspondance.* Volume III. Paris: Poussielgue, 1902.

Le Clère, Bernard, and Vincent Wright. *Les Préfets du second Empire.* Paris: Colin, 1973.

Lefebvre, Georges. *La Naissance de l'historiographie moderne.* Paris: Flammarion, 1971.

Lefèvre, A. *Sous le second Empire: chemins de fer et politique.* Paris: Société d'Edition d'Enseignement Supérieur, 1951.

Leguay, Pierre. "M. Seignobos et l'histoire." *Mercure de France* 88 (1910), 36–52.

————. *La Sorbonne.* Paris: Grasset, 1910.

————. *Universitaires d'aujourd'hui.* Paris: Grasset, 1912.

Léon, Paul. *Mérimée et son temps.* Paris: Presses Universitaires de France, 1961.

Léon, Pierre. "Les Grèves de 1867–1870 dans le département de l'Isère." *Revue d'histoire moderne et contemporaine* 1 (1954), 272–300.

Leonard, Charlene. *Lyon Transformed: Public Works of the Second Empire.* Berkeley: University of California Press, 1961.

Leroy, Maxime. *Histoire des idées sociales en France.* Volumes II and III. Paris: Gallimard, 1954.

————. *La Politique de Sainte-Beuve.* Paris: Gallimard, 1941.

Levasseur, Emile. *Histoire des classes ouvrières et de l'industrie en France de 1789 à 1870.* 2d ed. Paris: Rousseau, 1904.

————. "Le Mouvement des salaires." *Annales des sciences politiques* 23 (1908), 709–730, and 24 (1909), 38–61.

Lévy-Leboyer, Maurice. "Les Processus d'industrialization: le cas de l'Angleterre et de la France." *Revue historique* 239 (1968), 281–298.

Lewis, David. "Emmanuel Mounier and the Politics of Moral Revolution." *Catholic History Review* 56 (1970), 266–290.

Lhomme, Jean. *La Grande Bourgeoisie au pouvoir, 1830–1880.* Paris: Presses Universitaires de France, 1960.

————. "Le Pouvoir d'achat de l'ouvrier français au cours d'un siècle: 1840–1940." *Mouvement social* 63 (1968), 41–68.

L'Huillier, Fernand. *La Lutte ouvrière à la fin du second Empire.* Paris: Colin, 1957.

Liard, Louis. *L'Enseignement supérieur en France.* Volume II. Paris: Colin, 1894.

Lorwin, Lewis. *Syndicalism in France.* 2d ed. New York: Columbia University Press, 1914.

Lorwin, Val. *The French Labor Movement.* Cambridge: Harvard University Press, 1954.

Loubère, Leo. *Louis Blanc.* Evanston: Northwestern University Press, 1961.

Loubet de Bayle, J. L. *Les Non-conformistes des années 30.* Paris: Seuil, 1969.

Louis, Paul. *Histoire du mouvement syndical en France.* 2 vols. Paris: Valois, 1947–1948.

Lucas-Dubreton, J. *Le Culte de Napoléon.* Paris: Michel, 1960.

McKay, Donald. *The National Workshops.* Cambridge: Harvard University Press, 1933.

McNeil, Gordon. "Charles Seignobos." In *Some Historians of Modern Europe,* edited by Bernadotte Schmitt, pp. 477–494. Chicago: University of Chicago Press, 1942.

Magen, Hippolyte. *Mystère du deux décembre.* London: Jeffs, 1852.

Maier, Charles. "Between Taylorism and Technocracy: European Ideologies and the Vision of Industrial Productivity in the 1920s." *Journal of Contemporary History* 5 (1970), 27–61.

———. *Recasting Bourgeois Europe.* Princeton: Princeton University Press, 1975.

Mann, H. D. *Lucien Febvre: la pensée vivante d'un historien.* Paris: Colin, 1971.

Manuel, Frank. *The New World of Henri Saint-Simon.* Cambridge: Harvard University Press, 1956.

Marbo, Camille (Madame Emile Borel). *A travers deux siècles: souvenirs et rencontres.* Paris: Grasset, 1968.

Marcilhacy, Christianne. "Les Caractères de la crise sociale et politique de 1846 à 1852 dans le département du Loiret." *Revue d'histoire moderne et contemporaine* 6 (1959), 1–59.

Margadant, Ted. "Modernisation and Insurgency in December 1851: A Case Study of the Drôme." In *Revolution and Reaction: 1848 and the Second French Republic,* edited by Roger Price, pp. 254–279. New York: Barnes and Noble, 1975.

Marion, Marcel. *Histoire financière de la France.* Volume V. Paris: Rousseau, 1928.

Maritch, Sreten. *Histoire du mouvement social sous le second Empire à Lyon.* Paris: Rousseau, 1930.

Marlin, Roger. "Les Elections législatives de 1869 dans le Doubs." *Cahiers d'histoire* 7 (1962), 65–83.

Martin, Marc. "Presse, publicité et grandes affaires sous le second Empire." *Revue historique* 520 (1977), 343–383.

Marx, Karl. *The Civil War in France.* New York: International Publishers, n.d.

———. *The Class Struggles in France.* New York: International Publishers, n.d.

———. *The 18th Brumaire of Louis Bonaparte.* New York: International Publishers, n.d.

———. *Herr Vogt.* 2 vols. Translated by J. Molitor. Paris: Costes, 1927–1928.

Massa-Gille, Geneviève. *Histoire des emprunts de la Ville de Paris (1814–1875)*. Paris: Imprimerie Municipale, 1973.

de Maupas, Charlemagne. *Mémoirs sur le second Empire*. 2 vols. Paris: Dentu, 1884–1885.

Maurain, Jean. *Un Bourgeois français au XIXe siècle: Baroche*. Paris: Alcan, 1936.

———. *La Politique ecclésiastique du second Empire de 1852 à 1869*. Paris: Alcan, 1930.

Maurois, Simone André. *Miss Howard and the Emperor*. Translated by Humphrey Hare. New York: Knopf, 1957.

Mayer, J. P. *Political Thought in France*. Rev. ed. London: Routledge and Kegan Paul, 1949.

Mayer, P. *Histoire du 2 décembre*. Paris: Ledoyen, 1852.

Mellon, Stanley. *The Political Uses of History*. Stanford: Stanford University Press, 1958.

Merley, Jean. "Les Elections de 1869 dans la Loire." *Cahiers d'histoire* 6 (1961), 59–93.

Michel, Henri. *Les Courants de pensée de la Résistance*. Paris: Presses Universitaires de France, 1962.

Milward, Alan S. *The New Order and the French Economy*. Oxford: Clarendon Press, 1970.

Mitchell, Allan. "German History in France after 1870." *Journal of Contemporary History* 2 (1967), 81–100.

Mohrt, Michel. *Les Intellectuals devant la défaite: 1870*. Paris: Correa, 1942.

Moissonnier, Maurice. "La Section lyonnaise de l'Internationale et l'opposition ouvrière à la second Empire." *Cahiers d'histoire* 10 (1965), 275–314.

Monod, G. "Du progrès des sciences historiques depuis le XVIe siècle." *Revue historique* 1 (1876), 5–38.

de Montalembert, Charles. *De l'avenir politique de l'Angleterre*. 4th ed. Paris: Didier, 1857.

Morazé, Charles. *La France bourgeoise*. 3d ed. Paris: Colin, 1952.

Moreau, Pierre. *L'Histoire en France au XIXe siècle*. Paris: Belles Lettres, 1935.

———. *Le Romantisme*. Paris: Duca, 1957.

Moss, Bernard. *The Origins of the French Labor Movement, 1830–1914*. Berkeley: University of California Press, 1976.

Mounier, Emmanuel. *Mounier et sa génération*. Paris: Seuil, 1956.

———. *Le Personalisme*. 12th ed. In the Que sais-je? series. Paris: Presses Universitaires de France, 1971.

Muret, Pierre. "Emile Ollivier et le duc de Gramont les 12 et 13 juillet 1870." *Revue d'histoire moderne et contemporaine* 13 (1909–1910), 305–328, and 14 (1910), 178–213.

Namier, Lewis. "The First Mountebank Dictator." In *Vanished Supremacies*, pp. 54–64. New York: Harper, 1963.

Napoleon III. *History of Julius Caesar.* 2 vols. New York: Harper, 1866.

———. *Napoleonic Ideas.* Translated by James Dorr. New York: Appleton, 1859.

———. *Oeuvres de Napoléon III.* 4 vols. Paris: Plon, 1856.

———. *Political and Historical Works of Louis Napoleon Bonaparte.* 2 vols. Reprint. New York: Fertig, 1972.

Naudad, Martin. *Mémoires de Leonard.* Edited by Georges Duveau. Paris: Egloff, 1948.

Nora, Pierre. "Ernest Lavisse: son role dans la formation du sentiment national." *Revue historique* 228 (1962), 73–106.

Ollivier, Emile. *L'Empire libéral.* 18 vols. Paris: Garnier, 1895–1918.

———. *Histoire et philosophie d'une guerre.* Edited by Pierre Guiral. Paris: Martineau, 1970.

———. *Journal.* 2 vols. Edited by Theodore Zeldin and Anne Troisier de Diaz. Paris: Julliard, 1961.

———. *Principes et conduite.* Paris: Garnier, 1875.

———. *Solutions politiques et sociales.* Paris: Bellier, 1894.

Ollivier, Marie-Thérèse. *Emile Ollivier, sa jeunesse.* Paris: Garnier, 1919.

Oster, Daniel. *Histoire de l'Académie Française.* Paris: Vialetag, 1970.

Ozouf, Jacques and Mona. "Le Thème du patriotisme dans les manuels primaires." *Mouvement social* 49 (1964), 5–31.

Ozouf, Mona. *L'Ecole, l'église et la République.* Paris: Colin, 1963.

Pailleron, Marie-Louise. *François Buloz et ses amis: les écrivains du second Empire.* Paris: Perrin, 1924.

Paléologue, Maurice. *The Tragic Empress, a Record of Intimate Talks with the Empress Eugenie.* Translated by Hamish Miles. New York: Harper, 1928.

Paxton, Robert. *Vichy France: Old Guard and New Order.* New York: Knopf, 1972.

Payne, Howard C. *The Police State of Louis Napoleon Bonaparte, 1851–1860.* Seattle: University of Washington Press, 1965.

Pelletan, Eugène. *Nouvelle Babylone.* 3d ed. Paris: Pagnerre, 1864.

Perrot, Michelle. "Grèves, grévistes et conjoncture." *Mouvement social* 63 (1968), 109–124.

Persigny, Fialin. *Mémoires du duc de Persigny.* Edited by the comte d'Espagny. Paris: Plon, 1896.

Phelan, Edward. *Yes and Albert Thomas.* London: Cresset, 1936.

Picard, Alfred. *Les Chemins de fer français.* Volume II. Paris: Rothschild, 1884.

Pierce, Roy. *Contemporary French Political Thought.* New York: Oxford University Press, 1966.

Pierrard, Pierre. *La Vie ouvrière à Lille sous le second Empire.* Paris: Bloud et Gay, 1965.

Pilant, Paul. "La Réforme militaire sous le second Empire." *Revue des études napoléoniennes* 6 (1935), 71–104.

Pimienta, Robert. *La Propagande bonapartiste en 1848.* Paris: Cornély, 1911.

Pinkney, David. *Napoleon III and the Rebuilding of Paris.* Princeton: Princeton University Press, 1958.

Plessis, Alain. *De la fête impériale au mur des fédérés, 1852–1870.* Volume IX in *Nouvelle Histoire de la France contemporaine.* Paris: Seuil, 1973.

Ponteil, Félix. *L'Opposition politique à Strasbourg sous la Monarchie de juillet.* Paris: Hartmann, 1932.

Pottinger, E. Ann. *Napoleon III and the German Crisis, 1865–1868.* Cambridge: Harvard University Press, 1966.

Pouthas, Charles. *Démocraties et capitalisme 1848–1860.* 3d ed. Volume XVI in the Peuples et civilisations series. Paris: Presses Universitaires de France, 1961.

———. *Histoire politique du second Empire.* Paris: CDU, 1955.

Pradalié, Georges. *Le Second Empire.* In the Que sais-je? series. Paris: Presses Universitaires de France, 1957.

Prélot, Marcel. *Histoire des idées politiques.* Paris: Dalloz, 1961.

———. "La Signification constitutionnelle du second Empire." *Revue française de science politique* 3 (1953), 31–56.

Prévost-Paradol, Lucien. *La France nouvelle.* Paris: Lévy, 1868.

Price, Roger. *The French Second Republic: A Social History.* London: Batsford, 1972.

Prost, Antoine. *Histoire de l'enseignement en France, 1800–1967.* Paris: Colin, 1968.

Proudhon, P. J. *Contradictions politiques.* Edited by Georges Duveau and J. L. Peuch. Paris: Rivière, 1952.

———. *La Révolution sociale démontrée par le coup d'état.* Edited by Edouard Dolléans and Georges Duveau. Paris: Rivière, 1937.

Quinet, Edgar. *La Révolution,* 2 vols. Brussels: Lacroix, 1865.

Raphael, Paul, and Maurice Gontard. *Un Ministre de l'Instruction publique sous l'Empire autoritaire: Hippolyte Fortoul.* Paris: Presses Universitaires de France, 1975.

Ratcliffe, Barrie. "Napoleon III and the Anglo-French Commercial Treaty of 1860: A Reconsideration." *Journal of European Economic History* 2 (1973), 532–613.

Rauch, William. *Politics and Belief in Contemporary France: Emmanuel Mounier and Christian Democracy.* The Hague: Nijhoff, 1972.

Rebérioux, Madeleine. "Histoire, historiens et dreyfusisme." *Revue historique* 518 (1976), 47–73.

Rebérioux, Madeleine, and Patrick Fridenson. "Albert Thomas, pivot du réformisme française." *Mouvement social* 87 (1974), 85–98.

Reichert, Robert. "Anti-Bonapartist Elections to the Académie Française during the Second Empire." *Journal of Modern History* 25 (1963), 33–45.

Rémond, René. *La Droite en France de 1815 à nos jours.* Paris: Aubier, 1954.

Renan, Ernest. *La Réforme intellectuelle et morale de la France.* Paris: Lévy, n.d.

de Ribeyrolles, Charles. *Les Bagnes d'Afrique.* 2 vols. London: Jeffs, 1853.

Richards, Edward. "Louis Napoleon and Central America." *Journal of Modern History* 34 (1962), 178–184.

Ridley, F. F. *Revolutionary Syndicalism in France.* Cambridge: University Press, 1970.

Ripoll, Roger. "L'Histoire du second Empire dans *La Curée.*" *Revue d'histoire moderne et contemporaine* 21 (1974), 46–57.

Rist, Marcel. "Une Expérience française de libération des échanges au XIXe siècle: le traité de 1860." *Revue d'économie politique* 66 (1956), 908–961.

Rohr, Jean. *Victor Duruy, ministre de Napoléon III.* Paris: Librairie Générale de Droit et de Jurisprudence, 1967.

Rothney, John. *Bonapartism after Sedan.* Ithaca: Cornell University Press, 1969.

Rougerie, Jacques. "La Première Internationale à Lyon, 1865–1870." *Annali dell Istituto Giangiacomo Feltrinelli* 4 (1961), 126–161.

———. "Remarques sur l'histoire des salaires à Paris au XIXe siècle." *Mouvement social* 63 (1968), 71–108.

———. "Sur l'histoire de la première Internationale." *Mouvement social* 51 (1965), 23–45.

Rouvier, Gaston. *L'Enseignement public en France au début du XXe siècle.* Stockholm: Aktiebolaget, 1905.

Roy, Joseph-Antoine. *Histoire de la famille Schneider et du Creusot.* Paris: Rivière, 1962.

Rubel, Maximilien. *Karl Marx devant le bonapartisme.* Paris: Mouton, 1960.

de Ruggiero, Guido. *The History of European Liberalism.* Translated by R. G. Collingwood. Boston: Beacon, 1959.

Saint-Marc, Pierre. *Emile Ollivier.* Paris: Plon, 1950.

Sainte-Beuve, Charles A. *Causeries du lundi.* 15 vols. 3d ed. Paris: Garnier, n.d.

———. *Nouveaux Lundis.* 13 vols. Paris: Lévy, 1864–1870.

Salomon, Henry. "Une Expérience politique en 1870 et ses conséquences." *Revue de synthèse historique* 32 (1921), 15–140.

Sand, George. *Correspondance.* Volumes III–VI. 4th ed. Paris: Calmann-Lévy, 1883–1895.

Schaper, B. W. *Albert Thomas: trente ans de réformisme social.* Paris: Presses Universitaires de France, n.d.

Schapiro, J. Salwyn. *Liberalism and the Challenge of Fascism.* Reprint. New York: Octagon, 1964.

Schefer, Christian. *La Grande Pensée de Napoléon III.* Paris: Rivière, 1939.

Schnerb, Madeleine. *Mémoires pour deux.* Privately published, 1973.

Schnerb, Madeleine, ed. *Robert Schnerb.* Clermont-Ferrand: Volcans, 1964.

Schnerb, Robert. *Les Contributions directes à l'époque de la Révolution dans le département du Puy-de-Dôme*. Paris: Alcan, 1933.

——. *Le XIXe Siècle*. Volume VI in the *Histoire générale des civilisations*, under the direction of Maurice Crouzet. Paris: Presses Universitaires de France, 1955.

——. "Finances proudhonniennes." *Revue socialiste* 7–11 (1947), 169–179.

——. *Ledru-Rollin*. Paris: Presses Universitaires de France, 1948.

——. *Libre-échange et protectionnisme*. In the Que sais-je? series. Paris: Presses Universitaires de France, 1963.

——. "La Politique fiscale de Thiers." *Revue historique* 201 (1949), 186–212; 202 (1949), 184–220.

——. *Rouher et le second Empire*. Paris: Colin, 1949.

——. "Napoleon III and the Second French Empire." *Journal of Modern History* 8 (1936), 338–355.

Schoelcher, Victor. *Histoire des crimes du 2 décembre*. 2 vols. London: Chapman, 1852.

Scott, Joan. *The Glassworkers of Carmaux: French Craftsmen and Political Action in a Nineteenth-Century City*. Cambridge: Harvard University Press, 1974.

Scott, John A. *Republican Ideas and the Liberal Tradition in France, 1870–1914*. Reprint. New York: Octagon, 1966.

Sechaud, Pierre. *L'Académie Française et le second Empire*. Lyon: Bosc, 1952.

Sée, Henri. *Histoire économique de la France*. 2 vols. Edited by Robert Schnerb. Paris: Colin, 1939–1942.

Seignobos, Charles. "Les Conditions psychologiques de la connaissance en histoire." *Revue philosophique*, 24 (1887), 1–32.

——. *Le Déclin de l'Empire et l'établissement de la 3e République*. Volume VII of the *Histoire contemporaine*, under the direction of Ernest Lavisse. Paris: Hachette, 1921.

——. "L'Enseignement de l'histoire dans les universités allemandes." *Revue internationale de l'enseignement* 1 (1881), 563–601.

——. *Etudes de politique et d'histoire*. Edited by J. Letaconnoux. Paris: Presses Universitaires de France, 1934.

——. *Histoire sincère de la nation française*. 6th ed. Paris: Presses Universitaires de France, 1946.

——. *La Méthode historique appliquée aux sciences sociales*. 2d ed. Paris: Alcan, 1909.

——. "Les Opérations des Commissions Mixtes en 1852." *La Révolution de 1848* 6 (1909–1910), 59–67.

——. "L'Organisation des divers types d'enseignement." In *L'Education de la démocratie*, edited by Ernest Lavisse, pp. 92–132. Paris: Alcan, 1903.

——. *A Political History of Europe since 1914*. Translated by S. M. Macvane. New York: Holt, 1900.

——. *Le Régime de l'enseignement supérieur des lettres analyse et critique*. Paris: Imprimerie Nationale, 1904.

————. "La Révolution de 1848 et la réaction en France." In Volume XI of *Histoire générale du IVe siècle à nos jours,* under the direction of Ernest Lavisse and Alfred Rambaud, pp. 1–37. Paris: Colin, 1899.

————. *La Révolution de 1848—Le second Empire (1848–1859).* Volume VI of the *Histoire contemporaine,* under the direction of Ernest Lavisse. Paris: Hachette, 1921.

————. "La Troisième République." In Volume XII of *Histoire générale du IVe siècle à nos jours,* under the direction of Ernest Lavisse and Alfred Rambaud, pp. 1–51. Paris: Colin, 1901.

Seignobos, Charles, Emile Borel, and Jules Jeanneney. *Jean Maurain.* Paris: Presses Universitaires de France, 1939.

Seignobos, Charles, and Charles Langlois. *Introduction to the Study of History.* Translated by G. G. Berry. New York: Holt, 1926.

Sencourt, Robert. *Napoleon III: The Modern Emperor.* New York: Appleton-Century, 1933.

Senior, Nassau William. *Conversations with Distinguished Persons during the Second Empire.* 2 vols. Edited by M. C. M. Simpson. London: Hurst and Blackett, 1880.

————. *Conversations with M. Thiers, M. Guizot and Other Distinguished Persons during the Second Empire.* 2 vols. Edited by M. C. M. Simpson. London: Hurst and Blackett, 1878.

Sewell, William H., Jr. "Social Change and the Rise of Working-Class Politics in Nineteenth-Century Marseille." *Past and Present* 65 (1974), 75–109.

Sherman, Dennis. "Governmental Policy toward Joint-Stock Business Organizations in Mid-nineteenth Century France." *Journal of European Economic History* 3 (1974), 149–168.

Shorter, Edward, and Charles Tilly. *Strikes in France, 1830–1968.* London: Cambridge University Press, 1974.

Siegel, Martin. "Henri Berr's *Revue de Synthèse historique.*" *History and Theory* 11 (1970), 322–334.

Siegfried, André. "Charles Seignobos." *Revue historique* 193 (1942–1943), 193–203.

————. *Tableau politique de la France de l'Ouest sous la IIIe République.* 2d ed. Paris: Colin, 1964.

Simiand, F. *Le Salaire, l'évolution sociale et la monnaie.* 3 vols. Paris: Alcan, 1932.

Simpson, F. A. *Louis Napoleon and the Recovery of France.* 2d ed. London: Longmans, 1960.

————. *The Rise of Louis Napoleon.* London: Longmans, 1925.

Soltau, Roger. *French Political Thought in the 19th Century.* Reprint. New York: Russell and Russell, 1959.

Spitzer, Alan. "The Good Napoleon III." *French Historical Studies* 2 (1962), 308–329.

————. *The Revolutionary Theories of Auguste Blanqui.* New York: Columbia University Press, 1957.

Spuller, Eugène. *Histoire parlementaire de la seconde République suivie d'une petite histoire du second Empire.* 2d ed. Paris: Alcan, 1893.

———. *Figures disparues.* 3 vols. 3d ed. Paris: Alcan, 1894.

Stearn, Peter. "French Historians in the First World War." Paper delivered at the Society for French Historical Studies, March 21, 1970.

Stearns, Peter. "British Industry through the Eyes of French Industrialists (1820–1848)." *Journal of Modern History* 37 (1965), 50–61.

———. *Revolutionary Syndicalism and French Labor.* New Brunswick: Rutgers University Press, 1971.

Stern, Daniel. *Histoire de la Révolution de 1848.* 4 vols. Paris: Charpentier, 1862.

Stoianovich, Traian. *French Historical Method: The Annales Paradigm.* Ithaca: Cornell University Press, 1976.

Suleiman, Ezra. *Politics, Power, and Bureaucracy in France.* Princeton: Princeton University Press, 1974.

Swart, Koenraad. *The Sense of Decadence in Nineteenth Century France.* The Hague: Nijhoff, 1964.

Talbott, John. *The Politics of Educational Reform in France, 1918–1940.* Princeton: Princeton University Press, 1969.

Tchernoff, I. *Le Parti républicain au coup d'état et sous le second Empire.* Paris: Pedone, 1906.

Témime, Emile. "Une Journaliste d'affaires: Gabriel Hugelmann." *Revue d'histoire moderne et contemporaine* 18 (1971), 610–629.

Ténot, Eugène. *Paris en décembre.* Paris: Chevalier, 1868.

———. *La Province en décembre.* 3d ed. Paris: Chevalier, 1868.

Ténot, Eugène, and Antonin Dubost. *Les Suspects en 1858.* Paris: Chevalier, 1869.

Thibaudet, Albert. *Les Idées politiques de la France.* Paris: Stock, 1932.

Thiers, Adolphe. *Histoire du Consulat et de l'Empire.* 20 vols. New ed. Paris: Furne, Jouvet, 1874.

Thirria, H. *Napoléon III avant l'Empire.* 2 vols. Paris: Plon, 1896.

Thomas, Albert. "The Liberal Empire (1859–1870)." In Volume XI of *The Cambridge Modern History,* pp. 467–506. New York: Macmillan, 1909.

———. "Napoleon III and the Period of Personal Government (1852–1859)." In Volume XI of *The Cambridge Modern History,* pp. 286–308. New York: Macmillan, 1909.

———. "La Pensée socialiste de Babeuf avant la conspiration des égaux." *Revue socialiste* 40 (1904), 226–236, 513–528, 696–712; 41 (1905), 58–77, 179–202.

———. *Le Second Empire.* Volume X of the *Histoire socialiste,* under the direction of Jean Jaurès. Paris: Jules Rouff, 1907.

Thompson, James Westfall. *A History of Historical Writing.* Volume II. New York: Macmillan, 1942.

Thompson, J. M. *Louis Napoleon and the Second Empire.* Oxford: Blackwell, 1965.

de Tocqueville, Alexis. *The Old Regime and the French Revolution.* Translated by Stuart Gilbert. Garden City: Anchor, 1955.

————. *Recollections.* Edited by J. P. Mayer. Translated by Alexander Teixeira de Mattos. New York: Meridian, 1959.

Touchard, Jean. "L'Esprit des années 1930: une tentative de renouvellement de la pensée politique française." In *Tendances politiques dans la vie française depuis 1789,* pp. 89–120. Paris: Hachette, 1960.

Toynbee, A. J. *A Study of History.* Volume III. 2d ed. London: Oxford University Press, 1955.

Tudesq, André-Jean. *Les Grands Notables en France (1840–1849).* 2 vols. Paris: Presses Universitaires de France, 1964.

————. "La Légende napoléonienne en France en 1848." *Revue historique* 218 (1957), 64–85.

Vauthier, G. "La Souscription Baudin." *La Révolution de 1848* 24 (1927), 111–119.

de Viel Castel, Horace. *Mémoires sur le règne de Napoléon III.* 6 vols. Paris: Tous les Librairies, 1883.

Vier, Jacques. "La Comtesse d'Agoult, Emile Ollivier et le ministère du 2 janvier." *Information historique* 5 (1961), 190–195.

Vigier, Philippe. *La Seconde République dans la région alpine.* 2 vols. Paris: Presses Universitaires de France, 1963.

Villermé, René. *Tableau de l'état physique et moral des ouvriers.* 2 vols. Paris: Renouard, 1840.

Vincent, Gérard. "Les Professeurs de l'enseignement secondaire dans la société de la 'Belle Epoque.'" *Revue d'histoire moderne et contemporaine* 13 (1966), 49–86.

————. "Les Professeurs du second degré au début du XIXe siècle." *Mouvement social* 55 (1966), 47–73.

Wallon, Maurice. "Les Saint-Simoniens et les chemins de fer." *Annales des sciences politiques* 23 (1908), 514–528; 24 (1909), 83–100, 220–229.

Watson, D. R. "Educational Reform in France, 1900–1914." *Past and Present* 34 (1966), 81–99.

Weber, Eugen. *Action Française: Royalism and Reaction in Twentieth-Century France.* Stanford: Stanford University Press, 1962.

————. *Peasants into Frenchmen: The Modernization of Rural France, 1870–1914.* Stanford: Stanford University Press, 1976.

Weill, Georges. "L'Anticléricalisme sous le second Empire." *Revue des études napoléoniennes* 8 (1915), 56–84.

————. *L'Ecole Saint-Simonienne.* Paris: Alcan, 1896.

————. *Histoire de l'enseignement secondaire en France.* Paris: Payot, 1921.

————. *Histoire du mouvement social en France.* 2d ed. Paris: Alcan, 1911.

————. *Histoire du parti républicain en France, 1814–1870.* New ed. Paris: Alcan, 1928.

————. *Le Journal: origines, évolution et role de la presse périodique.* Paris: Renaissance du Livre, 1934.

————. "Les Journaux ouvriers à Paris, 1830–1870." *Revue d'histoire moderne et contemporaine* 9 (1907), 89–103.

————. "Les Saint-Simoniens sous Napoléon III." *Revue des études napoléoniennes* 4 (1913), 391–406.

White, Hayden. *Metahistory: The Historical Imagination in Nineteenth-Century Europe.* Baltimore: Johns Hopkins University Press, 1973.

Williams, Roger. *Gaslight and Shadow: The World of Napoleon III.* New York: Macmillan, 1957.

————. *Henri Rochefort, Prince of the Gutter Press.* New York: Scribners, 1966.

————. "Louis Napoleon: A Tragedy of Good Intentions." *History Today* 4 (1954), 219–226.

————. *Manners and Murders in the World of Louis-Napoleon.* Seattle: University of Washington Press, 1975.

————. *The Mortal Napoleon III.* Princeton: Princeton University Press, 1971.

Winock, Michel. *Histoire politique de la revue "Esprit," 1930–1950.* Paris: Seuil, 1975.

Wohl, Robert. *French Communism in the Making.* Stanford: Stanford University Press, 1966.

Wolf, Donald. "Emmanuel Mounier: A Catholic of the Left." *Review of Politics* 22 (1960), 324–344.

Wright, Gordon. "Public Opinion and Conscription in France." *Journal of Modern History* 14 (1942), 26–45.

Wright, Vincent. *Le Conseil d'Etat sous le second Empire.* Paris: Colin, 1972.

————. "The Coup d'état of December 1851: Repression and Limits to Repression." In *Revolution and Reaction: 1848 and the Second French Republic,* edited by Roger Price, pp. 303–333. New York: Barnes and Noble, 1975.

————. "La Loi de sûreté générale de 1858." *Revue d'histoire moderne et contemporaine* 16 (1969), 414–430.

Zeldin, Theodore, ed. *Conflicts in French Society.* London: Allen and Unwin, 1970.

Zeldin, Theodore. *Emile Ollivier and the Liberal Empire.* Oxford: Clarendon Press, 1963.

————. *France, 1848–1945.* Volume I: *Ambition, Love and Politics.* Volume II: *Intellect, Taste and Anxiety.* Oxford: Clarendon Press, 1973, 1977.

————. "Government Policy in the French General Elections of 1849." *English Historical Review* 74 (1959), 240–248.

————. "Higher Education in France, 1848–1940." *Journal of Contemporary History* 2 (1967), 53–80.

————. "The Myth of Napoleon III." *History Today* 8 (1958), 103–109.

————. *The Political System of Napoleon III.* London: Macmillan, 1958.

Zévaès, Alexander. "Les Candidatures ouvrières et révolutionnaires sous le second Empire." *La Révolution de 1848* 29 (1932), 132–154.

Index